The Concise Guide to Becoming an

Independent Consultant

The Concise Guide to Becoming an
Independent Consultant

Herman Holtz

John Wiley & Sons, Inc.
New York · Chichester · Weinheim · Brisbane · Singapore · Toronto

Library of Congress Cataloging-in-Publication Data:

Holtz, Herman.
    The concise guide to becoming an independent consultant / Herman Holtz.
        p.   cm.
    Includes index.
    ISBN 0-471-31573-7 (paper : alk. paper)
    1. Business consultants—Vocational guidance.   2. Consulting firms—Planning.   I. Title.
    HD69.C6H6199   1999
    001'.068—dc21   98-44989

Printed in the United States of America.

10 9 8 7 6 5 4

Contents

mass marketing. The marketing database. Networking for clients. Brokers, job shops, subcontracts, and the IRS. IRS and Section 1706. Technical services firms.

Preface

Consulting, as a career, has been one of the major beneficiaries of our explosively expanding high technology. The mainframe computer was responsible for creating a great many computer consultants, for example. Then the personal computer came along and multiplied the number of independent computer consultants many times over. Then came the Internet and Web sites, and that spawned a great many new consulting specialties.

Consultants who rely on high-tech skills and knowledge are among the most rapidly proliferating types and classes of consultants, but they are not the only ones for whom consulting has become a career. We have consultants today in every field—wedding consultants, dress consultants, telephone solicitation consultants, even automobile parking consultants! Whatever the need or problem, there is probably a consultant expert who can help.

Through years on CompuServe and now through several years on the Internet, I have been in constant and continuous communication with a great many consultants. Some are highly experienced old-timers, some are relatively new to the field, and some are either just embarking on a consulting career or preparing to do so. The words of one man who is employed as an internal consultant by his firm were especially rewarding. He reported that he did not aspire to launch his own, independent consulting venture, but he found certain principles enunciated in our Internet conversations and in some of his reading "made the lights go on" for him and were "liberating eye openers." These are some of the specific ideas he found to be so illuminating:

- Consulting is not itself a profession, rather it is how one practices a profession.
- Consultants need to market their services proactively as a planned part of their business and not as an afterthought.
- The client's perception is what defines the "truth" or reality of a consulting situation.
- Consultants need to make a profit in addition to making a living, that is, there should be something left over after paying themselves a salary.

- A consultant must be a specialist and a generalist at the same time.
- A proposal is a sales presentation. (Too often we write proposals as displays of erudite technical knowledge or proficiency in clever phrasings.)

I learned and I continue to learn more and more about consulting from other experienced practitioners. I have incorporated input from real live, practicing consultants whose comments reflect practical experience, rather than theory. I also learned of the problems independent consultants are encountering, and what help is needed to cope with these new problems in a changing world.

A NEEDED RESPONSE TO GREAT CHANGES

With all respect to Ben Franklin and his observation about the inevitability of death and taxes, I must point out that he neglected to mention another thing that is inevitable in this world: Change. Change is inevitable, it is constant, and it is, in the broad view, beneficial, although the immediate effects may not appear so. Many things about consulting have remained the same over the years, but much has changed. In this book, I will strive to reinforce that which is constant, but I will also focus attention on the significant changes that must be recognized and taken into account to continue succeeding as an independent consultant.

Some of the changes are minor and of only minor importance, while others are of great importance, and critical to one's success as a consultant. Professional practices and other businesses often fail because they become obsolete: Their principals fail to change when change is necessary. An old dog *can* learn new tricks, and often must do so to survive. We will look at independent consulting today, with all its opportunities and problems, some of them no different than they were yesterday and others totally new and different.

THE PERIPHERAL REQUIREMENTS OF TODAY'S BUSINESS

In our complex society, we must all be covered by insurance, especially hospitalization and general medical coverage. Few of us can handle the costs of today's routine medical costs, let alone the costs of medical emergencies, without insurance coverage. Large corporations can get group coverage without great difficulty; independents often have a problem in doing so. In this book, we will consider insurance and offer some ideas on how to obtain coverage.

Credit is also a problem for independents. Clients expect to be billed for services, even if they furnish a retainer to initiate a project. For small projects, they may want to pay with plastic—any of the popular credit cards. But credit card issuers—banks and others—do not welcome independent consultants, especially those who are home-based. This, too, is a problem we will address.

THE IRS VERSUS THE ON-SITE SUBCONTRACTOR

One of the problems facing consultants who undertake to function as independent contractors working on clients' premises, under subcontracts to brokers, is the attitude of the IRS: The IRS has questioned the contractor status claimed by independent consultants who work on the client's premises and on long-term contracts. On the other hand, many consultants, those employed in large organizations and those functioning as independent consultants, work on their own premises or on both the client's and their own premises, usually under contract to do a specific job, rather than under an indefinite-term agreement to work for the client. Some independent consultants have short-term assignments because of the nature of the work, but many consultants have long-term contracts and assignments. Thus, the IRS' position can be a serious problem, and it will be discussed in these pages, with suggestions for overcoming it.

THE PLIGHT OF TODAY'S RETIREES

Early retirement and second careers have been an increasing trend influenced by the great increase in retirement plans and employees' vested interests in such plans. There are also a significant number of military retirees, the majority of whom retire at relatively early ages. With the pressure of high costs of living today added to the natural energy and vigor of men and women who retire early, many launch second careers, and consulting is a popular option.

THE TECHNOLOGY EXPLOSION

The technological revolution has greatly amplified your capabilities for expanding your profit-making services and your resources for satisfying clients' needs. The computer age is many decades old, but the era of the desktop computer is barely a decade old. It was explosively revolutionary, even more so than its predecessor the mainframe computer age, reaching swiftly into every corner of our lives and changing the way we do many things. The desktop computers of 1988, for example, are primitive, compared to the personal computer today. Portable computers are more and more popular, so that even away from one's office, whether in one's automobile, an airplane, or a hotel room, all computer services and facilities are at hand. With the widespread use of modems, computer owners have ready access to other computers and public databases—information services.

You can't be a consultant today without using a computer. The facsimile machine (fax) has become almost as popular and common as the telephone. Cellular telephones enable an increasing number of private individuals, as well as consultants and other businesspeople to be in touch with their offices and their clients wherever they are.

THE NEED FOR ENHANCED MARKETING

In these times of general business slowdown and increasing competition, marketing becomes a more critical need than ever. We have given it more attention here than previously, with discussions of and suggestions for more efficient promotional schemes and materials. We'll offer additional and new insights into methods for marketing your services successfully. A large part of this book will focus sharply on specific marketing ideas and methods to consider and use, for those are the true ingredients of your success as an independent consultant.

These are all matters to be addressed in these pages, along with many other new developments and current conditions. The book is organized for your convenience in finding specific coverage and, more important, specific help for the solution of problems and exploitation of opportunities to expand and increase your success.

HERMAN HOLTZ
Wheaton, Maryland

The Concise Guide to Becoming an

Independent Consultant

Introduction

The definition of consulting is controversial. The profession and the term are often misunderstood by practitioners and misrepresented by critics. *Consulting* has become a term of convenience, used freely by independents of one sort or another and providing services based on expert, often specialized, knowledge. Applications—methods and vehicles for providing services—are so diverse that the need for definition, even a simplified one, arises frequently.

INCREASING NEED

Consulting is not new. It probably started as a necessary support service to tribal chiefs and others of earliest societies. We can imagine the first man who learned how to sharpen and point a stick to make a spear was soon besieged by others who wanted him to teach then how to do the same or do it for them. Few consulting situations are that simple now.

The growing complexity of society, technologically and otherwise, increases the need for consultants and the services we offer. Individuals and organizations everywhere find it increasingly difficult to cope with modern problems without expert help. I found it necessary to switch from a typewriter to a computer to do my own work 15 years ago, but although I have become computer literate, I often find it necessary to turn to a computer consultant for help. The need is not confined to technology: To obtain one's Social Security benefits often requires the help of a lawyer specializing in the field—a consultant in fact, if not in name. Consultants show companies how to take advantage of the new telephone services available. Consultants improve office organization and procedures, provide better inventory management, train staffs in writing effectively, and many other tasks. Most businesses use consultants at least occasionally.

In my local telephone directories there were virtually no listings under the heading *Consultants*. The emphasis is on the adjective that identifies the profession in which one consults—*Business Consultants* and *Engineering Consultants*. And under those general headings are more specific listings:

Business Consultants
  Career & Vocational Counseling
  Child Guidance
  Color Consultants
  Educational Consultants
  Engineers—Consulting
  Human Resources Consultants
  Image Consultants
  Immigration & Naturalization Consultants
  Infrared Inspection Services
  Marriage, Family, Child & Individual Counselors
  Movers
  Personnel Consultants
  Printers
  Tax Return Preparation
  Travel Agencies & Bureaus
  Wedding Consultants

We thus have marketing consultants, editorial consultants, management consultants, and others, again subdivided into more specific types: proposal consultants, direct mail consultants, advertising consultants, etc. Bear in mind that consulting is a viable means for practicing any profession. We refer to the consulting profession, but remember that consulting is in fact a way of practicing a profession.

Many practitioners who regard themselves as consultants are reluctant to identify themselves as such because of sneers and epithets from critics and opponents of consulting. Lawyers, physicians, dentists, architects, and many other professional or technical experts do not call themselves legal consultants or medical consultants to describe their professions, even when they are highly specialized practitioners. In fact, although physicians are often called on to consult with other physicians and recognize the term *consulting* as describing this activity, others (e.g., lawyers) never use the term, even when asked by another lawyer to participate as an adviser. The words *associate, co-counsel,* and *second chair* are the preferred terms in the legal profession. Even when bringing in someone to depose or testify, the expert becomes an *expert witness,* not a consultant, although consultants are often called upon to be expert witnesses. There are independent consultants specializing in being expert witnesses and performing related support services. (Expert witnesses usually do much more than appear and testify on the stand.)

A reasonable inference is that consultants are primarily specialists within a profession. That is how consulting appears to others, and how consultants themselves regard what they do. Thus, I am first a marketing specialist, second a specialist in marketing to government agencies, and third a consultant to those requiring assistance in marketing, especially to government agencies and especially with regard to writing proposals. I might also regard myself as a writer who consults with those requiring assistance in writing proposals. Even those are only two of several ways in which I might identify and define what I am and what I do. The differences are more than semantics; they have a great deal to do with how successfully I market my services, especially my success in helping clients perceive the benefits of what I do for them.

Note that in the listing on page 0, many services are not technical or professional. Included are movers, printers, tax return preparers, and travel agencies and bureaus. Again, it is not the technical nature of the service that makes it consulting, but the circumstances of the delivery. A surgeon does not become something other than a surgeon when he or she acts as consultant. Nor does a lawyer, an engineer, a marketer, an interior decorator, or any other specialist change the kind of work he or she does when acting as a consultant.

Independent consultants are defined by the kinds of services they provide or the means by which they provide services as much as by their special career fields. You may be known as a computer consultant, but that only identifies a general field, not what you specialize in doing in that field, such as databases, desktop publishing, software maintenance, user training, or other, even a subset of one of these.

HOW CONSULTANTS SPECIALIZE

Consultants work in many ways. Consulting itself is not licensed or controlled, although a consultant's profession may be licensed and controlled. Many organizations who supply technical/professional temporaries identify themselves and their temporaries as consultants. Many independent consultants contract independently on the same basis (as temporaries), bypassing the broker. Some brokers undertake contracts for on-site work and subcontract to independent consultants who will work on the client's premises and bill the broker. The effect is the same for the client, but legally there is a wide distinction between being an employee and being an independent contractor.

What is the importance of this? Why trouble ourselves about defining what we do if we are completely free to name it, define it, and practice it however we wish?

The definition and the fact that consulting is not itself a profession but a way to practice a profession is important in marketing your services. Later, when we probe the problems of marketing your services and methods for doing so, this will become more evident. You need to know what business you are in if you are to succeed in marketing your services. It is therefore *marketing*, more than anything else, that identifies and defines what this book is all about, for that is what business success is all about. You must *compete* successfully to survive.

The independent consultant needs help in marketing, that is what inspired the original idea for this book. While most beginning independent consultants are capable in their chosen fields, many—perhaps most—need help in mastering the art of marketing themselves and their services.

THE CONSULTING MARKET HAS GROWN AND CHANGED

Career prospects for independent consultants continue to grow: There is a steady increase in the number of business opportunities for independent consulting. The Internet alone has created many new consulting specialties. More and more specialists see independent consulting as the optimal way of practicing their specialties. The demand for consulting services has grown in both public and private sectors. Federal, state, and local governments continue to rely on consultants to serve many of their needs and solve many of their problems. Significant events, especially major technological advances, create new consulting specialties and greater need for them. The literature—articles, newsletters, and other publications—recognize this and are devoted to covering the subject as a matter of popular interest.

Many firms become consultants without changing anything, except their description. They change a few words on their business cards, letterheads, and other literature, but they continue to do what they have been doing—serving clients in a variety of ways as advisers and service vendors.

Individuals and organizations providing services to clients realize that they win and keep clients as much because they render good advice as because they carry out the services that are the basis of their business. That is, they begin to realize that their marketing appeal is that they are consultants in the classical sense.

How you define yourself as an independent consultant depends on what kinds of assignments you choose to accept and on how you deliver your services. You can accept only problem-solving jobs, if you wish, although you will probably limit your market severely if you do so. You can refuse assignments that require you to write lengthy formal reports or make formal presentations to the client's assembled staff, if you rebel at writing or public speaking. You may confine yourself to assignments in your local area, if you dislike travel. You can establish whatever rules, policies, and procedures you wish. In so doing, you define what that title *independent consultant* means for you and your own practice.

THE MORE IMPORTANT VIEW: THAT OF THE CLIENT

However you view yourself and your practice, it may not match how a prospective client perceives you and your services. Does that matter? It does, if you are to market your services successfully. You can sell only to the client's perception and the client's *expectations*. Perhaps you can shape the client's perception and expectations to some extent. Marketers do that—or try to—

constantly, sometimes with success, sometimes without it. But it can be risky to try to modify the client's perception to any significant degree. It requires great skill to do so, if it can be done at all, and the cost of failure may be loss of the contract and or even the contract you won earlier. It is usually more practical to determine what the typical client expects you to be, do, and deliver, whether that is scholar, expert, trainer, troubleshooter, mentor, guide, hard worker, resident sage, father confessor, trainer, writer, and/or other functionary, and try to conform to that image. (Note, too, that the same client may have different expectations in different situations, depending on what the client perceives the immediate need to be in each situation.) Your success in marketing yourself as a consultant depends largely on these factors:

1. How accurately you assess the image you must project and how effectively you project that image.

2. How well you estimate what your prospective clients want, including how they perceive their needs and problems.

3. How effectively you convince the prospective client that you are exactly what he or she is looking for.

4. How effectively you disseminate that image—make enough prospective clients aware of you, your image, and your capability to help them solve their problems and magnify their success.

Although they are important to winning clients, these factors are equally important to satisfying clients with your work after you have the contract (itself a factor in marketing). Everything you do after getting an assignment must confirm and reinforce your original image and expectations. In all marketing, truth is whatever the client perceives as truth. You must understand the client's perception. It is no less important to create a favorable impression generally. You will always have difficulty satisfying a client who has an adverse impression of you; it is much easier to please the client who has a favorable image of you. Clients tend to see what they expect and want to see.

There are many hazards in consulting independently, many of them peculiar to being a one-person show, for example, the feast-or-famine nature of consulting. It is difficult—frequently impossible—to backlog consulting assignments, and yet there are only so many hours a day available. How do you smooth out those peaks and valleys? Some jobs that come your way require several people; how do you cope with that successfully so that you do not lose the contract? Some clients cannot afford your regular, direct rates, although they have need of help. How can you help them (and yourself) without resorting to the destructive practice of cutting your rates?

Three especially noteworthy aspects of consulting include:

■ Consulting has more than its share of detractors, critics who question the merits of and necessity for consulting in general, and the capabilities and integrity of its practitioners.

- Consulting remains difficult to define; the debates and controversies over what it is (and what it is not!) continue to rage, although not as vigorously.

- Despite these problems, the markets for consulting—the *use* of consultants, that is—and the number of consultants in everyday practice continue to grow.

The need for specialists of all kinds keeps growing. Nor are the two trends—the growth in markets for consulting and in numbers of specialists hanging out their shingles as consultants—unrelated; they are the logical and inevitable consequence of forces such as the increases in technological, political, economic, and industrial complexities of society; and the rapidly rising average level of education.

WHO ARE THE CLIENTS?

Identifying typical consulting clients gives us another clue to the nature of consulting and consultants. We can divide clients into two broad classes: peers and others. Most consultants serve one or the other, and some consultants serve both. The physician invariably serves his or her peers, other physicians, when called on to consult. But a public relations (PR) consultant would most often—almost invariably—serve a client who is a layperson at PR. An engineer might serve other engineers as clients, but could easily be called upon by a client who is not an engineer.

This is an important point. It has a great deal to do with how you conduct your practice and especially how you do your marketing. But it also has a great deal to do with defining what you do as a consultant.

What Does (Should) a Consultant Do?

Better be proficient in one art than a smatterer in a hundred.

—*Japanese proverb*

There is nothing about the services provided by typical consultants that distinguishes them from other contracted-for services, such as those provided by an interior decorator, image counselor, or financial advisor. The differences between these specialists and consultants who provide similar services are principally in the titles and connotation of the word *consultant.* In this chapter we'll briefly review the titles and have a look at some of the most active fields for consulting and at several aspects of the consulting industry, especially as it pertains to independent consultants. (Counseling and advisory services are often fields where practitioners do not use the word *consulting.*)

Independent consultants are often independent contractors, but many consultants are specialists who work as temporary employees of service firms who assign them to work on a client's premises to augment the client's staff. High-tech consultants predominate among those employed in this way. Colloquially, they are referred to as "job shoppers," but are more formally referred to as "contract professionals." That kind of employment blossomed in staffing government contracts with skilled people during the Cold War and the high-tech arms race. Probably the most numerous class of contract professionals were and are the computer specialists.

COMPUTERS AND DATA PROCESSING

The desktop computer is now as common as the electric typewriter. Mainframe computers spawned many consultants and consulting specialties. Their number swelled rapidly, many independent, others building consulting companies. There were programmers, systems analysts, designers, engineers, technicians, writers, computer operators, and others identified by various degrees of experience and qualifications. Specialization was forced on consultants by the rapid growth of diverse new technologies.

The accelerating use of the personal/desktop computer and other applications were made possible by the development of new computer chips. Despite a decline in defense contracts and in the manufacture, sale, and use of mainframe computers, the growth in numbers of computer consultants continued, as did the use of contract professionals in general.

THE RISE OF THE PERMANENT TEMPORARY

The term *temporary* originally referred to office workers who were a convenience for employers with temporary needs for extra help. Temporary agencies were a boon to women who didn't want or couldn't find full-time jobs. They soon began to place engineers, writers, illustrators, and others who sought temporary jobs. "Temp" jobs normally pay a higher hourly rate than does "captive" employment, since fringe benefits are minimal or non-existent. A population of workers arose who preferred to work on higher pay temporary assignments and provide their own benefits. Contract professionals are virtually a subculture. Although many are independent contractors to clients, the majority work for one of the "job shops," a colloquial term for suppliers of the markets.

The situation can be more complex, and a third arrangement is possible: Instead of contracting with the client on whose premises the specialist will work, he or she may work on client's premises as a subcontractor to a broker who is a prime contractor to the client. Unlike a job shop, who actually employs the temporary and assigns him or her to a client's premises for work, the broker subcontracts with each individual for work on the client's premises, so the individual is an independent contractor.

Originally consultants were hired as temporary employees because it was the only way to staff a project rapidly enough with qualified specialists. Today many companies hire contract professionals because it makes better economic and business sense. It is far less expensive to staff up with temporaries than to hire and train new employees. Contracting imposes virtually no obligations on the client beyond paying the contractor for providing the contract labor. Temporaries can be hired quickly, with little paperwork and little legal obligation, since they are employees of a contractor, not of the client, and they can be terminated easily when the need ends. If a temporary employee proves unsatisfactory, there are no complications in having that individual's services ended, in contrast to the legal problems in discharging a permanent employee for cause.

The sizes of programs for temporaries—numbers employed and duration of assignments—vary widely. NASA has used large temporary forces, notably in engineering and computer-related work, and General Electric Company (GE) employed large numbers of temporary engineers in their missile and space programs. Where the project requires large numbers of temporaries, it is not unusual to have a half-dozen or more firms working together on the premises.

Duration of assignments also varies from a few days to several years. A consultant may be employed on an indefinite basis and be kept on for one project after another. At the Philadelphia-area plants of the GE missile and space systems, many consultant temporaries were "temporary" for as long as five years, as were temporaries at the large training center Xerox Corporation established in Leesburg, Virginia. These training technologists were all "hired"—placed under contract—as self-employed individuals or independent contractors working on the client's premises.

It is usually not by design that these assignments last so long. Frequently the assignment starts as a relatively short-term one, but new contracts come in and the consultants are asked to remain. This can continue indefinitely, the client always acting on the reasonable assumption that the need is temporary. (The word *temporary* thus becomes a flexible term.)

The practice of bringing in whole staffs of specialists, whether called consultants, contract labor, professional temporaries, on-site contractors, or contract labor, has become widespread in many sectors—major government contracts, commercial or nongovernment industry, and the government itself. Many federal institutions and facilities are staffed and operated by such personnel, especially by agencies doing technical work—NASA, EPA, and DOD, for example—but not exclusively so. The Air Force contracted with private industry to manage and operate a warehouse where it stores technical documents. The Postal Service Training and Development Institute contracted with a private firm to administer its correspondence courses in Norman, Oklahoma. The General Services Administration hired a private firm to run a chain of stores selling personal computers to government buyers. The NASA Scientific and Technical Information Facility in Maryland is staffed and run by a contractor. There are many government owned, contractor operated (GOCO) contracts, where it is more expedient or efficient to contract out management and operation of a government facility.

Clients who hire consulting specialists as contract professionals have the common problem of needing a temporary force of specialists, usually to staff a special project. But some clients have more classical problems; problems that are solved by a staff of specialists—consultants. A computer division of Sperry Corporation had such a problem, having built a custom-designed computer for the U.S. Navy. The Navy rejected the user manuals and demanded an acceptable set of manuals. The company contracted for a crew of technical publications specialists to assist their publications staff in making the manuals acceptable to the customer.

The number of computer consultants is still growing, along with the number of computer owners and computer technologies. When IBM entered the desktop-computer market, its IBM PC quickly became a dominant design influence, and the entire industry began a rapid conversion to the production of IBM lookalikes, advertised loudly as "IBM compatible," or "IBM clones." But IBM and the rest of the industry went from the original PC to ever-faster and more sophisticated systems so rapidly that the original PC became a Stone Age computer almost overnight. The universe of possible configurations into systems is so great that even experts can't keep up with all of it, but must choose an area in which to specialize.

Sometimes the client has a problem so highly specialized that solving it requires finding the right consultant. One of my clients had need of a specialist in Tempest and EMP-hardening technology, areas concerned with data security and system survival under nuclear attack. There are many engineering people who know a great deal about these technologies, but this case required precise compliance with highly detailed and sophisticated military technical specifications. Esoteric although this subject is, there is enough demand to keep an expert in the subject quite busy advising electronic companies, even the largest ones, about this. They managed to find one such expert who turned in an excellent performance, but there are probably not a half dozen others quite as knowledgeable about this specialized lore.

A few years ago NASA commissioned a venerable Japanese scientist to write a definitive work on celestial mechanics because he was considered to be the world's leading authority in the subject, and he was so well along in years that NASA feared the loss of his great knowledge if he did not soon record it.

There are many consulting specialties that are not in common supply. My own specialty is one of these. I write, lecture, and consult on marketing generally, but especially on government marketing. Clients call on me often to help them write proposals, the key to government contracts. There are not a great many consultants with an impressive track record of writing winning proposals—good proposal writers must be sought out—but the skill is not so highly specialized that the talented proposal writer is a rare and much sought-after expert. But everything changes. Once there was only a relative handful of proposal consultants. But that is changing rapidly as a result of high-tech developments and the Internet, which have led to an increase in the number of proposal consultants.

During the 1930s, there were consultants known as "efficiency experts." They claimed an ability to raise operating efficiency and reduce costs in companies. Businesspeople succumbed to the lure of relieving some of the economic pressure of those hard times, so more than a few companies brought teams of efficiency experts aboard to work their magic.

How good were they? It's hard to say because they ran into a buzz saw of opposition from employees and labor unions, many of the latter struggling then to establish and justify their very existence. They understandably saw efficiency experts as the enemy determined to eliminate jobs. (That has not changed a great deal!) Efficiency experts vanished into history or, more accurately, evolved into *industrial engineers* and *methods engineers.*

THE CONSULTANT ORGANIZATION

There are at least two distinct types of consulting organizations, although there are the inevitable hybrids. One is the supplier of technical/professional temporaries. The other is the consulting organization that undertakes a project, generally under a contract, with a defined end-product or service to be delivered, and with work done most often on the consulting organization's own site, but if necessary on the client's site or on both sites.

The Job Shop or Supplier of Temporaries

Typically, the job shop must submit a bid for each contract to supply on-site consultants. In most cases, the job shop offers resumes of those who are their potential employees, to be employed by the job shop only as long as the job shop has a client to send them to and bill for their services. Employment by a job shop is a technicality and coincides exactly with assignment to a client.

Normally, clients do not simply order a number of anonymous warm bodies, but review resumes of available individuals and often interview the candidates as well.

Typically, the job shop quotes consultants by classes, asking the same rate for each person in a given class, although not necessarily paying each person in a given class the same rate. (Beginners in this kind of work almost always sign up too cheaply, but they soon learn what to demand.) Fringe benefits are scant, if they exist, consisting of a few paid days off and perhaps a group hospitalization plan. And the employee often qualifies for paid days off only after employment for six months or a year, which is far from certain in that work. (Most "job shoppers" change employers frequently, as contracts end and new opportunities arise.)

This arrangement permits the job shops to operate at minimal overhead, an absolute necessity for survival in that field. Typical overhead rates are about 35 to 40 percent, which must cover insurance, taxes, miscellaneous costs, and profit. However, when the job shop is fortunate enough to hire on some well-qualified beginners, they may earn considerably more than their usual profit on those individuals.

There are many hardy individuals who savor the frequent changes of jobs and locales, the financial benefits of job shopping, and the many vacations they are able to take between assignments so they make a career of such work, earning at least half again as much as they would on salary, and in many cases considerably more than that. There are also some individuals who choose that mode of working because they are unable to obtain jobs on the regular payroll of a company, either because they are too old or can't pass a medical examination. Job shopping is also a boon for people who are retired but still active, alert, capable of a full day's work every day, and eager to have a second career.

Although there are many hardy perennials in the field, there are a great many who turn to that mode of working for a short while, attracted by the money or unable temporarily to find a job. Many tire of the uncertainty and the constant moving about necessary to work steadily in that field. Seasoned by the experience of a few assignments, they move on to work they find more satisfactory as employees or as independent contractors. It is not at all uncommon for job shoppers to be offered permanent employment by clients. All of this results in a steady turnover in the field, making it relatively easy to break into it as a training ground, or a starting point in a career.

W2 CONSULTANTS VERSUS 1099 CONSULTANTS

The distinction between the individual on an agency's payroll but assigned to work for the agency's client and the individual contracting directly with a client or with a prime contractor is drawn by identifying the first one as a W2 consultant, and the second one as a 1099 consultant. The W2 is the IRS form kept by the employer and furnished to the employee at the end of the year as an accounting of relevant taxes (withholding and FICA) paid to IRS. The 1099 is a form the client must furnish to a contractor showing the money paid during the year to that contractor.

THE CONSULTANT COMPANY

Many people do not consider job shops to be true consulting organizations nor contract professionals to be true consultants. But that is part of the difficulty in defining consulting. For example, among the many procurement categories the government employs to classify and organize its purchasing, there is **H: CONSULTANT AND EXPERT SERVICES.** One might expect that anything listed here would be consulting without question. Among the services requested here are real estate appraisals, computer software programming, technical writing, surveys, and other chores that we may not normally conceive of as consulting.

On the other hand, there are a great many services firms offering management consulting, among other services, because that term appears to encompass and include virtually any kind of service a business or any other kind of organization might need.

Prominent among these are the major accounting firms. Accounting firms apparently find it expedient—perhaps easier than others do—to make the transition to management consulting and conduct major operations under that business umbrella.

It is not only accountants who find that a useful transition. Engineering firms, such as Booz Allen and Hamilton, have also migrated into management consulting, as have firms in training development, public relations, and other specialized businesses. Nor is it only established companies who make such transitions. Individuals launch their independent consulting practices from a base of experience in some given industry because the potential for practicing as a counselor or consultant in any of today's many specialized fields is almost unlimited. Although such practitioners do not list themselves under a main heading of "consulting" as their basic category, they make it clear that they offer consulting services, whatever their listing. (See the list offered later in this chapter.)

HYBRIDS

There are two basic types of consulting, which may be at the extremes, *classic consulting*, recognized even by the purists, and a second type, which qualifies as consulting only dubiously. But the world is not black and white, and a great many consultants and consulting firms fall between these extremes having at least some characteristics of each.

There is a distinct difference between supplying technical/professional temporaries and carrying out projects on the client's premises. In providing technical/professional temporaries, the provider is selling hours of professional effort, normally at a per-hour rate. The supplier is obligated only to supply qualified personnel, as agreed to and contracted for, and does not incur responsibility for success of the project. It is up to the client to make best use of this labor—to manage the effort and the people. It is the client who is responsible for the result and who must pay for every hour worked by the temporaries, regardless of result, just as with internal, direct employees. On the other hand, the client may summarily terminate the services of the supplying firm or of any individual supplied. In contracting to carry out a project, however, regardless of where it is to be done, the contractor must assume responsibility for the end-result, which means also for the management of the staff, regardless of where they do their work. It's a critical difference.

Some firms who specialize in supplying professional temporaries also have in-house capabilities for staffing, managing, and carrying out projects on their own premises. But many of the firms whose main enterprise is handling projects in-house are equally willing to carry out projects on the client's premises or to supply professional temporaries, so that distinctions between the two tend to disappear.

THE CONSULTANT AS A SELF-EMPLOYED, INDEPENDENT

The individual independent consultant—the independent contractor—must be aware of the various organizations available, the markets for services, and the distinctions in obligations. As a temporary, you are responsible for best efforts, as directed. As an independent contractor, no matter where you work, you must be project-oriented and manage your project.

Whether you work mostly on clients' premises or in your own office depends on the kind of service you provide, the nature of your clients and their needs, and your own choices. If you counsel individuals in personal matters, it is likely that you will have to arrange to meet them in your own offices for at least two reasons: One is that in that situation fees are generally by the hour, usually running to only an hour or two per consultation and by appointment. That means that you must see several clients a day, making it impractical to call on clients. Another is that it is usually necessary to have a controlled environment—privacy and quiet, for example—something often difficult to achieve in a client's space. And in at least some cases, you will need direct access to certain resources on your premises, such as a computer, a library, or files.

On the other hand, if you serve organizations and the nature of your work is such that most of your assignments last at least several days and are billed by the day, you may work largely and perhaps entirely on the clients' premises.

However, consulting is a custom service and therefore must be tailored to each assignment. Even when dealing with large organizations, clients may visit you and work with you on your premises. In fact, except for presenting seminars, it is rarely that I do not carry out at least part of my consulting projects in my own office.

This does not necessarily mean that you must rent offices in a downtown location or in an office building. Although I did just that for some years, I subsequently discovered that even major companies who were my clients were not concerned to find that my offices were in my home, and they were entirely willing to call on me and work with me there. (In fact, many appreciated the wisdom of minimizing overhead costs by working from an office at home.)

Overhead reduction and other benefits of working from an office at home are obvious. However, you must decide for yourself whether it is a desirable alternative for you—whether you have suitable facilities for an office at home, whether it is appropriate to your practice, and whether there are local ordinances that you must consider.

FIELDS AND SERVICES SUITABLE FOR CONSULTING

Anyone who enters into independent consulting gets an education: My own early experience in presenting seminars reflected the common problem of underestimating the value of what we offer.

The "Graduate" Course Seminar

We all have a tendency to assume that what we ourselves know well is common knowledge. The first time I conducted a seminar on writing proposals for government contracts, I assumed that it would be a waste of time to teach the rudiments and such coverage would not attract registrants. I thus planned to focus my presentation on the grand strategies that distinguish the great proposals and brush hurriedly by the basics that I assumed were common knowledge to everyone with an interest in proposals and marketing to the government. I even stipulated in my advertising that I offered a "graduate" course, not at all suitable for beginners in proposal writing.

To my surprise, a generous portion of the 54 attendees who registered for that first session proved to be beginners, lured by my promises to reveal a number of inside tips, techniques, and strategies I had learned or developed over the years. (In fact, the cautionary note that it was not for beginners proved to be more an attraction than anything else, and undoubtedly was at least partially responsible for the extraordinary results I got from the uncertain groping of my first seminar venture.) But there were also a few experienced people, including two senior executives who were in the process of forming a new division of their large corporation. They had come to the seminar to see if they could pick up a few useful ideas.

Until I conducted that session, I had doubts that I could reveal enough little-known information to justify the cost and the full day's time spent by each attendee. (I seriously underpriced that first seminar because of this fear.) I was amazed to discover that even senior, experienced people were unaware of many basic facts that I thought to be quite fundamental and even obvious about proposal writing, facts that I would have expected senior executives to know as well as I knew them. (Later, I had the satisfaction of having a senior executive of one large company bring groups from his staff to two successive sessions of my presentation, remarking that he found just one of the ideas I imparted to be worth the entire day's cost in dollars and time.)

Let the Client Choose the Services

We make the mistake too often of trying to decide for ourselves what our clients need and want, when we should be "asking" the clients. That is, we should be experimenting by offering services and concentrating on listening and observing client reactions, to discover what works best in satisfying them.

I was surprised by the reaction to my first seminar's coverage of cost estimating—those cost analyses and presentations required in most proposals. I had originally planned to do little more than mention these briefly. To my amazement, that portion of my presentation proved to be one of the greatest "hits." Even senior people, I found, tend to be somewhat confused and uncertain about *direct* and *indirect* costs, *overhead, other direct,* and many other basic cost elements and concepts, let alone the more esoteric jargon and concepts such as *G&A* and *expense pools.* I had originally thought that even if the attendees did know something of the subject, they would be intensely bored by it.

This experience has been repeated in almost every seminar I have conducted, and I am always surprised by it. Aside from my difficult-to-shed feeling that accounting is a boring subject to most people, I am always surprised that experienced proposal writers have so little understanding of and interest in what costs are, how they are generated, how they proliferate, how they are classified, what they really mean, and how they must be analyzed and presented. Many years ago when I first became involved in proposal writing, I was not content to surrender the accounting portion of the proposal effort to accountants. I decided that costs were too serious a matter to be left to the accountants! I would work out the costs and let the accountants review them. I insisted that I would not submit (and be responsible for the success of) a proposal until and unless I personally approved of everything in the proposal.

It's a common error to assume that our peers know exactly what we know. Not so: You can probably sell your services to your technical/professional peers too, once you learn in what areas they most need help or what special knowledge or skills you have in your field that is helpful but not widely known or available in your profession.

Following is a list of just a few of the many fields/areas in which consulting services are offered. Even these are mostly generalized items, with various specializations in each. Study this list. You may find yourself qualified to consult in more than one field!

Even these descriptors are often too general. One security consultant, for example, may be a specialist in security devices—locks, alarms, barriers, safes, surveillance equipment, and other such items, while another is a specialist in guard forces, patrolling, background checking, and other security measures based on direct human surveillance, and still another in computer communications security. Most categories have subcategories. Career and vocational counselors, for example, may easily specialize in at least a half-dozen areas. There are many kinds of engineers—civil, construction, mechanical, electrical, electronic, stress, and industrial, and these are all subdivided into many narrower specialties. Designers likewise fit into all kinds of categories—package designers, lighting designers, presentation designers—as do most of the specialists listed here. In fact it is a rare field today that will not support a well-experienced specialist as a consultant in that field:

Accounting	Computer advisory services
Administration	Convention, conference, meeting planning/arrangement
Advertising	
Agriculture/farming	Data processing
Arbitration	Design
Audiovisual presentations	Drug and alcohol abuse
Auditing	Editorial services
Automation	Educational counselors
Aviation	Engineering, general
Business	Executive search
Business writing	Financial management
Career and vocational counseling	Food preparation
Communications	Gardening
Club management	Grantsmanship

Hotel management

Human resources

Industrial engineering

Industrial methods

Insurance

Labor relations

Lighting, interior/exterior

Management

Marketing

Municipal services

Organizational development

Payroll management

Personal security

Public relations

Publishing

Recreation program counselors

Restaurant management

Safety

Sales promotion

Strategic planning

Taxes

Training

Transportation

Weddings and social affairs

Word processing services

Writing services

Seizing Opportunity:
Capitalizing on Beginnings

A wise man will make more opportunity than he finds.
—Francis Bacon

Opportunities to become an independent consultant grow steadily in this technological and complex society. Almost anyone with specialized knowledge and ability can turn those skills into a consulting specialty. Here are a few examples:

- A former bookstore manager, Hubert Bermont, built a successful consulting practice as a specialist in book publishing, then went on to build The Consultant's Library, a publishing venture specializing in books for consultants. Today, he is the Executive Director of the American Consultants League, an association for independent consultants, and serves also as a senior member of The Consultants Institute, which offers consultant certification via a correspondence course.

- Author and publishing consultant Marilyn Ross of Buena Vista, Colorado, also conducts seminars and sells books by mail (Maverick Mail Order Bookstore). Marilyn started in such a remote part of Colorado that she was unable to get a telephone installed unless she was willing to pay about $25,000 to have a line run. She resorted to a radiotelephone, but can now be reached on the regular Bell system.

- Dottie Walters, well-known public speaker, writer, publisher, and public speaking consultant, is an outstanding example of personal versatility and diversified services. She stumbled into public speaking and consulting, as many do, overcoming obstacles that would have defeated anyone less determined and persevering. When she is not traveling the world on speaking tours, she is producing her bimonthly speakers publication, *Sharing Ideas,* writing and publishing, conducting seminars, and serving as an executive, board member, and advisor to national associations, one of which she founded.

■ Many individuals who started resume-writing services, have gone on to develop their resume writing into counseling and guidance as career consultants. They guide clients in organizing and presenting their qualifications, with related counseling.

The locksmith can become a security consultant, the accountant a tax consultant, and the beautician a makeup consultant. The principles are the same for all. What requires special skill or knowledge can be a consulting specialty. How you practice your consulting is highly individual. You must decide just how specialized to be, what services to provide, and how to provide them.

YOUR CONSULTING SPECIALTY VERSUS YOUR MARKETING NEEDS

There is a relationship between the degree of your specialization and your marketing requirements: The degree of specialization affects your appeal to prospective clients: In their eyes, you must be a specialist to qualify as a consultant. It is also a factor in how many competitors you have, and determines the size of your market: the number of people there are with problems and needs for which your services are appropriate. Choosing the right degree and kind of specialization represents the classical tradeoff, trying to find the right compromise.

It isn't entirely arbitrary. The kinds of clients and types of projects available influence your decisions. A resume writer in the Washington, DC, area specializes in resumes for law school students and law school graduates because there are many law students here and at least one prestigious law school. Were her resume service located where her clientele would not include many law school students and graduates, she would address another market.

Versatility Is the Answer for Some

Some individuals who have broad backgrounds of experience and are highly versatile have found an answer to the dilemma of finding the right specialty and services: They are able to change their specialties, chameleon-like, according to the market opportunities of the moment.

This is common among contract professionals. The typical methods for finding assignments and qualifying for acceptance make this viable. It requires the individual to have more than one resume or the ability to create the right resume spontaneously for each opportunity. Some multitalented individuals have a dozen resumes, none of which give false testimony, but each of which focuses on a different kind of experience and capability. One individual I knew, for example, was an electrical/electronic engineer who could double rather easily as a technical writer, draftsman, or designer, among other specialties for which he had resumes.

Client demands help to inspire this practice of the contract professional to have many resumes because many clients demand extremes of specialization.

Clients seeking technical writers, for example, have required that applicants be familiar with some given specification or specific kind of equipment. In fact, competent writers usually have no problem working to many specifications and with many kinds of equipment within the general technical field.

On the other hand, being a chameleon as a consultant may present an ethical problem for some. Is it honest to be different kinds of a specialist on different occasions? Is that versatility or is it opportunism? That is something you must decide for yourself.

It Isn't Always a Conscious Decision

Few people set out to become consultants; most enter the practice by chance. In some cases, the transition into consulting is so gradual that the individual hardly realizes that he or she is becoming a consultant. Often, there never is a specific decision to become a consultant; circumstances force the decision on the individual, perhaps even unconsciously, and propel him or her into the consulting profession almost before he or she realizes it.

My own case is an example. I was a freelance writer for government agencies and other clients after a career in high-tech companies where I had served in numerous capacities, from engineer and technical writer to marketing director and general manager. Friends, knowing of my success in winning government contracts, often asked my advice and sometimes even asked for assistance in writing proposals and other aspects of pursuing government contracts. I was so busy with my own work that eventually I was forced to decline. To my surprise, most requesters immediately offered to pay me for my time to consult with them as an expert! They wanted my help and wanted it badly enough to pay for it. I was thus launched into a new profession, almost involuntarily. Over time, the requests of clients dictated to me the kinds of services I offered, including seminars.

Many consultants are created by major developments. Technological revolutions of recent decades created many consultants in engineering and scientific fields. Lyndon B. Johnson's administration, with its War on Poverty and related programs, inspired many sociologists, psychologists, economists, educators, and others in social sciences and humanities to become consultants in education, housing, and other related fields. Programs launched to further the cause of civil rights and reduce racism inspired many other new consulting specialties, and the new communications media—TV and satellites—inspired the rise of a great many political consultants and image consultants. These and other programs have made consulting a growth industry.

WHAT DOES IT TAKE TO BE A CONSULTANT?

I am often approached by beginning or aspiring consultants seeking advice. Many of the questions are ingenuous, such as what do I need to be a consultant? How do I get started? How do I get clients?

These questions remind me of the joke about buying a yacht: If you have to ask the price, you can't afford it. There are no simple answers to any of these and similar questions. The answers that work for Smith are not the ones that work for Jones. Variables are involved, to about the same extent and nature as they are in determining the kind of specialization and services you ought to offer. I can't tell you what these ought to be for you: Only you can do that. To answer these questions, you need to make some lists:

■ What are your general and special skills?

■ What kinds of relevant markets (people and organizations) can you somehow reach?

■ What are their needs, general and specific?

■ What can you do to satisfy these needs?

These are, for the most part, dependent variables, not independent ones, but when they are identified and matched up, they define your consulting service, at least the beginning one. In time and with experience, you will modify it to satisfy the conditions you discover.

THE SEVERAL SKILLS OF A CONSULTANT

We have addressed only the identification of the basic skills and services you will offer your clients. However, as a consultant you need more than one set of skills. You need that set of skills that relates to your professional field—remember that consulting is not a profession itself, but is a way of practicing a profession. You also need the skills that any consultant normally needs—listening, analyzing, synthesizing, presenting—and those are as necessary to the client-relations side of consulting as they are to the technical side. And, if you are an independent consultant, that type we are addressing in these pages, you need a third and fourth set of skills, those skills relevant to (1) marketing your services and (2) administering your practice successfully.

I will not address specific professional skills. I assume here that you are proficient in your own professional field and need no help from me, nor would I be qualified to help you in your own profession. It is in the other three sets of skills, and especially in marketing, that I offer help in becoming a successful consultant.

Consulting Skills

As a consultant, you must have or develop skills and abilities that are necessary to consulting generally and to independent consulting especially, regardless of those professional skills you also require. You must, for example, be a good listener, a good analyst, and a good designer—able to analyze symptoms, understand and identify the problem, and synthesize solutions or approaches to solutions. But consulting also requires abilities to make effective presentations, in person, one on one, from a dais, and in writing reports and articles. Independent consulting also requires an ability to interface with a client, build an image of competence and authority, to win the client's respect, and to establish a relationship of mutual respect and, if possible, amiability.

All of these skills are necessary for success as an independent consultant. I have divided these sets of skills and functions into groups for discussion; in practice they are not so easily separated. They are intertwined and even interdependent. Some skills necessary to conducting a satisfactory consulting assignment are the same skills that help you market and administer successfully.

Management and Administration of the Independent Consultancy

Management and administration of your practice as an independent consultant are probably the least important of the four sets of skills and functions. They are not unimportant, but other skills, especially marketing, are even more critical. The reasoning is simple enough: It is a rare venture that fails when it is making enough sales at adequate prices. Profitable ventures can and do usually survive all other problems, even problems of poor management and poor administration. The reverse, however, is not true: No amount of highly able management and administration can save a venture that is not making enough sales to cover costs and produce a profit.

Nothing is black and white, and while it is useful in delivering explanations to segregate the functions and skills into separate classes, they overlap each other so much that it is difficult to know where (and whether) they are distinct and separate from each other. And if marketing is the most important set of skills for success—even for mere survival—as I have maintained consistently, it is also the olio of all the skills: for all must be brought into play in building and maintaining a successful consulting practice. The following example drawn from my personal experience illustrates this.

One of my valued clients is a conglomerate, headquartered in New York City and comprising 20 or more companies. (The number changes, as the corporation acquires attractive companies and divests unprofitable ones.) They had done some business with the government, rather casually, but never actively pursued government business. One day they decided to look into the prospect of chasing government contracts, and that led them to send two people to a seminar I offered in marketing to the government.

As a result, I was invited to have lunch with the executive appointed by the corporation to head up their new government-marketing division to discuss what I might do for them. As an immediate result of that luncheon meeting and my own aggressive follow-up, several things happened:

1. I was retained to help prepare a capability brochure for the corporation. (In fact, they provided a draft, which I was to critique and offer my own contributions.)

2. I wrote a proposal for one of the companies.

3. I delivered a custom, in-house seminar for a group made up of marketing people from a number of the companies.

4. I continued to help several of the companies prepare proposals.

5. I was called on periodically for miscellaneous chores.

All of this was because I was a good listener and analyst (consciously and deliberately because intent listening does not come to me naturally): I listened carefully to the client's views, analyzed his real and felt needs, and responded with offers I thought were relevant and would appear so to the client. It is critically important that you bear the client's orientation in mind, including any biases the client has, in making those recommendations. But compare that not atypical case with the following marketing rationale to which I find many subscribe.

Marketing Skills

Initially, the marketing challenge appears to be the simple one of winning clients for consulting assignments. Often, the beginning consultant is misled by the misfortune of gaining a first client or even several clients too easily. That is a misfortune because it misleads the new consultant, who will soon enough learn how much marketing effort is normally required to keep a practice growing.

Many beginning consultants believe that the main function of consulting is advising clients, whereas the truth is that in most consulting fields today, the client requires help in *doing* even more than he or she requires counseling help. That false premise also hinders effective marketing, which must promise prospective clients action and results at least as much as (and probably more than) advice and guidance.

Prospects often have a quite different view than the consultant does of what they need. They know they need help, but many approach consulting with some skepticism and apprehension. They are reluctant to agree to an hourly or daily rate on an open-ended arrangement, but want to know the total cost of the services offered. And even if you occasionally win a client who wants and needs only advice and guidance, you may find it more difficult to satisfy this client than it is to satisfy one who simply wants a job done and doesn't care about why and how, but only about results.

Take the case I cited of that major corporate client who started by retaining me to help write their capability brochure. They knew next to nothing of what a capability brochure should normally contain, and their draft, based on their corporate annual report, was all wrong for the purpose. Yet, to persuade them to change it to what it ought to be meant criticizing and condemning what they had done—not easy to do diplomatically. The conflict is immediately between treating the client with great care and doing your work honestly and ethically.

It calls for great tact to suggest and explain the need for drastic changes without condemning what has been already done.

Note, too, the variety of services I provided. Although perhaps the most valuable service I can render in many cases is actual proposal writing, I often find it necessary to spend a great deal of time selling the client on what I propose to do in the proposal. My typical client is a capable, and successful executive, scientist, or engineer, with ideas of his or her own, and requires me to be honest in my views, but also prepared to explain and justify my recommendations, especially when they clash with the client's ideas, as they often do.

In this case, had I stubbornly insisted that my consulting service was restricted to advising clients on government marketing, I would probably have gotten only about 20 percent of the volume of work with which I was blessed. Even if I had restricted my services to advising on and/or writing and leading proposal efforts, I would have closed the door on much of the work, and perhaps on all of it. The client might have decided to seek a consultant more amenable to meeting all of his needs. This brings up, once again, a marketing problem of a special kind: How specialized should you be?

Versatility versus Specialization

Your main specialty as a consultant may be some special knowledge, a special skill, or some combination of these. Most fields grow more diverse over time. In my own lifetime, I have seen radio, a hobby, become electronics, a serious field, and grow into computer and many other serious and highly respected engineering technologies and disciplines. No doubt this will continue and other new specialties will evolve, some within larger, established disciplines, others based on new departures and new fields.

THE AVENUES OF SPECIALIZATION

The degree to which consultants specialize varies widely. In my own case, I tend to generalize within the field of proposal consultation and writing, but I am the exception; most proposal consultants specialize in given subject fields—engineering and technical (NASA and military/defense projects, especially), social science projects, training development, health programs, or other specialized areas, based primarily on the consultant's prior career experience. I work almost invariably on proposals submitted in pursuit of contracts, whereas there are consultants who serve clients pursuing grants, which also usually require proposals.

As in all things, there are trade-offs—advantages and disadvantages—in versatility as there are in a high degree of specialization. There are no really good guidelines here: You must be guided in making your choices by your personal judgment, your objectives, your standards, your opportunities, and—perhaps most of all—by the lessons of your experience, which is really the final arbiter.

Many Consulting Specialties Evolve

Early decisions should be regarded as premises, to be tried and tested. What this means for most independent consultants is trial and error. You start at some position, and you make adjustments as your experience reveals the need for adjustments, until you achieve the point at which you are satisfied with the results. This means keeping an open mind. Set out at the beginning with the knowledge that your first premises are almost certain to be considerably less than perfect, and be prepared to learn and adapt.

For example, after I had begun to offer seminars on an open registration basis—available to anyone who wanted to come—I began to build a reputation as something of a specialist in this field and found myself drawing inquiries from large corporations who were interested in having me deliver a custom, in-house training seminar in proposal writing. Each time I received such an inquiry, I cheerfully calculated the costs for customizing my seminar to the individual client's needs and quoted accordingly.

The results were disappointing. I failed to win a single contract for an in-house seminar. Obviously I was doing something wrong, and my judgment was that these prospective clients were unwilling to pay the price for customizing a special seminar. I switched tactics: I began to respond to such inquiries with a proposal to deliver my standard seminar, customized for them insofar as I could do so spontaneously in my delivery, and principally through my choice of illustrative anecdotes and case histories, without extra cost.

I immediately began to win virtually all such contracts and thereafter presented many custom, in-house seminars. Moreover, whereas I began doing them at the equivalent of my daily consulting fee, I soon learned that this was a mistake and raised the cost. Interestingly enough, I soon learned an important fact: Clients did not object to the cost per se and apparently never had; they objected only to the idea of paying a special fee for customizing the seminar.

Flexibility—a Basic Requirement

It is only from experience that you learn these things. But there is another message here: No matter what your general specialty as a consultant is, be alert for opportunities to develop specialties within your consulting framework. It is not unusual for a consultant to come to practice a specialty quite different from that which he or she embraced originally. It is not unusual for any business venture to evolve into something quite different from its original nature and purpose. Many large companies today do not resemble their beginnings even remotely. Their ability and willingness to adapt to the conditions and needs they encounter often determines whether they survive or not.

A Special Case of Evolutionary Change

Change is inevitable, and is sometimes gradual and sometimes rather sudden. The ability to switch fields rapidly and frequently—having a number of different resumes on hand—was pointed out earlier as one way versatile consultants respond to targets of opportunity and maximize their prospects for assignments. Many consulting specialties are suggested by and spring out of new developments, such as equal opportunity and civil rights programs or new technologies. These conditions and circumstances do not always represent permanent change. Some programs and influences prove to be transient and fleeting. The vacuum tubes that once were the heart of electronics proved to be transient, giving way completely to solid-state electronics, and eventually to chips.

An important new situation was created by the establishment of the Postal Service as a government corporation. There were years of free-spending programs for consulting services to support the new Postal Service Training and Development Institute, and then harsh economic realities forced the sharp curtailment of the programs and especially of contracting out for services.

The effects of such changes are obvious. The consultant who has been highly specialized must move on or adapt in some other way, while those less highly specialized or diversified may well survive such catastrophes. For example the reading specialist—an educator-trainer in reading skills for the functionally illiterate—may be totally without resources in the face of an abrupt shutdown of a major government project, whereas the consultant educational-technologist—a developer of training programs generally—can probably turn to other government training programs, which abound generally.

The Basis for Specialization

A rather lengthy list of consulting specialties offered at the end of Chapter 1 tended almost entirely to classifying consultancies by general industries as fields of activity—accounting, taxes, travel, club management, and other such designations, rather than by individual occupations or skills, such as accountant, dietitian, housewares buyer, and conference arranger. A few such listings are offered here as a comparison with the earlier list to illustrate the difference:

Accountant	Contract administrator
Architect	Drug prevention specialist
Auditor	Editor
Copy writer	Fire-fighting equipment
Soils chemist	specialist
Appraiser	Grants writer
Arbitrator	Hotel manager
Automation designer	Insurance expert
Banquet planner	Merger advisor/negotiator
Career counselor	Municipal services expert

Office procedures designer   Researcher

Public relations writer   System Analyst

This focus on individual skill is quite important in resolving your own definition of what you offer to do for clients, for that inevitably becomes the chief focus of all your marketing. Even so, these latter listings are rather broad, in most cases, and could be narrowed further in their focus on individual skills you offer. A technical writer, for example, must sometimes demonstrate to a prospective client that he or she is a radar writer or computer writer, because many clients are convinced that it is necessary to be that highly specialized.

That points up another important factor: Truth is a subjective quantity, and in marketing the only "truth" that counts is the client's truth. No matter what you do, it is highly likely that the client will mentally tag and label you. I am a marketing strategist, in my own view, but some clients tend to perceive me as a proposal writer or as a lecturer on the subject, depending on their own needs and what they retain me to do for them. Moreover, most of my clients associate me with government marketing only. That is understandable, considering my extensive experience in that field, but the real reason for the perception is that most of my clients do not perceive a need for help in marketing commercially. Government marketing, however, is conceived as something of a mysterious and complicated project, in which they need help.

Here is another factor: Many prospects, especially those in marketing and sales, would resist retaining me to help them in marketing commercially because they would see that as an intrusion and admission of weakness in their own marketing skills. But government marketing is different, and it is not a blow to their egos to admit to a need for help in this special and difficult field. So in the end it does serve my own best interests to encourage that view of my special abilities.

You are always the victim—and occasionally the beneficiary—of the client's own biases. One problem is that clients pigeonhole you according to their needs, regardless of how you define your skills and specialties. But one problem I (and other writers) encounter when doing any kind of writing for engineers or other professional people and executives is the opinion many have that they can write as well as I can. Many refuse to recognize writing as a special skill or talent, and thus tend to treat the professional writer's work casually and almost with disdain. (Sometimes it seems as though everyone in the world wants to be an editor, even more than a writer, and is convinced that he or she is quite a good editor.)

One prospect was outraged at the consulting fee I asked for. "That's too much money for a hired writer," she stormed.

"But you did not retain me as a writer," I explained. "I am a specialist in developing marketing strategies for proposals to win government contracts. The writing is incidental and not what people retain me for at all."

It was futile. I was unable to make my point because my prospect was simply unwilling to accept it. She insisted that I was a writer for hire and asking too much money for my services.

Recognize that you do not always have an entirely free choice in deciding what you are and what you offer, as the *client* sees you. You must work at understanding the client's mindset and prejudices, and you may have to tailor yourself and your offerings accordingly, to win the client over.

In short, how you represent yourself and what you offer are not decisions to be made without analysis and deliberation, especially an examination of how clients tend to perceive you and what you do and—even more important—how clients prefer to view you and what you offer.

That is not as cynical as it sounds, and it is not an exhortation to mislead or deceive your clients. It is simple realism to structure your presentations to complement your prospective clients' attitudes.

Consulting as a Second Career

For many, retirement is not an ending, but a beginning, as they opt for a second career. Consulting offers a variety of opportunities for a second career.

—Herman Holtz

WHAT IS A SECOND CAREER?

Having a second career is a popular option today. Even with two incomes in a household, many couples and family heads need to supplement their retirement income. Too, many people are forced to change careers, as modern conditions and developments—mergers, acquisitions, shutdowns, downsizing—wipe out their jobs or force them into involuntary retirement. An increasing number of men and women retire at relatively early ages, while still energetic and capable of being gainfully occupied. With the end of the Cold War and increasing automation, early retirement is often encouraged as a means of cutting back workforces with as few layoffs as possible.

The American Association of Retired Persons (AARP) estimated that nearly 25 percent of all retired persons work full- or part-time. They noted also that about one-third of their own members would prefer to be working, for emotional satisfaction—feeling useful again—even if they have no great need or desire for added income. Kathryn and Ross Petras, writing in their *The Only Retirement Guide You'll Ever Need* (Poseidon Press, 1991), reported the findings of a retirement counseling firm, Drake Beam Morin, Inc., that of a group of slightly over 4,000 retired people they counseled, 49 percent became consultants or worked part-time, with 12 percent venturing into independent enterprises, and only 25 percent retiring from all work. So you are certainly in good and abundant company if you choose to have a second career.

Not everyone wants to be idle in retirement, entirely aside from the financial considerations. Many people who retire from initial careers today simply don't want to sit and rock, but want to do things that challenge them and make them feel useful and productive. In sum, that means that in today's complex society a second career can mean many things, including:

- A spare-time activity you pursue for added income or amusement.

- A career change you voluntarily undertake for any of many possible reasons.

- A new and different kind of career experience you choose after retiring from an earlier career.

Consulting lends itself to all of these applications. Not all career alternatives are suitable for part-time work, but many are, so there are many spare-time workers and entrepreneurs.

Modern conditions are a factor, with many people forced to change careers. Automation has ended many jobs and careers. The migration of heavy industries to other countries—the Orient and the Third World—has contributed to the trend. Changing business and industrial conditions in general have compelled many people to go in search of new careers.

The youthfulness of retirees is significant: The average age of retired people has declined sharply in recent decades. Where once 65 was considered to be the retirement age, many people today retire as early as age 50 or 55. That is relatively young in a society where life expectancy has increased considerably, and that alone is one reason more and more people retiring from long-term jobs choose to embark on new careers. Some relish the challenge of starting a new career, and they do so with great enthusiasm. Others choose to launch second careers because their retirement income is not great enough to satisfy their needs. There are also many published stories of people who contemplated retirement with great glee, envisioning a life of doing only what was enjoyable, but finding themselves bored beyond endurance after a few months and driven to find something to do as a career undertaking.

The number of retirees has been increasing steadily, with former military careerists forming a large percentage of today's retirees. The situation on the private side of the economy is not greatly different, since the peak of the downsizing trend seems to have passed. Still, the number of youthful retirees seems to be rising.

There is actually something of a crossover or hybrid situation. Some individuals embark on a spare-time second career while still working at a job, anticipating the time when they will retire, preparing for a smooth and easy changeover to a new career after retiring from a primary career. Some who pursued a spare-time career for added income or as something of a hobby choose to continue that combination hobby-career on a full-time basis after retiring or being forced to change careers.

More than a few observers have recommended consulting as an attractive second career. *Sylvia Porter's Planning Your Retirement* (Prentice Hall, 1991), for example, is one of many sources that suggest this choice for those who wish to continue working after retirement. Kathryn and Ross Petras, in their book, already cited, also note some advantages in this choice, advantages that appear rather obvious and have been cited by many writers on the subject: In a great many cases, the new independent consultant's first and most important client is the very organization from which he or she has just retired. That is a quite common condition, since it offers advantages and benefits to both parties, with an inesacpable logic: Who is better qualified to understand and serve the interests of an organization than the individual who spent 25 or more years there and knows the organization thoroughly? Thus, a great many newly established independent consultants find their former employers highly receptive to the proposition of retaining them as consultants.

Aside from that, in a great many cases, especially where the individual has completed a long career in specialized work or a senior position, the individuals have excellent credentials for a consulting career, including the following:

- Many years of experience and highly specialized knowledge in relevant fields.
- Mature judgment supplementing that special experience.
- Wide knowledge of the common needs and problems in the industry or business.
- Knowledge of related industries, businesses, and professions.
- Acquaintanceship with many other senior professionals and executives in related industries, businesses, and professions, providing valuable contacts.
- Versatility in many relevant skills, highly developed and honed.
- Better listening skills, partly due to the greater patience that many of us develop with advancing maturity, but also due to greater understanding of the problems, needs, and various situations common in the industry.

COMPANIES FOR SENIORS

The availability of second careerists is noted: There are a number of national, multi-office labor contractors who have designated certain of their offices to specialize in the placement of retirees and other older workers—senior citizens.

ALMOST ANY SKILL/KNOWLEDGE/EXPERIENCE CAN BE THE BASIS

Consulting is essentially a service, even when products are involved. It is giving advice and assistance to clients in doing things at which you are skilled and knowledgeable and in which the client wants your help for whatever reason. Even if you sell a product or line of products, service is still a significant factor, for it is what your product or products *do* for the client that is important to him or her. It doesn't matter if it is a highly technical matter or a more mundane one; the principle is the same. It also does not matter if one calls it consulting or by some other name—freelancing or contracting. Thus, one can become a consultant specializing in any service or set of services, with or without products, for which there is demand—for which clients, individuals, and organizations, feel a need for help. That sense of need may be based on any number of possible causes: the client lacks or feels a lack of adequate knowledge or skill, lacks the time or manpower to do the job, has a need to feel the security of having a professional expert/specialist handling the job, or simply treasures the convenience of having a professional do it. (Never underestimate the power of these latter two considerations as powerful motivators in selling.)

Many consultants are unusually skilled and often unusually well-credentialed in their fields, with several advanced academic degrees and impressively high former positions in government or business. These can be the principal bases for consulting practices, but these kinds of credentials are not a requirement. As you read earlier, the very term *consulting* has many diverse meanings. It is counseling, advising, instructing, and doing on a direct, face-to-face basis, but it is also profitable as the basis for creating useful products and corollary services, such as newsletters, monographs, audiotapes, videotapes, manuals, seminars, lectures, and training courses. In today's complicated world, the demand for advice, help, and convenience is so great that even the most mundane of skills can be put to work as the basis for a successful independent consulting practice, if you structure your service and marketing properly. Individuals and organizations will retain independent consultants for even relatively simple functions for a variety of reasons. Being a retiree may confer on you a special benefit not readily available to many other independent consultants.

If you are retired from a long career in some field, you have a certain advantage in that you are a voice of authority. Your years of service are credentials. You don't have the problem of so many young people entering the consulting profession of lacking a lengthy record of accomplishment. Even if you cannot point to a great deal of specific experience doing whatever it is that you now propose to do, you will command respect for your years regardless of the service you now offer.

One of the frailties from which many of us suffer is overestimating the knowledge of others. So often we have extensive knowledge of things that we believe everyone knows. You may assume, for example, that everyone knows how to organize a formal luncheon or dinner party. You may think that it is perfectly obvious that the words "black tie invited" appearing in an invitation to a wedding are intended to indicate that the wearing of tuxedos would be entirely proper and is encouraged. You may believe that anyone with a high school education knows how to apply for a birth certificate or passport, or how to write a resume or postgraduate thesis or dissertation. You may be shocked to learn the truth, that many people do not know how to do many of the things you and I assume are common knowledge. Of course, it is even less likely that they know how to do more complex things. Many do not know how to begin to research a subject, no matter how abundant the information is. Entrepreneur Matt Lesko made a business of helping people find information by founding Washington Researchers, and then went on to form a publishing enterprise that specializes in reference data in many fields of general interest.

This need for know-how in even some simple things applies to many small business owners, as well as to individuals. A surprisingly large number of business owners do not know many of the things you or I might assume "everyone" knows. Nor is that confined to small business owners: I have encountered many executives of rather large corporations who were sorely in need of help in reading and understanding official pronouncements, preparing bids, and writing help-wanted advertising. One executive was enormously impressed with my great wisdom in counseling his marketing people to be sure that they protected their positions by quantifying whatever they were bidding, something I thought to be quite obvious and was mentioning only in passing. I have met senior executives in major corporations who could not understand clauses in contracts written in what I thought was simple English. I have known business executives who did not understand the common practice of "discounting paper" or "selling their paper" at a local bank or qualifying for a line of credit.

That is why consulting practices may be and often are based on what initiated executives consider rather mundane and simple services. It is necessary only that they be services you can perform quite capably. The following is a list of just a few examples of the many hundreds of opportunities for employing your skills, knowledge, and experience as an independent consultant, even if they are not based on unusually specialized knowledge and training. (On the other hand, do not underestimate the appeal or the value of your knowledge and skills.) Many individuals have built successful practices providing such services as the following:

- Menu planning—a service for individuals and organizations planning luncheons, award dinners, social dinner parties, or other events.
- Personal financial management—cost control, investments, long-term planning, solving financial problems.
- Automobile buyer's service—assistance in buying new or used car, getting the right price, making a mechanical check in case of used car, and related services.
- Job counseling—advice and assistance in planning the job search, writing the resume, handling the interview, and other elements necessary to success in job hunting.
- Recruiting—employees or members—advice and assistance in planning and organizing membership drives and other campaigns.
- Party planning—advice and assistance in ideas for parties, planning and organizing, arranging for pranks and/or other entertainment.
- Public speaking—counseling others in public speaking and/or writing speeches.
- Convention and meeting service for business organizations—advice and assistance in arranging for meeting places, programs, speakers, equipment, refreshments, and whatever else may be needed.

- Expert witness service (litigation consulting)—much more than taking the witness stand. Usually the expert witness is a consultant to the client but often does not appear in court.

- Bureaucratic guidance and services—advising and assisting clients in navigating the bureaucracy to get information, apply for various programs, and respond to official requirements.

- Letter writing—the day of the public scribe is not entirely ended. Many people pay gladly to get assistance in writing letters of various kinds.

- Using a computer—set the computer up, install software, design networks, and teach others how to use the programs.

- Information specialist/broker—do research for clients who lack time, patience, knowledge, or desire to do so.

- Dress for success—advise others, men and women, how to dress most effectively for various positions, and functions in the business and professional worlds.

- Marketing specialty—advise clients on advertising, writing sales materials, setting up exhibits for conventions and trade fairs, other aspects or specialties of marketing.

- Office systems organization—organize office functions, filing systems, job duties, other necessities for an efficient office operation.

- Real estate adviser—help individuals find the right house at the right price and guide them through the mortgage and closing/settlement processes.

- Scholarship counselor—help students and their parents find scholarship opportunities, loan programs, and other assistance for getting into college.

- Quality control counseling—help companies set up quality control programs, especially today's total quality control.

- Security guidance—advice on security systems, including locks, fences, alarms, guard services, and other aspects of security.

MARKETING—WINNING CLIENTS

To make any business succeed, effective marketing is necessary. Consulting is no exception, and what has been pointed out earlier about marketing applies here. If you are retired from a primary career, do take advantage of that track record you have of serving successfully and earning retirement. Study the items just listed and note those that represent your own greatest strengths. Use them as your primary sales arguments in developing brochures, sales letters, and in-person presentations. Stress not only experience, but *successful* experience. Develop a narrative of your most notable achievements that are relevant to the consulting services you offer. Make this a boilerplate reference, narrative and even tabular for some applications. (You may have to remind your former employer that it was you who developed and installed that much more efficient inventory control system, while you must also explain it to strangers.) Make sure to stress your achievements, even more than the years of experience. That is one of your most valuable assets as a consultant: They are credentials, and they are important whether you market to organizations or to individuals. Try to quantify. In my own case, the fact that I was once a manager and a director of marketing are not nearly so important nor so impressive as the fact that I wrote proposals that won over $360 million in contracts for my former employers and clients. Find the impressive numbers and cite them.

WHAT KINDS OF CLIENTS TO PURSUE

You can decide in advance what kinds of clients you want to pursue and then choose services suitable for that kind of client, but in most cases we start with a class of services and then seek out the right clients for them. Many services are suitable for both individuals and organizations, while others are more appropriate to one than to the other, or the service is usually tailored to one or the other. Although that identifies two broad classes of clients, each must be further subdivided. There are many kinds of organizations, but there are also many kinds of individuals, in terms of their interests and wants as clients.

Services for Business Organizations

The following are just a few examples of services that are most appropriate to organizations—businesses, large or small, clubs and associations, government agencies, and others: Accounting, personnel, taxes, investments, mergers and divestitures, marketing, seminar planning, publications guidance, expert witness/litigation services, and information brokering.

Many of these kinds of services have many possibilities for further specialization. Marketing, for example, may be retail, mail order, direct mail, discount, or even otherwise specialized; few marketing consultants attempt to know or do it all. Of special interest now is databased marketing, an improved method for marketing via any of those methods by increasing the sharpness of targeting prospects.

Services for Individuals

Many individuals go to specialists for help to satisfy personal needs or would be glad to get such help if they knew that it was available. Examples include letter writing, guidance through bureaucracies, buying new or used automobiles, buying new or used houses, making optimal arrangements for relocation, party planning, private dinner party catering, job-hunt counseling and assistance, cooking courses for brides and brides to be, guidance and counseling on house repairs or modernization, and many others.

Services for Both Organizations and Individuals

Many services have appeal and usefulness for both individuals and organizations—help in financial planning, social event planning for groups, writing and editing services, and computer services, for example. You can specialize in any of these, however, and you may choose to target individuals, organizations, or both as clients.

A Special Market

More and more individuals are becoming self-employed today, usually working from home, with the assistance of computers, modems, fax machines, laser printers, voice mail, and many other electronic devices. They are in many enterprises, and many need help. In fact, many seek help in choosing a field and getting started, and will pay consulting fees for expert guidance. This is a kind of hybrid, a business service and yet a personal service. Among the kinds of help they seek are these: Help in analyzing their assets and suggesting possible businesses they may turn their assets to, guidance in starting mail order businesses, selecting products, marketing products, creating brochures, finding suppliers, and other services relevant to launching a small business.

MARKETING YOUR SERVICES

If you are a recently retired worker, you may enjoy special advantages in getting a new consulting practice started. Your former employer may be your first client. You can argue the immediate advantages: You know the people in the organization and they know you. You know the organization's needs, wants, and problems. You know your way around in the organization. For these reasons, you have a great advantage in marketing, and you have the argument that you need no learning time: You are ready to start doing what has to be done without delay. You also can make a highly credible argument that it is less costly to retain you to help as a consultant than it would be to hire someone to learn the job you retired from.

You may also be familiar with other organizations and people in the field from which you have just retired. You have similar advantages vis-à-vis marketing to these other organizations, even if to a somewhat lesser degree. You know the people and can get in to see them far more easily than you can get in to see those who are strangers.

In general, if you choose to consult in the field where you have worked, you have opportunities in networking because you know many people in that field. You can and should maintain whatever memberships you maintained while active in that field, attend meetings and conventions, and remain actively in touch with old friends in the business.

For these reasons alone, you do well to stick to what you have been doing and to the industry, business, or profession in which you were employed.

Success will almost surely come easier there than in some new field. Still, you may be one of those who wants to try something entirely new and different.

PLOWING NEW FIELDS

Many people, on retiring, want to get into a new field. They are tired of doing what they have always done, and they want a change. They are ready, they believe, to tackle something new and different. Or they want to try to realize an ancient ambition they were never able to attempt before.

Many individuals have long-cherished ambitions to be consultants. They have long believed that they can help others and that it would be pleasurable to do so as an occupation. Consulting would be a new occupation, but they want also to consult in a different area than the one in which they have worked. The expert accountant, for example, may have become expert with computers, and wish to tackle computer consulting as a second career. (One consultant I met is an accountant who specializes in helping accountants get computerized.)

Breaking into a new field as a consultant is not all bad as an idea. There are advantages, as well as disadvantages. For one thing, you are likely to bring to it a fresh outlook and some new ideas, whereas there is always a tendency to keep doing things the same way when you continue on in the same field in which you have worked for many years. Too, there is a certain exhilaration in learning a new and interesting field of work. Obviously, it can't be a field in which you do not know the work at all: You can't decide to be a computer consultant if you know nothing about computers. However, you might be a consultant in editorial matters or training in the computer field, or you might apply your skills in other industries than the one in which your worked. For example, you might use your years of experience as a bank official to advise industrial companies in financial matters, counsel individuals in managing their finances, or advise clients on investments, to name just three ways in which you can put your broad experience to work. (Bear in mind that consulting is inherently usually highly specialized in the subjects it addresses and the services it provides.)

There are various other ways in which you can diversify. One is by adapting your specialized knowledge. In my own case, the bulk of my proposal writing was in response to U.S. government RFPs—Request for Proposals—and quite often for military organizations. With the decline of government procurement, I found it necessary to turn to the private sector for this work. However, I also found that my experience in writing proposals in response to RFPs worked equally well in responding to private firms who solicit bids and proposals for subcontracts, and to foreign governments who issue tenders, rather than RFPs.

Most people have more than one skill and area of expert knowledge. One man I know is an expert woodworker—he can turn out furniture of professional quality—and he has used that hobby as the basis for a second career in which he trains others in that craft and, more recently, has begun writing books on the subject. Many people are as expert in some spare-time hobby as any professional. You need not be expert across the board, either: Being expert in some aspect may be enough. Many of today's computer consultants are young people who had no formal training in computer technology, but became quite expert without the benefit of that preparation. (In fact, computer technology has long been dominated by youth.) Or you may be a collector of antiques and become expert enough to offer a service to others who need help in finding genuine antiques. Or you may have become an expert collector of art, stamps, coins, or other hobby, and be able to turn that hobby to account as a consultant.

On the other hand, you may wish to plow a new field in terms of how you turn your knowledge and experience to helping others. For example, you might want to pass on your years of experience as valuable knowledge to younger people—more in a training mode or group presentation than in a one-on-one service. There are several ways to do this (as noted in other chapters), such as by writing and lecturing.

Lecturing and Seminars

Public speaking is itself a major field in which a great many consultants diversify their talents. You can develop a seminar (or even several seminars) to impart what you know about your specialty. You have the choice then of offering it to the public at large, as described, or offering to present your seminar to interested groups under contract. That latter option has two aspects itself: There are seminar production companies who will produce your seminar and offer it to the public. They will hire you for a guaranteed minimum and percentage of the proceeds or for a flat sum to present your seminar. They will do the marketing, prepare all the materials you prescribe, and handle all the arrangements. You need only show up and deliver the presentation. But there is another way: Many organizations will retain you to present your seminar as an in-house event. I have presented my government marketing/proposal writing seminar many times to corporations, colleges, and associations, as well as to registrants drawn from the general public.

As an alternative, you can lecture at local colleges and universities. Most have extension courses of various kinds and will entertain a proposal to add a lecture course. I have found this not at all difficult to sell.

Selling Custom Seminars and Training Courses

You usually need a proposal to sell yourself as a lecturer, seminar leader, or instructor. Chapter 12 is devoted to this topic, but you may not need anything quite as formal and extensive as the proposal approaches described there. You probably will need a rather informal letter proposal, explaining your presentation, your qualifications, and a reasonably complete description, including a detailed outline of your proposed presentation or lectures.

Publications

Publications—monographs and, especially, newsletters—are another way to pass on to others what you have learned. With today's computer hardware and software resources, you can turn out a professional newsletter or monograph without being a publications expert.

In that connection—publications—there is another possibility: serving publishers as a consulting expert. Many writers offer publishers manuscripts—books and articles—on specialized subjects. The typical publisher has no internal means—in-house staff experts, that is—for checking these manuscripts for technical accuracy, but relies on outside consultants for help. You can make your name and specialties known to publishers and in time begin to win some of these assignments.

Classically, consulting contracts are project oriented. That means that you contract with a client to solve some specific problem, create a product, or otherwise to pursue a defined goal or objective. You may be paid by the hour, by the day, or by some agreed-upon flat fee for the project. (Hourly or daily rates are probably the most common basis for billing clients.) However, today a great many consultants work as temporaries, albeit in a technical, professional, or executive staff capacity. Modern business conditions arc such that they encourage this as rewarding for both the consultant and the client.

CONSULTANTS AS TEMPORARIES

It is not as well known as it ought to be, perhaps, but temporary help is a major force in the business world today. We all know about the office temp, that typist/clerk/secretary you hire for a few days to help you out of a bind in your schedules, but you may not be aware that you can hire an engineer, comptroller, lawyer, physician, or other technical/professional specialist for a few hours, a few days, a few weeks, or a few months. Few people are aware that it is possible today to hire virtually all kinds of technical and professional specialists as temporaries. Viewing this from your viewpoint, you can probably find temporary employment—as a W2 employee, that is—in whatever field you specialize, as many consultants do. It is the nature of our economy today that not only is this a desirable alternative but it is sometimes the only viable alternative. Many consultants have long accepted temporary assignments as a natural and appropriate mode of consulting, and there are those who prefer to work in this manner, for a number of reasons.

In the trade today, working as a temporary is discriminated from working as a classic consultant by referring to temporary employment as W2 employment (assignments that result in your being issued a W2 form certifying your earnings and taxes paid) versus being a 1099 consultant (referring to the 1099 form that is sent to you and the IRS in January when you work as a contractor).

Technical and Professional Temporaries

This special kind of consulting has long served the needs of government and industry and offered special opportunities to retired people who want to go on working but prefer temporary or part-time employment. In the post-World War II era, when the Cold War inspired a huge program of weapons developments, the majority of such placements was in the offices and plants of major defense contractors who needed engineers, physicists, programmers, drafters, technical writers, designers, and hordes of other technical and professional workers. The industry has matured greatly since then, and today offers opportunities to workers in a much wider variety of fields. As you will see shortly, some of the companies in the industry even cater to retirees and older workers, recognizing their increasing presence in the markets.

The Temporaries Industry

By far the majority of temporary workers are actually on the payrolls of companies who place them in clients' offices under contract. The U.S. Census Bureau reported more than 1,100 companies providing such technical and professional temporaries from 11,000 offices, representing about 6.5 million temporary workers in all categories. Recent figures from the National Association of Temporary and Staffing Services show 54.8 percent of this market is in the industrial, professional, and technical areas, 36.8 percent in office/clerical occupations, and the remainder in marketing, health care, and other occupations.

There has been a steady growth of this industry, with many old-timers, such as Volt Technical Services, a division of Volt Information Sciences, Inc., a company that dates back to 1950, when it was one of many companies specializing in placing technical-professional workers in defense plants and government offices. (Government has been a heavy user of such services.)

As employers have come to recognize the advantages of hiring temporaries in many situations—it costs them less, in many ways—the scope of this field has expanded widely, not only in terms of numbers of temporary placements and companies offering this, but also in terms of the great variety of kinds of work for which temporaries are hired. Some occupations, such as nursing, have long been by their nature well suited to temping, as have been those highly technical occupations already identified. Today, however, even top-gun executives—chief executives, comptrollers, and marketing directors, for example—are being hired as temporaries. The trade has taken to referring to these as interim executives, while the more general term is contract professionals.

Pros and Cons of Being a Contract Professional

Temping is an expedient for many, especially older workers who believe, rightly or wrongly, that it would be difficult for them to find a regular job or actually want only temporary employment. They may even consider temping with some distaste. However, temping turns out to be a pleasant experience for many, especially those who have specialized skills of some sort and no desire for the rigors of a mandatory nine-to-five job every day. Here is what a writer friend, Judith Anderson, says about temping:

> As for me, I was laid off this summer, and have discovered the joys of temping. It's unbelievable to me that everyone around me (except my sons, who have all loved temping at one time or another) thinks I should be searching for a permanent job. I think that, as long as there's temporary work to be had, and as long as I can afford insurance, it's the more pleasurable path. Certainly, these days there's not much in the way of job security in a permanent job. And, I meet the nicest people, and work at places I might not see otherwise. I get to go new places and meet new people, and even have an occasional day off. I feel totally refreshed in body and spirit. But, it takes a certain temperament to truly enjoy temping. Of course, the consulting temperament is akin to the temping temperament.

That is not an unusual reaction of those who undertake temping for the first time. The reward for many is in an interesting variety of work and frequent change of scenery—an end to the typical boredom of many jobs after they have settled into a set routine. I once accepted an assignment to help a company respond to a tender from a South American government. Before I had finished that assignment, I was asked to conduct seminars in consulting for the company's engineering staff. Ultimately, I was also asked to conduct seminars to train the staff in proposal writing. I have also worked as a technical writer in many companies located in many places, and there I enjoyed the variety of locations, but also the variety of assignments in terms of the equipment about which I wrote, including missiles, space voyages to the moon, radar and systems reminiscent of Buck Rogers and other science fiction.

FINDING ASSIGNMENTS

By far the majority of consultants and others working as temporaries are placed by the companies who specialize in doing that. However, many consultants place themselves on clients' premises as temporaries. That is, they seek out clients who will hire them under contract at some hourly rate, rather than by the project, and they function more as employees than as contractors. Both methods for winning assignments are thus open to you.

Some consultants disdain temporary assignments or accept them only reluctantly when they find it necessary. They may do so because they believe that they are compromising their principles and confessing failure as independent consultants when they accept temporary job assignments. They view that as being placed on someone's payroll as employees, even if they have placed themselves there. Many, however, embrace temping, via some broker or firm specializing in placing temporaries as a means for utilizing their full time in an earning capacity because they need not do any marketing. The firm that places them handles the marketing. Or they may favor such employment because it represents a temporary commitment, one from which it is easy to disengage.

Finding temporary assignments is relatively easy, especially if you are willing to travel and to be placed by one of the firms specializing in this work. Some of these firms do this kind of work only; others, such as employment agencies and other corporations, have a separate division that does this kind of work.

There are a great many firms who advertise in the yellow pages and in the daily newspapers. You will need a resume, of course, and basically it will be the same resume you would use if you were in pursuit of a permanent, full-time position. However, because you are a consultant, as well as a temporary, you are likely to be hired for specialized work, and those who work regularly as temps tend to tailor their resumes for the specific assignment. In fact, it is likely that the firm seeking to place you will offer help in writing or revising your resume suitably. Many who work always as temps by preference have several standard resumes, each for a slightly different specialty—an engineer might work also as a computer programmer, designer, technical writer, or marketing executive. With experience, you will probably develop several resumes of your own. As a general modus operandi, you ought to follow a regimen along the following lines to maximize results:

- Develop a list of placement firms.
- Send each a resume for their files. Be sure your address and telephone number, especially the latter, are listed prominently. (Fax number and e-mail address also, if you have them.)
- Monitor the help-wanted advertising in newspapers every day, note placement firms you do not have on your list and add them. Note, also, the needs they list.
- Be flexible and consider assignments that may be corollary to your regular specialty, but well within your capabilities.
- Call the firms with advertisements of special interest. They may not perceive in your standard resume your qualifications for the assignment unless you point it out and are willing to revise your resume to stress the special abilities called for.

Networking

If you prefer to do your own marketing and place yourself directly with clients (whether on an hourly basis or by the project), you will have to establish some kind of marketing plan. Networking is a popular concept that many consultants use today, and about which much has been written elsewhere, describing and prescribing it as a highly organized and formal activity.

Networking is a rather modern development in marketing one's services. It consists of pursuing activities that will provoke and encourage word-of-mouth recommendations, although even that does not fully explain the concept. It is perhaps more precisely defined as marketing via the grapevine. That is, to put it into the most common terms, winning clients from those who have heard of you or have heard good things about you. To turn the idea to your own application and purpose, you must identify and pursue the various means available to you to see to it that prospective clients will have heard of you.

There are many ways to accomplish the goal of being heard about via informal and even involuntary activities. The latter are the indirect result of something you did not control—a friend had the opportunity to recommend you to someone and did so—while others are most deliberate, results you have been at pains to provoke—you addressed a group and made your services most clear to everyone. (Many of my consulting assignments result from individuals learning of me through my books, although I write them as a freelance writer and not to publicize my consulting service.)

Other informal methods are simply doing all the things that raise your general visibility—public speaking, joining associations and being active in them, attending conventions, and making sure to meet many people, letting them know what you do, and handing out many business cards and brochures. Join as many associations and write and lecture as much as possible because these activities produce clients and assignments. They raise your professional image and make people aware of you and what you offer. In time, a great many consulting assignments will come to you spontaneously.

Today, there is a special means for networking effectively—supernetworking, in fact. It is the Internet. Without leaving your desk, you can write and chat with people all over the world via your keyboard and the Internet. There are discussion groups, associations, and numerous other facilities. By all means, spend some time on the Internet getting acquainted and becoming known.

A FEW RELATED CONSIDERATIONS

Consulting is a word with a broad definition: it means a great many things in today's society. Basically, however, it means making your broad knowledge and ability available to aid those with less knowledge and experience. As we use the term, it means helping clients via any means and media possible. It means reaching your clients via any or all of many possible means: face-to-face doing and advising; training via lectures, seminars, and formal classrooms; and/or guiding via printed materials, audiotapes, or videotapes.

Many consultants use a broad mix of these methods to help their clients, while they earn reasonable profits from their labors. The production of these various means of communication and help are legitimate elements of a consulting service. Later chapters will deal with these subjects, and you can refer to them for guidance. You may prefer writing and lecturing as your consulting work, in fact, and you may be able to confine your practice to them.

Why Do So Many Consultants Fail? How to Succeed

Nothing in the world can take the place of persistence. Talent will not; nothing is more common than unsuccessful men with talent. Genius will not; unrewarded genius is almost a proverb. Education will not; the world is full of educated derelicts. Persistence and determination alone are omnipotent.

—Calvin Coolidge

THE SHADOW OF FAILURE

It is a sad observation, but I admit to both surprise and delight when I find a newly established independent consultant still in independent practice a year after its founding. That I am surprised is itself tragic because it points out the high rate of failure among new consulting practices. Unfortunately, that high casualty rate is a fact: Quite a large number, possibly even a majority, of new practices perish within a year or less. The real tragedy is that most failures are avoidable with just a little foresight and caution. Most of those who fail could as easily have survived that critical first year and all the succeeding years.

Every year I receive many handsomely printed and dignified announcements of new consulting practices, with embossed business cards, brochures, letters, and other trappings of the new practices. I receive many telephone calls from new independent consultants, advising me of their new ventures and offering to be available to me for future support and/or co-ventures in consulting. And today, in the era of cyberspace, I see many new Web sites announcing new consultancies.

Every year brings many resumes and letters from these new consultants, almost pleading in their offers to support my own consulting projects. Most such offers are thinly disguised appeals for help (they have an undertone of desperation). I am saddened to get such appeals because they suggest that the individual has no active clients or current work assignments, and therefore has no income and few prospects for new assignments. It means that survival of the individual as an independent consultant is in question.

In many cases, I learn ultimately that the individual has joined the salaried staff of some organization, often that of a former client. That is not necessarily a tragic fate; often it is good news: Many consultants win excellent positions that way and are quite content with the result. In fact, some independent consultants never intend to remain in private practice permanently, but enter into consulting as an expedient to serve them until they find a permanent post somewhere. But most of the failures I refer to here are those of individuals who intended to build a solid independent consulting practice and pursue it from that time forward. Being compelled reluctantly to admit failure is almost tragic and is, at the least, a traumatic experience.

Despite this, it is only fair to observe that in a more global sense, such events are not always failures. For those individuals with an aggressive, upbeat attitude, that of the indomitable entrepreneur, there are no failures, but only temporary setbacks. For the true entrepreneur, each such experience is an important lesson learned, another step leading to ultimate success.

THE ROOTS OF FAILURE

There are many reasons for the failures of independent consultants, some applicable generally to the failures of other kinds of businesses and professional practices. The U.S. Small Business Administration and almost anyone else with substantial entrepreneurial experience will agree quickly enough that the first year of a new venture is almost always the most critical, the one that witnesses by far the majority of business failures. That does not make you safe after that, but your probability of success is much greater if you survive the first year. Many venture capitalists regard the third or fourth year as the watershed year; survive that, they believe, and you can count yourself a probable success for the long term. (In evaluating a prospective venture, they often calculate, as a major criterion or viability, its probability of starting to produce a profit by the end of the third or fourth year.) The IRS is similarly influenced, agreeing that it is not unusual for a venture to produce little or no profit for the first three years, but having serious doubts that a venture is truly a business venture and not a hobby if it fails to produce a profit after three years. Paul and Sarah Edwards, two of the country's best-known experts, lecturers, and authors on small business (especially working-from-home ventures), appear more comfortable with the first five years as the trial by fire for small business, with survival then indicative of the probability of long-range success.

Even for those who do not survive these critical years, the experiences are not always lost opportunities, as witness a thoughtful observation reported by the late Howard Shenson. He was a prominent lecturer and writer on the subject of consulting, regarded by many as the consultant's consultant. He recounted the experience-based wisdom of a consultant who faltered three times, but was back on his feet and trying again a fourth time. This individual,

Shenson related, observed that his first failed effort taught him the lesson of accounts receivable or too much easy credit extended. His second try foundered too, but, he said, taught him the lesson of accounts payable or failure to manage spending well. And his third unsuccessful run taught him the lesson of overhead—the disastrous effects of having too much of it. Now, trying for the fourth time, he was hopeful that the education he had paid so much for—the mistakes he had learned not to repeat—was complete and he would now succeed.

He was not alone in that wisdom; a great many others have observed that what so many commonly refer to as failures are not that at all; they are simply lessons or experiments to discover what will and won't work. Edison conducted thousands of such experiments to find the right material for his incandescent-lamp filament; Charles Kettering tried many approaches before he solved the problem of building an automobile self-starter that would be small enough to be practicable; Milton Hershey's hugely successful chocolate-candy corporation was not his first effort to launch a successful candy business; and U.S. success at putting a satellite into space orbit required the education of several unsuccessful earlier efforts, as Werner von Braun and our other space scientists learned what not to do, as well as what to do. Succeeding without experiencing and overcoming setbacks is rare. Beware of the early success that comes sometimes without great effort or simply by chance: It sends up the wrong signals and can mislead you into making truly disastrous mistakes. It's Murphy's Law working in a truly insidious fashion.

There is a great deal of evidence that most successful entrepreneurs are individuals who failed a time or two—usually several times—before they found their major successes. It appears that this is the school that teaches success. There are many successful people, some quite well known, who firmly believe that without the education of a few failures, true success is not possible. This is not surprising: Formal education cannot teach success in the business world. Here the education that works most reliably is the education of experience. Despite the exceptions, such as those who are born successful or have success thrust upon them, the secret of success is usually the experience of and learning from various tries or mistakes. There are bad guesses, inaccurate estimates, and misfortunes, but there is no universal and unfailing formula for success. There really is no failure as such, but there are the normal mistakes, sometimes painful, usually costly, but always educational, if you use the experience wisely.

Whatever we call these experiences, they are education. It helps to remember that education is never free; it has a cost. But then all success has always had a price and required a willingness to pay that price.

WHAT IS FAILURE?

There is no such thing as failure, other than the voluntary one of quitting the battle. There are setbacks, there is experience, and there is education, but these are taken in stride as anticipated events, resulting in a constant movement toward the eventual success you must experience if you accept the lessons of your education and apply them to your future.

If that sounds like positive thinking, it most certainly is. It is England losing every battle except the last one, and thereby winning the war. It is Edison with 10,000 victories in finding the materials that will not work and eliminating them. It is Elisha T. Otis striking out on every ill-fated venture until he invents the safety system for elevators and founds the company bearing his name today. It is Chester Carlson, rejected for years by everyone to whom he offers his invention, until he meets tiny Halide Corporation, which soon became mighty Xerox Corporation because they listened sympathetically to the inventor of xerographic copying and understood its significance.

The converse of this is to win all the battles and yet lose the war; that happens, too, especially to those who concentrate on winning battles and not on winning the war.

Failure is easy to define: It is quitting, giving up, surrendering to obstacles and setbacks. It is almost certain that you will have setbacks while you are learning what works and what does not work. It is illogical to believe that you can succeed without being floored and picking yourself up each time, digesting what you have learned in that latest encounter, and going on. Success results from knowing that you must eventually learn what does and does not work for you (for *you,* not necessarily for someone else) and thus find the right methods and practices. Early unexpected, unearned, and undeserved success—winning your first client or first project without effort through some stroke of luck—is itself a kind of failure: It misleads you and in so doing sets you back in your quest to learn what you need to know for your eventual, long-term success.

THE COMMON MISTAKES OF NEOPHYTE CONSULTANTS

I do not suggest that you, experienced and highly capable in your profession but perhaps, less experienced in the world of business, will not encounter disappointments and frustrations in abundance; you almost surely will. Still, while setbacks can be positive influences in building a practice, many can be avoided when you know what they are and how they are caused. Let's look at a few typical cases. These are all based on real people—they are factual accounts, suitably disguised—but they are absolutely typical of the mistakes a great many consultants make, usually the result of inexperience.

*   *   *

Jerry T. came to Washington from the Midwest, fresh out of college, with his attractive new wife. Making the rounds of government offices here, he soon ran into an official in the State Department who took an immediate liking to Jerry and offered him an assignment as a training consultant because he didn't have a slot open to offer him a job. The assignment was to set up and conduct a seminar for some State Department staff. It went quite well and led to other consulting assignments as his new friend recommended him to other government agencies. Before long, the volume of work expanded to a point where Jerry could not handle it alone. He then rented a suite of offices in downtown Washington and hung out his shingle as a training consultant. But he wanted to do things right, so he bought a stock of impressive stationery, had beautiful (and expensive) brochures printed, furnished his suite handsomely, and hired a secretary.

It was wonderful while it lasted, but government budgets have their ups and downs. The next year Jerry's friend had no funds to continue his training program, and Jerry had no other clients of any importance. He soon closed his downtown office suite and went in quest of a job again.

*   *   *

Bobby S. is a fine illustrator. He worked for a major engineering firm, doing everything from detailed schematic drawings to artist's concepts for employers' engineering projects, documentation, and annual reports, and soon was managing an entire department of illustrators and drafters. His work brought him into direct contact with clients, and occasionally some of the clients tried to get Bobby to moonlight with them, and even to start his own independent service. Bobby was always somewhat reluctant to do so, somewhat fearful of leaving his steady job. But he was finally persuaded to do so when his wife became pregnant and he was faced with a great many extra expenses. But it still bothered him, and he did not relish stealing so much time from his home life, so he soon began to consider acting as a consultant. He set up a work area at home and quit his job.

Suddenly, all those former clients who had encouraged Bobby to go out on his own evaporated. They had all kinds of apologetic excuses, but little work to offer. Bobby has survived, and is managing well enough now, but he had a couple of very lean and very difficult years. It will take more than a good year or two to make up what he lost.

*   *   *

John R. is a somewhat different kind of case. A Ph.D.—really Dr. John—he is a computer specialist and a bright fellow. A victim of downsizing, when his company's principal contract ended, John turned to consulting by letting his business friends and acquaintances know that he was now available on a consulting basis.

John is a technical/professional specialist who happens to write well. He also thinks well and can devise strategies, which makes him an excellent proposal writer. He soon found a number of clients eager to retain him to do just that, after a few telephone calls, and he was soon busy as many hours a week as he wished to work, at rates he stipulated. He even took in a partner to help him handle the workload, which had grown swiftly beyond his ability to handle it alone.

It lasted for several months. But proposal writing, while it is a year-around activity, also has peak seasons, when organizations who normally write many proposals need extra help, and those who do only occasional proposal writing do not have the expert skills on staff and must hire consultants. So the proposal consultant is as likely as others to experience peaks and valleys of business. The failure to recognize and plan for this was John's undoing. He neither diversified the services he offered nor did he do any serious marketing throughout those busy months: He was too busy writing proposals and invoicing clients to give even his thoughts, much less his time, to questing for new and additional clients or offering additional services. It was almost inevitably only a matter of time before he would be forced to seek a salaried position again.

*   *   *

Note the common mistakes, the most serious of which is the general failure to market until business slows or comes to a halt. But the failure to diversify a bit is also a severe handicap to a new consulting practice, which affects your marketing in several ways: It limits your market prospects to only those who need that single, special service you offer; it limits the size of your projects to that single service; and it handicaps you against competitors who offer a wider diversity of services than you do.

THE BASIC TRADE-OFFS

We make trade-offs throughout our lives, giving up one thing to gain another and otherwise compromising between alternatives—between what you wish for and what you can get. One of my consultant friends, for example, makes a great deal of money every year—over six figures, in fact—but has traded off having a normal home life because he must travel and be away from home more than 300 days a year to earn that much money. In my own case, I sampled that mode of professional life for a time, but eventually I refused to make that trade-off, despite the greater income possible.

Most trade-offs are deliberate decisions. You decide what are the options available and what you want. This applies generally to your practice as a consultant: The more highly specialized the expertise and services you offer, the more sharply targeted your marketing must be, and the higher the fees you can charge (theoretically, at least). But this usually means a smaller market, and thus a more difficult marketing challenge. Of course, the reverse is true: Making your offering a more generalized one—a range of services, instead of a single, sharply defined and highly specialized service—broadens its appeal and increases the number of prospects. It also increases the number of direct competitors with whom you must vie for your contracts, and may tend to decrease the size of the fees you can command.

A more subtle effect is psychological: Broadening your field of claimed expertise tends to lessen your credibility as a consultant because clients usually equate consulting with specialization, and so they are likely to regard the most highly specialized consultants as the most highly qualified experts. In today's world, the generalist is not highly regarded.

That is an important consideration because you must sell to the client's perception, not to your own. That is what makes your image a critical one. But the trade-offs you make sometimes affect that image. In my own case, I can offer clients a special knowledge of government contracting and extensive successful experience in it. I would dearly love to confine my consulting to thoughtfully stroking my beard as I counsel clients who are in pursuit of government contracts. But only rarely am I so fortunate as to have a client who wants only my advice: In practice, my consulting work usually requires me to supply that expert knowledge as actual participation in the writing and direct management of proposals, which may mislead prospective clients as to the real nature of what I do to help them. One prospective client had invited me in to discuss her proposal-writing need, but was stunned to learn my consulting fee. She insisted that my fees were too high for any writer, even a proposal writer, and refused to budge from her bias that I was "only" a writer and overpriced. I soon gave up the waste of my time. There are some arguments you can't win, and there are some that are not worth winning.

I find it necessary to trade off between the image of the scholarly expert counselor and that of marketer, writer, lecturer, seminar leader, trainer, researcher, and other roles I must play as part of what I offer. I see it all as consulting, and the failure to offer and provide a complete consulting service prevents many independent consultants from succeeding.

HOW SPECIALIZED OUGHT YOU TO BE?

There is more at stake here than the question of where to draw the line as a specialist. The mistake is trying to decide from your own viewpoint how specialized you ought to be as an expert consultant. You may have an opinion of what the logical specialties are in your field, and for what niche you are best suited, but you have to judge what will be most appealing to the prospective clients, who decide, finally, whether you will or will not succeed in your undertaking. Never forget that your success is in the hands of your prospective clients: If they cannot get what they want from you, they will go elsewhere.

The question of what to trade off is one you must answer for yourself because the right answer for someone else is probably not the right answer for you. When it comes to the breadth and diversity of the services you offer, you must be guided by what you need to survive, especially in the early months. Ultimately, you will establish a pattern, as you discover what services are most salable, which most profitable, and which most suitable to your own talents, skills, and desires. You will almost surely wind up eventually with a far different set of services than you visualized when you started your career as an independent consultant. (I had no intention of lecturing, offering seminars, or publishing a newsletter when I started, much less of lecturing in local colleges and conducting regular courses.)

HAVING IT BOTH WAYS IN SPECIALIZING

There are two kinds of specialization for you to consider: specialization in the subjects of your expertise and specialization in the modes in which you provide those expert services. I specialize in marketing to the government, especially in proposal writing, the key to custom contracts. But I generalize in the services I provide to those who want help in winning government contracts: I offer my personal services as a proposal writer, proposal manager, and proposal leader, but I also offer to provide proposal aid in other ways: One is study of requirements and advice on deciding to propose or not to propose on specific requirements. Another is the provision of counsel and strategy formulation to those who have adequate proposal-writing staffs. Another is proposal-writing training, usually in the form of seminars. And still another is an information service in the form of a newsletter and occasional monographs or manuals on the subject. I am thus able to maintain the image of a specialist who focuses on an area of great concern to clients, and yet diversify what I do without being constrained in revenue-producing activities.

This is an option open to every independent consultant: It is a way to have your cake and eat it too: You can be a highly specialized professional, with all that such specialization bestows in the way of benefits, and yet be diversified in sources of income based on that specialization.

MARKETING

One basic mistake many newcomers make is offering too narrow a range of services—overspecialization; equally common is the mistake of marketing to too narrow a range of potential clients. Even worse is failing to understand the role of and need for marketing in the consulting enterprise. So often an individual launches a consulting enterprise on the basis of a single client or two, and assumes that the quest for more clients need not be a concern until he or she needs more clients. Far too often it is only the promise of business from a single client or two that inspires individuals to establish independent practices. But whether the access to an immediate paying client is the result of good fortune or is itself the catalyst for establishing the new practice, it often deceives the new consultant as to the ease or difficulty of winning clients and assignments. Too often, it is only after leaving a job, making an investment, incurring serious debt, and dedicating many months of effort, that the new practitioner begins to discover the harsh truth: Most clients and contracts do not come as easily as that first one or two did or as easily as he or she thought they would.

Probably the deadliest of all marketing mistakes is the assumption that the right time to market is when business is slow and you have the time to market. This approach to marketing is based on the foolish assumption that you cannot afford to "waste" your time in marketing when you are busy serving paying clients, and the equally foolish idea that there is no need to market when you are busy.

Such reasoning fails to recognize that there is a considerable time lag between marketing effort and resulting sales. That is especially true in the field of professional services. Here the gap can be many months, for a variety of reasons. Even the most effective marketing of consulting services is likely to pay off substantially with contracts only months later, months during which income may be zero or near-zero. That is a period which most independent consultants have difficulty enduring and surviving. How long can *you* survive with zero income?

THE TEN LAWS OF SURVIVAL

This entire book is largely focused on survival, with marketing success as a basic need. You are almost certain to come face to face with disappointing and sometimes disheartening realities, such as Murphy's Law, which states as its basic premise that anything that can go wrong will go wrong. Various laws based on this make the premise appear almost optimistic! Here are some things that befall most of us, sooner or later:

- The deceptively easy first assignment turns out to be a real bear, and almost induces you to give up being a consultant before you get the job under control and completed.

- That pleasant fellow you accepted eagerly as a client without a written agreement because he was so obviously an honest and sincere gentleman fought you every inch of the way, constantly misrepresenting what you thought was a clear understanding, and making you fight to get paid.

- That struggling little company who was so unconcerned about the cost of your services proved to be unconcerned because they didn't have any money anyway, and you never did get paid or you settled for less than the full fee due and had to pay an attorney or collection agency a third of that for helping you collect even that much.

- One of those associates you brought in to help you handle a project that needed three people was a dud, and you wound up covering for him and working all kinds of extra hours to protect your own reputation. And the other one even tried to steal the client from you.

There were other problems. The accountant who set up your books billed you for a great deal more than his original estimate; he was full of long-faced and regretful explanations. The printer botched your stationery, and you had to have it all done over. The answering service lost several important messages—probably cost you a client or two. And almost everything you bought to furnish and equip your office cost more than you planned. (Your shopping was based on newspaper advertising and catalogs, and you trustingly believed the advertised prices when planning your budget.)

Here are ten laws of survival to help you avoid the worst of these problems:

1. Expect everything to go wrong and plan for it by having alternatives planned and ready to be implemented when needed.

2. Make $50 mistakes, not $500 ones. You need that education you get from mistakes, and you expect to make them, but you can learn as much from $50 mistakes as you can for $500 or $5,000 mistakes.

3. Avoid or delay every expenditure possible. If you don't get substantial prompt payment discounts, take 30, 45, or even more days to pay your bills, like the big companies do. Make the old computer and printer do a little longer. Type xxxxxx over the old telephone number and type in the new one on your old letterheads. Do your own filing. Get that downtown office next year. Don't be in a big hurry to order the new brochure. Shop around for a better price; printers' prices vary all over the lot, and you can do better. If you have a good laser or inkjet printer, print your own letterheads and labels; few customers will know the difference or care about it, and you can cut costs for these items by about two-thirds.

4. Never refuse a job on which you can earn a profit. Accept that small job that is offered, and never mind that big job you were promised; it may or may not—probably will not—ever materialize, anyway, and you will have lost the small one that you can have now. Forget those vague promises; only the bird in the hand counts, especially when the landlord, the butcher, and the baker approach with their bills in one hand and the other hand outstretched expectantly.

5. Never get so successful that you turn down jobs or fail to make time for marketing because you are already over-busy and overworked. (Failure to market when you are busy is the harbinger of ultimate disaster; tomorrow's contract is even more important than the one you are now working on because you don't have it yet.) The next time things are slow and you are desperate for a contract, you'll wish you had obeyed this Law.

6. Forget the clock, and the calendar, too. Forty-hour weeks and two-week vacations are things of the past, at least until you are firmly established (if then). You'll rest and vacation when business is slow, if you put in those 50-, 60-, even 80-hour weeks when you have the work. Work now and rest later.

7. Don't start believing your own press clippings: Don't overrate your own importance and become too much the discriminating specialist: Don't, that is, become a pompous ass. (Perhaps that is an occupational hazard, but some consultants booby-trap themselves this way.) You are never too big or important to earn a dollar doing honest consulting

work, even if you think the task is not as prestigious or upscale as that for which you yearn.

8. Remember that you are worth what you cost, and discounting your rates—bargaining and agreeing to different rates on each occasion, even when you are badly in need of the work—is not only unprofessional, but demeans you in the eyes of the client and even in your own eyes. It eventually damages you, as word gets around that clients can bargain with you for your best rate. There are other ways to help the customer economize and win the job without working for coolie wages or compromising your professionalism, ways we'll discuss. Especially, don't be led down the garden path by clients' promises of lots of business later, recommendations to friends, and so on. Those are bargaining tactics of some clients, and you are almost certain to ultimately regret acceding to or being influenced by them. (Word-of-mouth recommendations are almost invariably from people who never promised them to you or expected to profit from them in some way.)

9. Be totally businesslike in your dealings. Stick to your guns on your rate (see Law 8) and unless there is good reason to make exceptions (for example, a formal purchase order or letter of commitment from a large and well-established company with A-1 credit rating), do ask for a retainer as "earnest money" upon signing an agreement, and do ask clients to sign a simple agreement with you, explaining the commitments of both parties clearly.

10. In many ways, the most important Law is to be totally ethical. That means being completely honest, respecting and keeping confidences, safeguarding clients' proprietary information, doing an honest day's work, honoring your contracts scrupulously, and rendering honest bills for your services.

These Laws summarize most of this book, but before getting on to the later chapters, let's have a closer look at some of the key points and injunctions.

On Being Too Much the Specialist

At one extreme is the consultant who is so specialized that he or she has only one or two services or solutions and works overtime at trying to force-fit the client's problem to one of those services or solutions. It doesn't work. The client will not tailor his or her needs to your solutions. Consulting is tailoring your services to the client's need.

Consulting is a custom service. Never forget that. The degree of specialization is an inverse quantity: the more sharply you focus your specialization the less able you can customize your service to the client's needs. You must be highly flexible, if you are to be able to tailor your services to each client's need, as you should. Oddly enough, although the basis for consulting is generally specialized knowledge and skills in some area, consulting soon proves to be interdisciplinary and forces you to be something of a generalist within your field.

As a proposal consultant, for example, my broad objective is always to find the strategies for selling to the prospects, for example, the government agency. However, to do that, I find it highly useful and even necessary to have an extensive knowledge of the government in its procurement regulations, publication processes, writing and editing functions, sales and marketing principles, advertising, copy writing, and management, as well as the skills that are inherently necessary for any consultant. (More about those later.) In fact, my clients expect me to be able to advise them in all these matters. Weakness on my part in any of those areas would limit my usefulness and with it my market appeal and the scope of my services.

One problem is that clients often tend to force you into a mold. Because it is a normal human tendency to sort and classify everything and everybody, clients will often assign you a tag. As an engineering-support organization, we once wrote technical manuals for NASA's Goddard Space Flight Center. As a result, we were nearly passed over for a value-engineering project which we were well equipped to handle. The client had no idea we had a staff to handle such a job—in the client's eyes we were simply technical writers, rather than an engineering-support organization—and only vigilance and aggressive marketing on our part won us the project.

Experience, Education, and $50 Mistakes

It is probably apocryphal, although credited to department store merchant John Wanamaker, but he is reported to have said, "I know that one-half of my advertising dollar is wasted, but my problem is that I don't know which half it is."

The truth is that probably more than one-half of all advertising dollars are wasted because there is rarely a reliable means for measuring the result of advertising. Advertising is one of many areas where we spend money hopefully, usually without a means for measuring or even estimating the outcome to determine whether the expenditure is a worthwhile investment. It is hardly surprising that many of those expenditures do not pay off adequately, leading us to characterize those investments as mistakes, rather than as the price of education.

You are going to make many decisions that will not turn out as well as you hoped. Why not, therefore, knowing that you are buying an education, take a small advertisement in the Yellow Pages, rather than a large one, if you insist on trying that medium? If it works, you can always increase it next year. Why buy 1,000 expensive, two-color, embossed or engraved business cards and matching stationery when you don't even know whether you will soon be changing your address, telephone number, business name, copy, or services offered? You won't lose any clients by ordering 500 plain, white cards and stationery, tastefully printed on adequate—not costly—stock. Why buy a $5,000 computer system, when you can start with a $1,000 system?

You do well to establish your office in your own home, if at all possible. You do not need offices in the most expensive part of town or in the most recently built and most costly office building. You can almost always find something more modest, and yet adequate.

You never need to be self-conscious, apologetic, or self-deprecating about running your enterprise on a sound financial footing and economizing wherever you can. On the contrary, many of your clients will be impressed that you are levelheaded and practical. That is not a bad image to acquire.

There Are No Small Jobs

In the theater they say that there are no small parts. There are also no small consulting jobs. I don't have a $5,000 or $10,000 proposal-writing job every month. I have sometimes paid my office rent by helping a student polish a doctoral dissertation or ghost-writing a marketing brochure for an executive.

I have to this day clients who have adequate staffs to write their proposals, but they like to have me come in and help them analyze the request and recommend a strategy. Or they retain me to simply organize and lead their team, and possibly write or rewrite just a key section or two. And sometimes they have me back later to review and critique their proposal drafts. But I also have clients who ask me to come in and present one- or two-day training seminars to their staffs. I consider lecturing to be a part of my consulting service. (In fact, I enjoy doing it, aside from the fact that it also pays the rent.)

Jeffrey Lant, the well-known author and Internet entrepreneur, found a large market for the frequent books he writes and publishes to counsel and aid other businesspeople. He has continued to expand his activities and has built a large business.

Steve Lanning, a marketing consultant specializing in direct mail, founded and published the Consulting Opportunities Journal as an activity of his National Consultant Resources Center (now published by the New Ventures Publishing Group). He, too, has continued to diversify and grow, offering more and more services to others.

The list could go on and on, and we will come back to meet these consultants and others again and to listen to some of what they have to say in advising beginning consultants. The message here, however, is that successful consultants are individuals who are enterprising, versatile, and unafraid to diversify and exploit opportunities. They all agree that the independent consultant is well-advised to be conservative in expenditures, as well as in inflating his or her self-image.

THE CONSULTANT'S IMAGE

By now, I hope you understand that your own image of what you are is not the critical one; only the client's image of you really matters. The client often does not perceive the transaction as one of buying something from you, but rather as hiring you temporarily. Far too often, the client tends to regard you as a temporary employee, rather than as an independent entrepreneur selling a valuable service and entitled to function as an equal.

This misunderstanding of your role can lead to an unpleasant and unhappy consultant-client relationship. However, in most cases, the evolution of this client's mistaken perception of you as a temporary employee can be avoided, if you practice certain measures to establish and preserve the proper image.

First the Self-Image

First you must settle the relationship firmly in your own mind. You must think of yourself as an independent contractor and you must value yourself and your services properly. You are delivering a service of value to your client, trading your services and special abilities for money. You are fully competent to do everything the client requires of you, and you have complete confidence in yourself and in your ability. Unless you firmly believe that, you are unlikely to persuade anyone else to believe it: No matter how brave a front you put up, your convictions about yourself manage to shine through the facade and are perceived by the client and the client's staff or associates. Most of all, however, bear this in mind: Your true value, what you are being paid for, is not your time. That's a much mistaken notion that some have. Time is only the measure by which you calculate your charges. What you sell—or should sell—is results. You must help your clients understand that, too.

Through the Client's Eyes

The client does not have to like you, although that would be helpful. Clients do business often with individuals they do not particularly like, when the business relationship is a brief one. However, where you and the client must work closely together for a substantial period, amity helps a great deal, and if that is not possible, at the least you must avoid an abrasive relationship. You must see to it that your personality is compatible with the client's personality, at least to the degree that you do not strike sparks from each other.

The Roles You Must and Must Not Play

The don'ts of behavior are characteristics that may be acceptable in some places, but are definitely out of place in most places, in bad taste, or so offensive to many people that it is risky to exhibit such traits. In fact, we all play many roles in life, and most of us play more than one role—worker, father, mother, friend, confidante, supervisor. The consultant is a role too, but consultants often play the wrong roles in the client's office. Here are some roles to avoid:

- *Mr. or Ms. Personality.* They are full of good cheer and compliments for everyone in sight, memorizing everyone's name, bringing in doughnuts every morning, and otherwise buttering everyone up with overbearing cheerfulness and good will.

- *The Name Dropper.* Don't drop those names, not even if you really do know all those prominent and influential citizens.

- *The Militant, whether Male Chauvinist or Impassioned Libber.* These roles are akin to each other, all impassioned seekers after justice. Save these arguments, poses, and positions for another time and place.

- *The Supremely Confident Know It All.* Forget how stupid everyone who doesn't agree with you is; be patient with the unfortunate ignoramuses and forgive their ignorance if you want to get along.

- *The Hero.* Don't come on too strong—no braggadocio about your great feats of the past and your magnificent promises for the future.

- *The Night Club Comedian.* Don't tell racy, off-color stories, make ethnic jokes and slurs, be a back-slapper, or try otherwise to be a standup comedian. It's much harder than it seems, and even if you happen to be a good comedian, it doesn't help your image as a serious consultant.

- *The Great Polemicist and Orator.* Don't get into political, religious, or other discussions about which so many people get emotional—not even lengthy discussions of sports, which are often in that same category.

- *The Eager Beaver.* Don't rush about offering unsolicited help, especially in matters unrelated to the work you were retained to do. Be responsive if you are asked—you may occasionally be asked for your opinion on some matter not related directly to the effort for which you were retained—but wait to be asked.

- *The Irrepressible Marketer.* Important although marketing is, don't make the mistake so many make of trying immediately to fatten your part, as they say in show business, either by trying to expand the contract you have just won or by trying immediately to sell a next contract with the same client. (This can be related to the Eager Beaver problem, in which the consultant is busy poking into and involved with everything but the job for which he or she was hired, trying desperately to set up future business.) You can wear out your welcome very quickly this way.

On the other hand, there is a role you should play: Come as close as you can to playing the total and complete professional. That means quiet confidence, a courteous and friendly personality, but a subdued manner, dedication to doing the job as quietly and efficiently as possible, and a willingness to listen intently and actually hear what is being said. (So many people listen—apparently listen, that is, but never actually hear.) Learn people's names, acknowledge others pleasantly with a nod, a hello, "Good morning," or whatever is most appropriate, but then go about the business you are there for and forsake the morning coffee club. (You are probably not accepted by the regular staff, and they may very well resent your efforts to be one of them temporarily.)

A Few Keys to Success

There is no single secret of success in consulting. Consulting success is a mix of many skills and functions.
—*Herman Holtz*

THE ART OF LISTENING

Marketing is probably the most important function of any business because a business thrives or fails according to its success in finding buyers. In consulting, you must sell yourself; you must inspire confidence and trust. One skill that is critical in inspiring trust is listening. Although listening comes naturally to some, we can all learn how to listen better.

Much been made of the art of listening. Often we spend time thinking about what we are going to say next, rather than truly listening and grasping what the other person is saying. "The art of listening" is a catchy phrase, but it doesn't mean merely being silent while the other person is talking. Listening is hearing with full and complete consciousness of what the other person is saying, rather than hearing only sound.

Former U.S. President Franklin D. Roosevelt delighted in telling a story that demonstrated how little most people listen. He said he tried sitting in his wheelchair (he was a polio victim, although few knew this in those pre-television days) at White House receptions and greeting each visitor or pair of visitors with his typically brilliant smile, a warm handshake, and a murmured, "How do you do. I've just murdered my grandmother." Not a single visitor or guest ever turned a hair, he said, because no one really listened. They simply did not hear what he had said. They "heard" only what they assumed he had or should have said.

Not truly hearing polite pleasantries is one thing, and does no harm. Failing to hear what a prospective client is saying is expensive: It costs you sales. One highly successful salesman reports that his secret of success is listening. Once he gets his prospect going on a favorite topic, whether it is fishing, golf, or manufacturing ball bearings, prolonged listening and hearing on his part produces clients and contracts.

If this sounds a bit cynical, as though listening is simply a sales gambit, it is not. It is a courtesy, showing respect for the other person, but more important, it is the means for determining what the prospect really needs or wants, the key to making the sale.

We noted that many prospects cannot define their problem; they describe only the symptoms. Consulting requires analysis to determine what the problem is, before you can win the contract. It is the key to understanding the problem and synthesizing a solution. The client is the best and often only source of information you need to market successfully, and listening to the client is the way to gain that information.

Selling is itself consulting, and successful salespeople are always consultants in making sales presentations. Fuller Brush sellers show housewives how to solve housekeeping problems. Avon and Mary Kay salespeople help customers find the answers to beauty and makeup problems. Clothing-store salespeople help customers find clothes that enhance their appearance. Every successful salesperson helps prospects do something that is beneficial to the prospect. There is no other reason to buy from any salesperson.

As an independent entrepreneur, you sell, you are the salesperson. You will succeed only to the extent that you can help your prospects get what they want. And it is only by listening that you can learn (1) what the prospect thinks he or she needs and (2) what the prospect really needs.

DECIDING WHAT BUSINESS YOU ARE IN

In addressing groups, I often startle and even outrage many listeners when I charge that they do not know what businesses they are in. This accusation may startle and outrage you, too. Still, it is probably true: Unless you happen to have been exposed to the right kind of marketing indoctrination or have some unusual instinct for sensing the truth about marketing effectiveness, you are almost surely defining your business from your own viewpoint, in terms of what you sell, what, that is, you wish the client to buy. If you advise clients on organizing their office procedures or do it for them, for example, you may define your business as management consulting or even more narrowly as office management.

That seems logical enough, doesn't it? It describes what you do, and what difference does it make, anyway? Defining business is not an academic exercise; it is a critical question. The answer is likely to have a great effect on your success or lack of it. Your success in marketing depends on how wise you are in perceiving what business you are in from the client's viewpoint. You may or may not be able to change your decision as to where, how, and in what you will specialize after you have launched your practice, but you must be able to perceive your *offer* through the client's eyes if you are to sell your services effectively. It is the perception of the client that defines your business. The client is buying something he or she probably defines quite differently than you do. Thus, the answer to the question of what business you are in is not always arrived at easily. But let's consider some related ideas that may help.

Business Definition as a Commercial or Advertisement

The definition of your business is or should be a commercial for it. A sales appeal—your offer—is usually effective to the degree with which it explains what you *do* for the client. Keep that in mind; it explains the why, how, and what of defining your business.

A Common Denominator of All Businesses

Sophisticated marketers understand that every business is a service business because every customer buys what the business sells to gain some benefit— what the item or service will do for him or her. Some buyers of watches are buying only capability to see the time conveniently, while others may be buying jewelry. (You must decide whether the watches you sell are mere time-keepers or are also jewelry.) Everyone today has an electric refrigerator to store food safely and conveniently. We have TV receivers primarily for entertainment and automobiles to give us mobility at our convenience.

Yes, of course there are other motivations, but the principle is the same: People buy something, even manufactured products, to gain something it will do for them. Whatever the item, ultimately it is the service of what that item does for the buyer that we must sell.

What Customers and Clients Really Buy

Consultants are in the problem-solving business generally because clients call on consultants when they need help. Perhaps that is not true for every business, in the final analysis, but in any case it is a good place to begin analyzing what you sell.

A client normally wants the consultant to solve the problem by the most efficient and rapid means possible. But that does not always tell the story. Suppose the client is an executive who is in trouble, under great pressure to straighten out some troublesome situation. When he retains a consultant to help him or her off the hot spot, the consultant is in the rescue-service business! On the other hand, when the client is an executive who is trying desperately to establish himself or herself in the organization, to get recognition and become a hero or heroine, the consultant is in the hero-making business!

YOUR TRUE CLIENT

Clients are organizations, but they are represented by the individuals with whom you must do business. Perhaps your contract or purchase order says

PDQ Corporation, but your true client may very well be Harry P. Executive, for all practical purposes. To get PDQ Corp. to pay you and to do business with you again, you must satisfy client Harry P. Executive. Thus, you must know what Harry P. Executive wants and somehow demonstrate an ability to satisfy that want if you are to win the job. Moral: Be sure you know who your true client is, as well as what the client wants.

The Key to the Definition

Since your business is satisfying clients' wants, it seems obvious that finding out what your clients really want is the key to discovering what business you are in. There is almost certain to be a degree of variation among the wants of your clients, but there must be some common ground from which to start. All clients for my proposal-writing service wanted to win government contracts, and I could get the attention and arouse the interest of every one of them with my promise of assistance in doing just that. That interest established, we could move on to a more detailed discussion of what the client wanted and whether we could reach agreement.

Thus you begin with a general understanding of the client's want, and then work at defining that want more precisely. You cannot base your offer on a stated promise to get the client off the hot spot or to make the client a hero or heroine. Your appeal must be more subtle than that. But you must understand the client's true motive if you are to make the most effective offer, and it is quite often necessary for you to help the client understand and recognize his or her want.

In many cases, where the client does not consciously perceive his or her want in these terms (it may be an unconscious desire), you can help the client see one of these possibilities as the chief benefit of your services. It is safe to say that all organizations have problems as a fact of existence, and individuals have responsibility for solving the problems, so the basic appeal to solving problems is always a sound one. But it is not unlikely that every executive, but especially young ones who are still working at establishing their images, yearn at least subconsciously to gain special recognition by doing something heroic for their organizations. Many successful marketing campaigns are based on arousing the Walter Mitty that is buried in most of us.

Everyone wants love, prestige, ego gratification, security, success, recognition, and many other emotional satisfactions. They also need to be in on things, to belong, to be recognized as having worth, to be appreciated, to feel important, to be loved, to be admired, to be successful.

Clients Are People!

In marketing, all truth lies in the client's perception. You may be sure that you are bringing the client a major benefit, the ideal answer to the problem, or the means for making the client a hero or heroine in the organization, but it does not matter if you cannot persuade the client to see and believe it. You need to be able to see matters from the client's viewpoint and find the means for helping the client perceive the benefits you offer.

On the other hand, clients are sensitive and you must take care to avoid giving offense. You need to have regard for the client's pride. The fact that a client has called on you for help does not mean that he or she necessarily feels less competent than you to do the job. An amazingly large number of clients believe that they are perfectly capable of doing the job themselves but are just too busy to do it or find that it is not a wise allocation of their time. This may or may not be true, but what difference does it make? Ordinary diplomacy dictates that you must not flaunt your knowledge and ability. Even when and if the client is willing to admit to a need for a capability or knowledge he or she does not have, it is risky to appear to be patronizing or condescending. Remember that you will often be retained by a client who can, indeed, do the job as well as you but truly does not have the time to do the job personally. It can be hazardous to assume otherwise; some individuals are quite sensitive and will be offended.

Even when the client is wrong—perhaps especially when the client is wrong—you must exercise a great deal of tact. Many executives and professionals freely admit, for example, that they do not write well and are happy to turn the job over to a professional writer. Unfortunately, many others insist that they write as well as anyone, when they "have the time," but are too busy to do their own writing. However, there are countless cases where the client has called on a freelance writer, presenting a hopelessly inept draft of some document and asking for a quotation to edit and "clean it up a bit." The foolish consultant remonstrates that the manuscript is a mess and needs complete rewriting, a tactic that will probably cost him or her the job and any future work from that prospect. The smart consultant agrees that a heavy edit would help the piece, furnishes a quotation for the total rewrite he or she plans to do, and winds up with the job and a satisfied client. (There is nothing unethical or dishonest in using diplomacy and calling the job editing, if you are charging a fair price to do what you know must be done and then doing it.)

Most of us want to believe that we are the very best at whatever we do, and we think that the client ought to be able to recognize that obvious fact. The average client, however, has no way of knowing that one consultant is any better than the next consultant. All the consultants the client talks to claim total competence, so how is a client to know the difference? In those circumstances, a client may simply award the project to the lowest bidder.

To win, you must help the client perceive the difference: Educating the client is often a necessity in marketing. Even if you were willing to try to be the low bidder, generally a self-defeating practice in itself, it would not necessarily be the winning strategy. It is far better to market your services by demonstrating that you and your services are superior to others.

THE TWO BASIC SALES SITUATIONS

There are two basic sales situations: In the first case, there is a felt need: The client is aware of a specific need for consulting services to solve a problem, whether it is a technical problem that requires some special expert or a staff shortage that requires a professional temporary or two. In the second case, you must create a need for your services: The client may or may not be aware of a need, but even if conscious of a problem to be solved, has not yet decided that outside services are needed.

These are two different selling problems. In the first case, you are selling against competition. The contract will be awarded to someone, and it's your task to convince the client that the contract should be awarded to you. In the second case, it is your task to convince the client that your services are needed and can provide valuable benefits. Of course, there is the hazard, usually unavoidable, that the client may decide to conduct a competition, rather than making the award directly to you, so that you will have created an opportunity for your competitors.

In either case, you are likely to be required to do some analysis and propose a specific plan and estimate of costs to satisfy the client's need—submit a proposal, that is. It is probably in your own interest to encourage the client to require this. The client will probably rate you on how well you understand and appraise the problem, as well as on how effective your plan appears to be.

Here is where the failure to listen carefully to what the client has to say can be fatal to your marketing effort and even to your entire company, as it was to Sam and his small, but growing engineering-services company. Sam was a former Navy employee, an engineer, and his company did business almost exclusively with the Navy. Unfortunately, Sam knew too many people in the Navy and was too familiar with their needs. He reached a point where he was sure that he knew more about what they needed and wanted than they did, and began to ignore their stated requirements in favor of his own mandates of what they would get from him. And he didn't hesitate to tell his clients that they need not tell him what they wanted him to do; he already knew all he needed to know.

This arrogance began to cost him the contracts he had once been able to gather in almost routinely, and it was not very long before his once prosperous service organization was no more. The Navy had no difficulty in finding other competent engineering consultants who were more compliant and responsive in listening to their statements and satisfying their needs.

THE INDEPENDENT CONSULTANT:
SPECIALIST OR GENERALIST?

Ironically, as an independent consultant, you must be both specialist and generalist: the specialist, technically and in the client's eyes, while also the generalist as a one-man band, a man or woman doing all or nearly all the things (technical, managerial, and administrative) necessary to run a small business. Even the functions on the technical side of a consulting practice are highly diverse.

The Independent Consultant as a Technical/Professional Specialist

Consulting requires certain technical/professional skills, which you, as an independent consultant must be capable of personally doing. Every consulting assignment requires at least some of the following six direct-support functions, and many require all of them:

1. Listening
2. Analysis and problem definition
3. Problem solving
4. Doing
5. Public speaking
6. Writing

Listening and Doing. Listening and doing are functions required for most consulting projects. You must master and practice the art of listening to what the client says, as well as to what those whom you interview and/or must work with have to say. And you must actually do the engineering, computer programming, office-procedures design, training development, and whatever else constitutes your services. Frequently, you are expected to lead and guide the effort. (Even in major proposal-writing jobs, where the client's staff must do much of the writing, the proposal consultant must lead, edit, supervise, write, and be totally responsible for the final result.)

Listening includes reading that requires paying close attention to all details, as in reading an RFP, which must often be reread many times to wring all the useful information from it.

Analysis, Problem Definition, and Problem Solving. Analysis, problem definition, and problem solving are normal consulting functions you must carry out almost as a routine. Even when clients identify their problems quite clearly and dictate the desired or required solution, you should be able to analyze the symptoms and verify the clients' statements or discuss them with the client if you find that necessary.

Public Speaking and Writing. There is frequent need for and always good use to be made of expert speaking and writing. You may be called on to make presentations or train members of the client's staff, but you will also find speaking before groups valuable as a marketing tool and as another income center. Writing falls into the same category, and is so often necessary that it perhaps ought to be included as a necessary function of consulting because for many types of consultancies you must write reports and proposals as part of all assignments. Thus, as in the case of speaking, writing may be the basis for an important income center in your practice.

The Independent Consultant as a Businessperson

Consulting is a profession but it is also a business, and you must be a businessperson to succeed. That means being a manager and administrator. The functions required for management of any business include at least these:

- Accounting and record keeping
- Cost estimating and pricing
- Scheduling and time management
- Financial management
- Marketing and sales

There are other elements of business management and administration for many kinds of enterprises. This list includes the main functions in managing and administering a consulting practice. The first four elements are the same in principle for all business enterprises. Marketing, as an independent consultant, however, is a special problem, and something of a gray area of management. It is not readily separated from the technical/professional side of consulting, and will therefore be discussed briefly here and in greater depth and detail later, since help in marketing your consulting services is the single most important objective of this book.

Accounting and Record Keeping. Many individuals entering into a small business immediately retain a certified public accountant to set up an accounting system for the enterprise and to handle all bookkeeping and accounting work. Non-accountants tend to the belief that accounting is something of a black art, a mysterious ritual that most of us cannot hope to fathom. This feeling is reinforced by fear of the Internal Revenue Service and the mistaken belief that the purpose of keeping books is to comply with the legal statutes and preferences of the IRS.

There is nothing wrong with retaining a professional accountant to handle your accounting needs. There are good arguments for doing it yourself, too, and it is far less difficult than you might imagine. In fact, there are several ways to compromise between the extremes of turning it all over to a professional accountant and doing it all yourself. (I tried both extremes and now use a compromise solution successfully.) Here are the basic alternatives:

1. The accountant sets up your books and a system for you to follow, so you do the day-to-day journalizing, check-stub maintenance, invoicing, and other routine chores. The accountant comes in periodically and does your formal postings, balancing your books, reconciling the bank statement, making up estimated tax returns and other tax forms when necessary.

2. The accountant sets up the system and instructs you in how to do postings and keep the books. Periodically, perhaps every quarter or half-year, the accountant goes over your books to do all your taxes and prepare the standard reports you should have.

3. You use one of the standard accounting systems designed especially for very small businesses. (You can buy the combination journal/ledger and instructions from almost any stationer.) It will have a tax guide, but you can get an accountant's help to do your taxes and prepare your standard reports, if you wish.

4. Use a computer program that does it all for you. (There are several excellent programs designed for small business.)

There are some variants on even these basic hybrids: You may find an individual accountant who will come to your office to work, but you are more likely to be dealing with an accounting firm who will want you to bundle up your books and all your papers periodically and carry them to their offices, where they will do the work. You may make various adjustments between what you will do and what your accountant will do, if you choose to use an accountant.

I use the third option listed, and my accountant does my end-of-year state and federal corporate and personal income taxes for me. I had tried having an accountant handle it all for me, and I was dissatisfied with the arrangement for several reasons, of which the most important was that I had to hold my breath, waiting to hear how I was doing. I decided that I needed to know immediately when things were going wrong, and I found that those little do-it-yourself systems actually let you know every day how you are doing if you keep up with it and pay attention. Moreover, it's a great deal less expensive and a great deal simpler. (Most consultants have simple accounting needs.)

The purpose of accounting is not to make life easier for the IRS, although the law requires you to keep some kind of record. The primary purpose of an accounting system is to furnish you information so that you can manage your practice to best advantage. You want that information while there is time to make adjustments—discontinue something that is costing you money, for example, or expand a marketing effort that is producing good results—not when it is too late to correct a mistake or take advantage of an opportunity. (It is quite easy to be entirely unaware of such things or to misread the signs if you do not have a system that alerts you.) To be useful and do what it ought to do for you, the system must furnish information that satisfies three requirements:

1. It must be accurate.
2. It must be timely.
3. It must be relevant information.

The need for accurate information needs no discussion. Timeliness is of the essence, as already noted. You need to know now how things are going in real time, while you can take corrective action. Only you know what information is useful or right for your purposes, and even you may not know that until you have had some experience using your accounting feedback. Keeping your own books and making your own postings helps you learn this and may be the only way you can learn it.

It is not possible for an accountant to do for you what you can do for yourself in this respect. Moreover, the accountant has a tendency to burden you with a system that is far more complex and sophisticated than you need, and actually tends to conceal the facts from you, rather than highlighting and dramatizing them, as it should. The simpler the system, the better it is for you all around.

In addition to this, remember that the accountant is simply not familiar with your profession, let alone the circumstances of your individual practice, and cannot possibly anticipate what you need. Those simple systems, however, give you absolutely up-to-date information, if you keep them up. In it you can usually identify every cost center you have, what it has cost you this past week (or month, if you prefer to keep records on a monthly period), and what it has cost you in total for the year to date. You have the same figures for all costs, and for all income, so that you can make comparisons as often as you like and you can spot changes in a trend immediately.

Some organizations also use their accountants or comptrollers as financial managers. I think this is a mistake. Accountants and comptrollers are concerned normally with day-to-day operations, maintaining records, making reports, verifying expenses, and getting the data to the managers who need the information. Financial managers, on the other hand are or should be concerned with future projects and overall management of many functions and processes affecting the organization's finances, such as the following:

- Cost analyses, to ensure that work is estimated and priced accurately. This is not a simple matter. It is not unusual for organizations to operate at a loss for a long time without realizing it because they have failed to make a realistic and accurate analysis of all their costs.

- Optimizing the organization's cash flow and financial position by ensuring prompt invoicing, taking advantage of all discounts, managing assets to minimize interest payments and maximizing return on investment.

- Cost control, including the use of available cost reduction and cost avoidance practices.

- Funding operations, including equity funding, debt financing, and other available measures.

- Scheduling and time management are executive functions that you will normally do for yourself. They can be complex in the large company but are usually quite simple in the small organization. However, if you get into work situations in which you must keep accurate time records, you will have to organize some sort of formal system for this.

Marketing. Marketing is rarely a simple function, and in the case of selling consulting services it usually gets quite complex because such services can rarely be sold through the conventional or traditional marketing methods. Many consultants who have tried such methods—media advertising, brochures, and personal calls on prospects—have been puzzled and dismayed to find that results are often zero and rarely more than minimal.

To some degree this reflects a failure to formulate a specific and detailed marketing plan in advance, especially the detail of identifying the specific benefits you offer via your services and the specific kinds of prospects to whom you wish to make offers. Many new consultants believe that if enough people are made aware that they (the consultants) are now ready to solve clients' problems for them, the telephone will start ringing.

The opposite is true. Rarely does a client choose a consultant casually as a result of a conventional advertisement or sales call. Quite the contrary, clients find consultants through indirect means, such as recommendations by friends, reading about consultants in articles, reading articles and books written by the consultant, meeting consultants at business meetings and conventions, and hearing consultants speak at such events. A retired friend of mine is now a computer enthusiast, but for several years he resisted all my efforts and those of his own son to get him interested in computers. He happened to attend a meeting at a resort hotel, where a spokesman from Dell Computers spoke. My friend placed his order for an upscale system at that meeting!

Many of these activities of consultants are marketing functions, and they call for the application of certain skills listed earlier as technical/professional skills. It is partly for this reason that the subject of marketing is handled separately here as a kind of gray area between the two sets of skills. The importance of marketing in consulting success is enough to justify treating the subject separately. The essence of this chapter is how to survive the first year and set the survival and success patterns for succeeding years. The secret of that survival and success has been for me and for a great many other independent consultants having more than one consulting service and/or related product to sell (other profit centers, that is) and effective marketing of all the services.

DOS AND DON'TS, ESPECIALLY FOR THE FIRST YEAR

The first year of a new venture is the most critical one. The sensible main objective of the first year is not success or profit: It is survival. The second and only slightly less important objective of the first year is education—learning what works and what doesn't work for you, what to do and what to avoid doing, and whatever else only experience can teach you.

General Suggestions for Minimizing Costs

Don't get carried away with the enthusiasm of a new venture. Enthusiasm is a great asset and will help you considerably, but it should not blind you to the reality of that first year, when it is quite possible that you will pay more money out than you take in, especially if you are not careful in what you pay out. Remember that what you spend this first year—and possibly even in succeeding years—is the cost of your education, but the education need not be disastrously expensive. Ross Perot, who today is reported to have assets worth billions, started Electronic Data Systems as a one-man enterprise in an office he rented for $100 a month, with only $1,000 in borrowed capital. He still has simple tastes and claims that no painting or lithograph in his office cost more than $25. The late Sam Walton, of Wal-Mart stores, reported to have built personal assets of between $7 and $8 billion, was also a man of simple tastes, drove a pickup truck, and kept modest offices.

Here are some suggestions for conserving your cash and minimizing your first-year expenses:

- Make no long-term advertising commitments, such as Yellow Pages advertising or an advertising term contract with a newspaper.

- Set up your first office in your home, if at all possible. If you must have an office outside your home, choose a modestly priced one in the nearest business district, especially where you do not have to pay monthly parking fees.

- If you must rent office space somewhere, rent a single office, not a suite, or sublease an office from someone with a suite. This can be quite inexpensive and comfortable.

- Consider desk space in a communal office. These are offices in which you pay a modest sum for your own desk in a large room, with answering service and access to a conference room, copier, stenographic services, and a mail room. This is a good arrangement if you will not spend much time in your office: It gives you a telephone number, business address, mail address, and place for the occasional conference with clients on your premises. It also saves you the cost of furnishing an office, minimizing initial investment.

- Be conservative in furnishing your office. You can buy a decent desk new for not more than $200, for example. But you can do even better by seeking out one of the companies who rent office furniture and sell used furniture. They often have great bargains in nearly new office furniture. Also watch the classified advertising sections of your newspapers for salvage sales: furniture slightly damaged in accidents of one sort or another, bankruptcies, and other bargain opportunities.

- Be modest in ordering your business cards and stationery. Plain white thermographed (raised printing) stationery (cards, letterheads, and envelopes) in black ink on good quality stock is entirely adequate. Expensive cards and stationery will not produce one extra dollar's worth of income for you.

■ Shop around. The market for most things is competitive. You can easily spend $3,000 to $5,000 for a computer, but you can also now get a quite adequate system for well under $1,000.

A Few Special Tips for Cost Avoidance

In the booming economy that we have enjoyed over recent decades, we seem to have forgotten that ours is a competitive economic system. We refers to both buyers and sellers but not all buyers and sellers. A few sellers still deal competitively, and a few buyers still seek out the best offers. It is easy to pay too much for things if you fail to be conscious of and take advantage of the competitive system. An example of what I mean follows.

When I made the move to my own home from a costly downtown suite of offices and monthly parking costs for my car, I had to seek out some new suppliers. Of special importance to me was a good supplier of printing, since I was at the time publishing a newsletter and otherwise using a great deal of printing regularly.

I turned to the Yellow Pages to get quotations and was dismayed by the exorbitant figures I was quoted. They were higher even than those of downtown Washington, which I had always thought to be rather high. I soon realized that I had been calling only those printers who had large advertisements in the Yellow Pages. Next I tried printers who had a mere one-line listing and no display advertisement. Immediately I began to find printers whose prices were much more reasonable. I soon chose one for my work and not only did this printer offer modest prices, but he gave excellent service and entirely satisfactory quality.

I learned a lesson from that and have since used the same philosophy in seeking out other suppliers. It is not foolproof; you must still exercise good judgment in your choices; but it is a sound basis, I have found, for beginning a search.

The same philosophy applies to other areas. Buying nearly new office items from renters of office furniture is a good practice generally, but that does not guarantee a fair price. I have discovered some renters of office furniture who wanted to recover the original price plus a profit, despite the fact that the item was no longer new and had probably earned back all its original cost for the merchant. And you need not be an expert to know what a fair price is: A little comparative shopping will soon educate you as to the proper market for any item so you can judge an offer properly.

I shopped very carefully in buying my first personal computer. I shopped by studying all the personal-computer advertising I could find, first of all. I reviewed articles in computer magazines to compare what the writers offered as advice on the subject. I had no illusions about what I wanted: I wanted a computer for word processing, nothing else. That any computer can do other work was irrelevant: I intended to buy a good word processor and not be attracted by other features, which would not be of any use to me and would cost me many dollars.

I wound up with a $1,900 system, which included a printer (I paid a few hundred dollars more than that for a bigger and faster printer.) at a time when most systems cost about twice that. I am now using my fifth computer, but each one was still running well when I decided it was technically obsolete. Because I was careful in that and subsequent investments in computers and related equipment, I did not hesitate long to "trade up" when it seemed the time to do so. Perhaps if I had invested more money in earlier systems, I would have been reluctant to upgrade and so would deny myself the advantages of the newer systems. That's another advantage of being conservative in what you buy; it's far less painful to write it off when it is time to replace it.

There are occasions when you win assignments you can't handle alone. Sometimes you need others with skills similar to your own, and sometimes you need others with complementary or supporting skills. At times, I have had to find other proposal consultants to help me handle a proposal task too big for one person. At other times I have needed specialists in logistics or some other discipline for which I have no skills, and sometimes I have had to have drafting or illustrating help to support me.

The results have often been disappointing and costly. More than once I have paid off the associates or hired help and worked late into the night to do their work over because I considered it not up to my own standard. Perhaps the client would have accepted it, but I would not, for a reputation is fragile and once damaged almost impossible to repair. I am unwilling to submit work I believe to represent less than my best effort. Consequently, I learned to follow certain principles:

- Require references and check them out. (An amazingly large number of people fail to verify references.)

- Don't hire people by the hour. Doing so compels you to pay them for each hour worked, no matter how productive or unproductive they are, no matter how satisfactory or unsatisfactory the result is. (Even when the result is satisfactory, why should you be penalized if the other person is a slow worker? Sometimes an hourly rate inspires slow work!)

- Do retain the other party as a subcontractor, not as an employee or even as an associate. Reach agreement on what is to be done, when it is to be done, what the quality standard is to be, and the price. And then write that agreement up in some simple letter form.

- Do make it clear that payment will be made when you accept the product as meeting the quality standard agreed on.

A great many people can "talk a good game"—speak knowledgeably and be quite convincing about how good they are at what they do, and yet turn out to be rather poor performers. I subscribe strongly to Pareto's Law, also referred to as the 80–20 Rule.

Vilfredo Pareto (1848–1923) was a French-born economist who did his significant work in Italy and is therefore mistakenly referred to as an Italian economist (and even as a Swiss economist sometimes!). He discovered that in the Italian economy a small proportion of the applied cause is responsible for a disproportionately large portion of the result.

Pareto's Law recognizes that there is a great disproportion in distributions, and it applies everywhere: A small amount of the cause accounts for the major portion of the effect. For example, 20 percent of any production team normally produces 80 percent of the output, and vice versa, unfortunately, the other 80 percent of the team produces only 20 percent of the output. Eighty percent of the money in a bank is deposited by 20 percent of the depositors. Twenty percent of the workers in a project produce 80 percent of the result. And, as value engineers have discovered, 20 percent of the parts in a machine do 80 percent of the work.

This demonstrates a law of inverse ratios, revealing horrible inefficiency and waste: 80 percent of the cost is incurred to produce 20 percent of the result, and 20 percent of the cost produces the other 80 percent of the result; in sales organizations, for example, it is not all unusual to find that 20 percent of the salespeople produce 80 percent of the sales, and the remaining 80 percent of the sales force produces only 20 percent of the sales. This has been found to be largely true in all sorts of applications and activities. Applied to people, I find that probably not more than 20 percent of the performers in any field are truly top notch at what they do, and the other 80 percent populate a spectrum ranging from acceptable to unacceptable.

The real hazard is semi-competence. It's easy to recognize the truly competent and truly incompetent, but it is usually difficult to be sure about the quasi-competent individual, who often gets away with substandard work for a long, long time before you are sure that the work is really not quite good enough for your needs. I found it in accountants who had good references and could say all the right things, but whose books never balanced, whose invoices were always being sent back to correct errors, and who could never come up with the right answers to ordinary questions asked by management. I found it in technical writers who diligently put in long hours, but who, in the end resigned when the time came to surrender a manuscript, leaving nothing but a large notebook filled with indecipherable notes and in some cases not even that. And I found it in engineers who discussed the work convincingly enough but whose designs and prototypes never met the specifications or matched the reports they wrote. In fact, I was grateful when I found someone whose work I heartily approved of because it assured me that I did have specific standards, when my disillusioning experiences were sometimes causing me to wonder whether I was not excessively and unjustly critical.

Beware of being deceived by appearances. Many of these quasi-competents are experts at creating the appearance of competence and success in what they are doing. But judge by results and by results only. It's the only way to be sure.

Even taking the relatively safe route of acting on friends' recommendations and doing business with large, successful vendors has its hazards. I undertook to develop a sales brochure for a rather large firm, who asked me to have a quantity of them printed after I had finished preparing the manuscript and final copy. A friend and subcontractor, who was handling art work and preparation of camera-ready copy, recommended a local printer who had a large shop and did fine work. My friend didn't tell me what kind of business ethics the firm practiced, however. I furnished a maximum estimate of the size of the final document, number of photographs, and so on, and was quoted a price. I delivered copy that was 10 percent smaller than my estimate, and the printer, who should have thereupon reduced his price, attempted to charge me 20 percent more than he had originally estimated! Only the fact that I had his estimate in writing and challenged him to sue me in court persuaded him to settle for his original estimate.

Finally, beware of moonlighters. I hesitate to condemn them as a class, but I have had many bad experiences. Many are excellent performers, but you would be wise to be cautious and check their references out carefully. Many are unreliable because they have regular, steady jobs and are not dependent on their moonlighting. They tend to get tired and begin fading long before the job is done. They take off time for a movie or a party at critical junctures. They balk at redoing their work when it is unacceptable. And sometimes they simply disappear and are not heard from again. I prefer to trust subcontracts to full-time self-employed individuals who depend on the work for their survival. They are almost invariably far more reliable.

The odds are therefore not exactly in your favor, and you will be wise to practice defensive tactics when entrusting some portion of your success to others.

Founding the
Consulting Practice

Well begun is half done.
—Horace

IF YOU HAD IT TO DO OVER . . .

- What were your mistakes or major problems when you started?
- How did you handle them?
- What would you do differently today?
- What advice would you offer beginners?

These are among questions I asked a number of experienced independent consultants. Some answers were gathered in CompuServe forums of independent consultants sponsored by the ICCA, the Independent Computer Consultants association, and in the work from home forum. Much information came to me via Carl Kline, of the National Referrals Center, and his own online reports on Internet, quoting letters from consultants. A summary of that wealth of experience and wisdom is offered here.

An early reaction of many participants was that the exchange of ideas resulting from my queries would have been greatly helpful when they were starting, but was pretty much a review of what they learned "the hard way." As the study proceeded, many participants discovered that they could still benefit by reviewing their early mistakes and reinforcing the lessons learned. Some admitted a tendency to forget the need to market continuously, for example, and needed to be reminded that one must market for tomorrow, not for today.

Let me note here that some of the advice and opinions from others were in variance with my own opinions and the counsel I offer in these pages. That is no surprise: Each of us mirrors his or her own experiences and draws conclusions therefrom. But none of us has experienced exactly what you will experience, so none of us can give you advice totally specific to your own need. Take from what follows, therefore, only whatever is relevant and helpful to you.

David Moskowitz was one helpful respondent. He is an independent computer consultant based in a Philadelphia suburb. He stated plainly that one should have enough capital to survive for a year before launching an independent practice. That is a piece of advice offered frequently, I found. Unfortunately, it isn't always possible: Many independent consultants confess that circumstances forced them to launch their ventures on short notice and without preparation, as did Moskowitz, and they were forced to manage somehow without reserves.

He stressed also the need to have some clear concept of just what you want to do as a consultant, rather than venture forth with some vague idea of what you will offer clients, and he agrees heartily on the need for marketing knowledge and sales training. He also noted a need to learn negotiating skills, which I regard as a sales skill.

Many agreed that the discussions gave them a new view and appreciation of accounting as a source of important management information. Esther Schindler, who chaired one organized discussion, admitted that she has always thought of accounting as an incredibly boring subject, but suddenly found it an incredibly fascinating one when it concerned her money and her business! Later, Esther admitted that she and her partner, husband Bill Schindler, had made the common error of the typical too-eager new entrepreneurs, accepting contracts with nothing in writing and suffering predictable consequences of being victimized by clients who demanded (and got) too much and sometimes failed to pay their bills even then.

A few participants offered rueful comments that they had suffered from failure to establish a suitable accounting system at the beginning.

I found consensus about the need for continuous marketing, even when one has a full schedule. Many had learned the hard lessons of failing to market for tomorrow's contracts, assuming that the time to market was when they were not busy doing paying work. They reported many experiences that stressed the need for more attention to marketing. One consultant, for example, was relaxing with what appeared to be a comfortable backlog of contracts, when he had three sudden contract cancellations and immediate gaps in his working schedules and income.

The need to do careful credit checks of clients and to get retainers up front was also a common lesson learned. The failure to verify credit and the fear of losing a sale by requiring a retainer have cost many consultants heavily. One reported a loss of over $5,000 in printing costs alone when a client simply refused to pay.

Several consultants agreed with the opinion of consultant Gerre Jones that incorporating as a Sub-Chapter S Corporation is a good plan, although some pointed out that this is a mixed blessing because not all states treat such a corporation benevolently—with tax breaks. Obviously, this is a matter to discuss with an expert accountant or attorney who is familiar with the relevant laws in your own state. Too, the tax laws undergo frequent change, and that is an influence on your decision as to the form of your business organization.

GENERAL CONSIDERATIONS SUCH AS LICENSING

Unless your basic profession requires licensing to practice or your local statutes compel you to have a mercantile license of some sort, you probably do not need a license of any kind. Consulting is not itself a licensed or regulated enterprise. If you are uncertain about it, seek information or guidance. Here are some sources:

- A local lawyer
- The local Chamber of Commerce
- Clerk of your county/city/town hall
- The business editor of the local newspaper
- Local business owners
- Discussion groups on the Internet
- The local U.S. Small Business Administration (district) office
- State or local government small-business office

Even where licensing of some sort is required, there may be special provisions. In Miami, I was required to have a mercantile license, but as a war veteran I was entitled to a much reduced fee. Moreover, the licensing authority was kind enough to give me permission to conduct my business without a license until the beginning of the new license year.

Small Business Administration (SBA)

The SBA operates about 90 district offices throughout the United States. Your local telephone directory will furnish the address of one nearest you. Among the services the SBA usually has available to small business owners are at least two free consulting services. One of these is furnished by members of SBA's SCORE (Service Corps of Retired Executives). The other is furnished under contract to SBA by private firms located where they can serve the country's large population of small businesses. Visit the nearest SBA office to see what they can offer you.

State/Local Government Programs

Many state and local governments have instituted socioeconomic programs to aid small businesses and minority-owned businesses. Among the services offered is general counseling. Check with these programs to see what they can offer to help you in getting started. Use the Internet search services to find out more about these programs.

THE MATTER OF A BUSINESS NAME

A government executive who reviewed many brochures and proposals remarked, "The bigger the name, the smaller the company."

He sighed and smiled when he made this observation because he applauded all enterprise and truly wanted to award contracts to new, small firms. Still, there was an ambivalence in his reaction because he was also an admirer of complete honesty. Because of that, he felt that a grandiose business name such as "International Computer Systems & Information Consultants Ltd." was an effort to impress and deceive him into believing that he was dealing with a major organization. That led him to wonder what else in the proposal, brochure, or other sales presentation was false window dressing and hyperbole.

There is great dignity in simplicity and understatement. Witness the names of many major corporations, even their original, full names, further simplified to acronyms or abbreviations, in many cases:

- RCA (Radio Corporation of America)
- IBM (International Business Machines)
- Xerox Corporation
- GE (General Electric Co.)
- GMC (General Motors Corp.)
- USI (U.S. Industries, Inc.)

Most of these supercorporations became so well known by their initials that many people do not even know the names for which these letters stand, although the original names are quite simple and straightforward. Obviously, a long and elaborate name is unnecessary to gain acceptance, and may be a disadvantage.

The two most popular ways that consultants name their practices is by their own names and what they specialize in, for examples:

- Gordon W. Honeycutt
- Honeycutt Marketing Consultants
- Gordon W. Honeycutt & Associates

Often, the consultant adds another line or two, in addition to an address and telephone number, elaborating a bit on the exact nature of the services offered such as Marketing Plans, Direct-Mail Services, and/or Market Surveys.

One immediate advantage of using your personal name in this manner is that you have no legal complications. On the other hand, if you use a trade name of some sort such as International Marketing Consultants, you do have to register that name ordinarily. If you incorporate, that business name is registered in filing your documents of incorporation, but if you are a sole proprietorship or partnership, you usually have to comply with state and local statutes requiring that you file fictitious or dba (doing business as) names. That is to give notice to all who it is doing business under that name and is the true and proper owner/s of the business operating under that name.

This is not an especially costly procedure, normally, and you can do it all yourself, if you wish, although most people retain a lawyer to handle it. (A clerk in the Philadelphia City Hall was able to advise me completely on proper procedures for doing this, even to exact wording of the required advertising.) It normally amounts to filing statements with the state and local governments and placing an advertisement in the local daily newspaper or in a special legal periodical *(The Legal Intelligencer)* for three insertions identifying yourself as the owner of the business.

Even if you use part of your own name (rather than your complete name) as part of the fictitious business name, for example, Honeycutt Marketing Associates, you may be required to file that name since it does not really identify you as the proprietor. (It is probably best to consult the authorities or a lawyer in such case.)

WHAT TYPE OF BUSINESS ORGANIZATION SHOULD YOU USE?

A large number of independent consulting enterprises spring to life as corporations, often because an accountant or lawyer so advises, but often on some mistaken notion of the new entrepreneur that incorporation lends prestige and is a must for success and a mandatory safeguard against liability.

There is nothing wrong with incorporating, of course, and it may well turn out to be the best route for you, but consider the several other ways to organize your venture.

Sole Proprietorship

If you own the business and all its assets in your own name, whether you work alone or have help, you have a sole proprietorship. The assets are entirely yours and you are entirely responsible for any liabilities. This is by far the simplest way to operate, but some consultants are increasingly apprehensive about the potential liabilities of being totally and personally responsible in these times of excessive litigation, and many find this a persuasive argument for incorporating.

Partnerships

A formal partnership is suggested when you have one or more partners. Proprietorship, in a simple partnership, is vested in all partners, shared according to whatever agreement exists between or among you and your partners. You share responsibility for all liabilities, and ownership of all assets. You should have a detailed agreement drawn up between or among you, properly notarized and witnessed. It is probably a good idea to have an attorney handle this for you. In fact, it is usually wise for each partner to have his or her own attorney. Even if you operate as a sole proprietor, however, you may find advantages in having your spouse named as a partner. It is best to consult an attorney to learn the pros and cons of doing this before making your decision.

Limited Partnership

A limited partnership is somewhat like a corporation, in that although it has the legal and tax characteristics of a simple partnership, the liability of the partners can be limited to the capital invested.

Corporations

Corporations are legal entities. The U.S. Supreme Court defined a corporation as "an artificial being, invisible, intangible, and existing only in contemplation of law," a definition echoed frequently in other courts and in legal texts.

The corporation is treated as though it were a person in many ways. That is why it is the corporation, not you personally, that is ordinarily responsible and liable for the obligations of the corporation. (LTD, standing for Limited, which some people use in preference to Inc. or Incorporated, refers to limited liability.)

There are a number of types of corporations. Some are public, accepting investors by selling stock in the corporation. Most independent consultants who incorporate, however, form close corporations. (You can sell stock privately, to the limits prescribed, in a close corporation, but you cannot offer stock to the general public. That is a far more complex proposition.)

You can incorporate also as a nonprofit corporation, but again that has many drawbacks, although it also has a few advantages. You can draw a salary and expenses, plus normal fringe benefits, and you can treat yourself quite well as an employee, but the corporation cannot accumulate a reserve of profits and you never have an equity position—a business you own personally and can sell. Some individuals opt for a Sub-Chapter S Corporation, an entity that does not have to pay corporate taxes. To qualify for this, you must have some limited number of stockholders and draw income from operations, not investment—an arrangement that may or may not be suitable for you. (You may have noted that one of the consultants quoted earlier, Gerre Jones, believes firmly that this is a must for the independent consultant, but conditions for an S Corporation vary from one state to another and from one tax year to another.)

Most individuals who incorporate tend to form a close corporation, one held closely with limited participation. It is possible, in fact, to hold all the offices yourself! Most who form corporations, however, bring in family members and sometimes close friends to act as other officers and directors of the corporation.

Pros and Cons of Incorporation

Accountants and lawyers tend to encourage you to incorporate. They are generally sincere in their beliefs that everyone in business ought to be incorporated; the nature of their work almost mandates that conviction. However, each stands to benefit directly if you incorporate—lawyers charge fees to do the paper work and accountants get much more work to do when you are incorporated—so there is always the question of whether they are objective in recommending that step.

There are pros and cons in incorporating, as in most things. Aside from the possible benefits of adding prestige to your professional image, there is the real consideration of limiting your liability: If someone sues your corporation and gets a judgment against it, your personal property is normally immune to that judgment. On the other hand, being incorporated adds a great deal of bookkeeping and accounting and a few extra taxes as well. Balancing this added paperwork burden is the use of a corporation as a tax shelter. Unless the tax code changes considerably—as it may very well—the corporation offers some opportunities to manage your affairs so as to lower your overall taxes. Many individuals believe that if they incorporate their businesses, they will immediately and automatically be allowed many more deductions for business expenses and thereby enjoy lower tax rates, as well as sundry other benefits.

That is partly true. You will still pay whatever your individual tax rate is on the money you draw from the corporation for your personal use, whether you pay yourself a regular salary or simply draw money from time to time. The lower corporate tax rate—assuming that it is lower, which may or may not be the case for you—applies only to the money left in the corporation, money that the corporation banks as profit or earned income.

The deductions you take for business expenses are essentially the same, whether you are incorporated or not. Your insurance, other taxes, interest paid, rent, and other expenses are deductible regardless of the type of business organization. However, as a corporation you may be able to give yourself certain benefits that are not taxable as income and are deductible business expenses for the corporation. (Your tax expert should advise you.) In general, the tax benefits begin to accrue significantly when you begin to earn substantially from your work much more than they do when you are earning only a modest income.

Contrary to the beliefs of many, incorporation does not add to your prestige or heighten your professional image. You can incorporate in most states today for less than $100. The forms are simple—an attorney may draw up a thick document to apply to the state, but there are usually simple forms you can fill in (a single page, in Maryland) for a simple, close corporation.

Even the bylaws and other necessary trappings of incorporation are not a problem. There are suppliers of all these things in all metropolitan areas. My local telephone directory has three names under the heading Corporation Supplies, offering supplies such as corporate seals, stock certificates, printed bylaws, resolution forms, and record books. These suppliers are expert in the whole matter of incorporation and can usually advise you as to where to go to get the necessary forms and how to go about filling them out and filing your application for incorporation. Nor is this procedure expensive. I paid only about $50 for my complete corporate kit when I incorporated.

Don't be misled. I have met individuals who believed that they could not incorporate because they worked from their homes. But the state really does not care where you conduct your business, as far as a legal address is concerned. That's a matter possibly for the local zoning commission, but it has nothing to do with incorporating.

Even if you wish to incorporate, you do not have to do so immediately. You can incorporate when you wish to. There is the disadvantage that you will have some additional taxes to pay and a good bit more accounting work to do when you incorporate, but you will also gain some useful options.

Where Should You Incorporate?

The State of Delaware has long been the favorite state in which companies incorporate because Delaware has made incorporation simple. Consequently, it enjoys by far the largest number of corporations, even though few of those corporations maintain headquarters in or even operate in that state! However, wherever they do operate, they are a foreign corporation and must register as such, which involves a few penalties, such as taxes. At the same time, they must keep a registered agent in the state of their incorporation.

Most states have liberalized their requirements for incorporation so that it is usually inexpensive and easy to incorporate in your own state. That eliminates the problems of being forced to register as a foreign corporation and being forced to pay someone to act as your registered agent in the state of your incorporation. (You are your own registered agent when you operate in the state of incorporation.)

Consider, then, your own needs, your own problems, your local laws, federal tax laws, and whatever else applies to your individual situation. In addition, consider the messages of the next few paragraphs.

DO YOU NEED A LAWYER?

There are many reasons to retain a lawyer. Some are good reasons; some are not. A good lawyer can ease your path in a number of ways, for example, by:

- Doing things for you that require legal expertise and/or familiarity with the system
- Advising you as a legal expert
- Advising you as an objective observer
- Representing you and your interests

You can do a great many things for yourself, thereby saving a great deal of money. Ordinarily you can handle your own incorporation, registration of business name, applications for licenses, drafting simple letter agreements, and similar do-it-yourself projects. There are many books available to help you learn how to do these things. These books include sample forms and guidance in how to handle corporate tasks (such as writing resolutions, holding directors meetings, opening corporate bank accounts, and deriving maximum benefits from incorporation). You can also get from these books a complete set of bylaws you may use, perhaps with some minor adaptations, as your own corporate bylaws.

One word of caution: Do not ask your lawyer to make your business decisions. Depending on the individual, some lawyers may make it clear that what they offer is advice and their best opinions to help you reach decisions, while others may urge their recommended courses of action on you, even prophesying dark and ominous events if you fail to heed their good advice. But even the best lawyer is only an advisor, no matter how sound the advice offered; you must make the decision, as a result of all advice and your own good judgment. But that good judgment depends on your own complete understanding. Require that your lawyer couch the advice and the rationale for it—and do insist on knowing the rationale—in language that you can understand.

DO YOU NEED AN ACCOUNTANT?

Everything said about needing or using a lawyer applies equally to your relationship with your accountant, who is also an advisor, and who may talk in a jargon you do not understand. Insist that your accountant also explain everything in plain English.

Strictly speaking, you do not need an accountant; it is possible to manage without one (especially if you use the simple proprietorship method of doing business). There is this to consider, however: You would probably make relatively extensive use of a lawyer's services in setting up and organizing your practice, but after that you would probably need legal services only occasionally, if and as legal problems arose. Accounting, however, you must do regularly, keeping records of every day's events and generating appropriate reports and tax returns, as required. Here is a list of the kinds of functions that must be performed in all accounting systems:

1. *Journalizing:* Entering bills, receivable, and other items into the daily journals spontaneously, as they appear.

2. *Posting:* Transferring journal entries to ledger pages and columns.

3. *Balancing and auditing:* Validating the correctness of the entries posted through balancing columns and checking specific items when columns do not balance.

4. *Calculating overhead:* Determining the cost of doing business as a mathematical rate—percentage of direct labor and/or of other direct costs.

5. *Generating reports and statements:* Preparing such items as the profit and loss statement, the balance sheet, net worth statements, and various periodic reports.

6. *Tax work:* Making out tax returns for the government agencies (federal, state, and local), with required forms, reports, and statements.

7. *Scheduling payables:* Listing invoices to be paid, with schedules for the payment dates, calculated for maximum cash-flow and other financial advantages.

8. *Invoicing receivables:* Sending out invoices for money due you.

9. *Miscellaneous:* Follow-up statements and notices urging payment of invoices, preparing special reports, making estimates, calculating and preparing payroll checks, and whatever other tasks arise.

These are the general tasks of accounting, although the functions and elements may vary from one organization to another, depending on the size of the organization, the nature of the organization's activities, and the nature of the accounting system itself.

Happily, this set of tasks is not nearly as formidable as this listing makes it appear, at least not for the independent consultant. Except for the tax work, keeping books via one of the simple commercial systems, such as The Dome Simplified Weekly Bookkeeping Record, a paper system printed as a loosely bound book, is quite simple. The system includes a general day journal (the left page) and a ledger (the right page). You journalize each event—expenditure, sale made, bill paid, and so on—as it happens, noting the number assigned to the type of item—3 for advertising, 21 for repairs, 30 for travel expense, and so on. At the end of the week, you total all the number 3 items and post them opposite number 3 on the right—ledger—side, and do the same for all the others. You keep running (cumulative) totals on everything, including income. You can determine—anytime and at a glance—how total outgo compares with total income, what cost items are your greatest ones, and just about anything else you want to know about dollars and cents in your venture. The ledger has three columns for all the cost items and the income or sales items: total this week, total end of last week, and total to date (Figure 6.1). You can see how easily you can detect changes in your costs. An equally simple form gives you an accounting of money received on the same basis—this month, last month, and total to date—to give you an instantaneous balance of income versus outgo, which is the essence of all accounting.

When I turned to this system, after suffering the frustrations of permitting an accountant to do it all and tell me what he wanted to tell me when he wanted to tell it to me—which meant as much as three months after the fact—I sought out another accountant. I wanted him to do my taxes only, but he wanted to do much more. I spent an hour arguing with him before he came to accept the fact that I was not going to pay him many hundreds of dollars to design a special system for me. In fact, when he came to the realization that he would have to accept me on my terms or not at all, he finally admitted that my

		Total This Month	Total to Last Month	Total to Date
8010	Accounting			
8020	Advertising/mktg			
8030	Auto expense			
8040	Books/mags/subs			
8060	Contributions			
8080	Health insurance			
	Dental			
8090	Entertainment			
8100	Car/office ins			
8120	Miscellaneous			
8130	Office expense			
8140	Postage			
8150	Promo/gifts			
8160	Office rent			
8170	Repairs			
8180	Payroll: Sher			
8180	Payroll: Herm			
8190	Subcontract			
8200	Supplies			
8220	Property tax			
8230	Unemployment:			
	IRS			
	MD			
8240	C&P/cellular/FAX			
8250	Travel			
8300	MD corp tax			
8310	FED corp tax			
3050	IRS withholding			
3060	SS/FICA/med with			
3070	State MD with			
3210	Computer/discover			
5030	Non-deductibles			
8110	Interest charges			
1020	Petty cash			
1040	Rec loans			
	TOTALS:			

Figure 6.1. Basic bookkeeping rationale.

decision to use the simple Dome system was probably a wise decision for me, and we have had no problems since, except that he complains that I give him too much detail at tax time. But I like the detail; it tells me how we are doing and allows me to take corrective steps in time to apply a cure when things are not going as they should.

Today, there is an abundance of simple, easy-to-operate accounting systems for your computer, such as the popular Quicken system.

DO YOU NEED A BUSINESS PLAN?

The question of a business plan comes up often as a problem for the newly launched or aspirant independent consultant, usually in terms of such questions as these:

- Do I need a business plan?
- What is it supposed to do for me?
- What should it look like?
- Where can I find out more about it?

The term *business plan* means different things to different people. For many, it is a euphemism for loan proposal. That is because there are two kinds of business plans—or, more accurately, there are two uses for a business plan, and thus two ways in which to slant it: It is designed to help the entrepreneur raise capital for a new enterprise (probably the most frequent reason for creating it) or it is designed to help the entrepreneur think out what must be done and make plans to do it—to create a road map to follow.

Actually, that is the thrust of a business plan regardless of whether it is actually a planning guide for a start-up or a prospectus to persuade bankers or investors to provide capital.

Neophytes are likely to think of a business plan as a firm guide for operating the business, but it is best recognized as a set of estimates and premises that should be compared with conditions experienced and revised frequently. Often, the original business plan should be scrapped and a new one drawn up, accommodating the inevitable changes that take place in the course of conducting a business and making needed corrections to earlier estimates.

Every business venture ought to be based on a business plan, but the enormous variability in business ventures mandates an almost equally enormous variability in the plans. Many features are common to all, but many others are peculiar to the industry or business and to the individual circumstances. These must be reflected in the two business plans.

A general outline is offered at the end of this chapter for your guidance. Study each element of the outline carefully and be sure that it is appropriate and fits the practice you plan. Make whatever changes are necessary to ensure that fit.

Consider business conditions of the moment and make any changes necessary to make your plan a sensible one vis-à-vis market and financial conditions. Be prepared to review the plan periodically to revise, update, and/or otherwise modify the plan to meet sudden or unexpected changes in conditions.

The model represented here would be adequate for launching a relatively large venture. To adapt it to a small venture, it is necessary to merely reduce the scope of the coverage, eliminate irrelevant/unneeded items, and so on.

SOME GENERAL OBSERVATIONS ABOUT BUSINESS PLANS

The executive summary is important. This is a brief summary—a page or two. It is an overview and a reminder of your major goal and major approach.

The plan must be highly *specific*. It must specify products and/or services to be developed and marketed, and where and how these things will be done. To whom will you sell? (Identify markets.) How will you reach your markets? Avoid vague generalizations here.

Shun *hyperbole*. Facts are much more impressive and much more convincing. Use nouns and verbs, not adjectives. Avoid superlatives and sweeping generalizations. Be rigidly factual and practical.

The chapters or sections normally found in even the simplest business plans intended to be operating guides include most or all of the following:

1. The service(s)/products
2. The organization
3. The market(s)
4. Marketing/sales strategy/plans
5. Administrative plans and projections

They are presented in this order here, but this is not necessarily the best order, which will vary from one case to another, according to what is most *important* in terms of the *purpose* of the business plan.

GENERALIZED OUTLINES

Here are some major items that should be covered:

- Start-up capital requirement.
- Start-up decisions:
  —Office location
  —Starting fixtures, furniture, equipment, supplies
  —Services offered

—Products offered

—Short- and long-term goals and objectives

■ Marketing plan/strategies:

—Client(s) profiles

—Competition

—Advertising

—Promotion

■ Rate structure

■ Potential for diversification/other profit centers

■ Contingency plans

Finances, Taxes, and Related Problems

Business is about money and problems related to money
as much as it is about what you sell and how you sell it.
                                                    —Herman Holtz

USING WHAT YOUR ACCOUNTANT TELLS YOU

Accountants have their own jargon, just as lawyers, doctors, engineers, and insurance people do. It is confusing because words do not always mean what you
think they mean. You may assume that cost of sales is what it cost you to get
the order, but it refers to all the costs incurred in filling the order. A sale is not
an order here; it is money received. Having your system on a cash basis
doesn't mean you sell for cash only; it means you post a payment when you pay
it and a receipt when you get the money.

I do not understand most of the jargon but I am not afraid to ask dumb questions. The fear of asking questions leads to trouble. As in dealing with your
lawyer, make sure that you understand what your accountant tells you. Ask all
the dumb questions you like, and make sure that you understand and agree
with the rationale before you accept your accountant's recommendation.

In short, use your accountant as a doer of things you can't or don't want to
do yourself and as a source of information whose opinions you consider and
value, but not necessarily accept as guidance. You, and no one else, make the
decisions.

ACCOUNTING IS A MANAGEMENT TOOL

The main purpose of accounting is to furnish information for management.
Management is probably second only to marketing as a topic of never-ending
interest in the business world. Books are published on the subject continually,

and it is discussed in countless periodicals, taught to thousands of college students, and offered in seminars and special training courses. Every few years there comes a new Messiah of Management with a new catchword to describe a revelation of some new theory and system alleged to make any fool a brilliant manager.

Management is not mystical or complex, nor is the mastery of it simple. Despite the popular notion that management is the art of directing others, it may or may not have anything to do with other people. Even the smallest enterprise, where one person does everything, must be managed. Management is the use of available resources to achieve goals. It requires qualities that cannot be reduced to mechanical functions nor conferred by simple tools. Even given the capacity to reason objectively and creatively, you need information upon which to base that thinking: No one can think objectively and make sound judgments without having the essential information. A decision cannot be any better than the information upon which it is based. Ergo, the information produced by accounting is essential to good management, and is therefore the major objective of and reason for accounting.

The Information You Need

Here are some of the kinds of information—the most critically important items—that your accounting system ought to deliver to you to put you in full and total control of your enterprise:

- *Overhead costs.* Rent, heat, light, telephone, advertising, postage, etc; what and how much they are and whether they are approximately constant or are trending up or down.
- *Sales figures.* Dollar figures, volume, frequency, and types of sales/clients; trends, if any.
- *Cost of sales.* Total cost of winning and completing every project/ assignment.
- *Markup.* How much you must add/are adding to estimated cost of each project to meet expenses and realize profit.
- *Profit.* Surplus above all costs for each job, total, and average.

Monitoring this kind of information regularly enables you to discover immediately any increases in costs, decline in sales, slippage in profitability, and relative profitability of each type of sale or project. These are all key factors in the success of your enterprise. Even in a small enterprise you can be so busily engaged that you can go on for a long time—months—losing money without being aware of it. Unfortunately, if enough time elapses before you discover that costs have gotten out of hand or you are marking up your costs insufficiently and losing money on your projects, it may be too late to recover. More than one business has succumbed to such unpleasant surprises. Hence the urgency of current information on the health of your enterprise.

When I required a great deal of printing, I kept a close watch over printing costs. If they climbed more than they should, I conferred with my printer or changed printers. Sometimes I found that one printer had the best price on one type of work, while another had the best price on another kind of work. When schedules permitted, I had printing done out of town, via mail order, if it reduced the cost.

Accounting feedback also told me clearly what activities were most and least profitable. This is guidance for planning future action—what types of sales and contracts to pursue and which to abandon. Sometimes we accept work we enjoy doing without checking on whether it is profitable: We need the reality check.

I was well aware of what were supposedly the typical seasons—peaks and valleys of sales volume—and I checked my own sales against this. Surprisingly often, I found that my own sales did not follow the pattern, but were sometimes even the exact opposite, peaking when conventional wisdom said sales should be down. Lesson: Conventional wisdom is only opinion; ledger figures are facts.

SOME COMMON MISTAKES

Business savants of institutions such as the U.S. Small Business Administration and Dun & Bradstreet frequently report and remark on the rate of small-business failures, often as high as 70 percent of new start ups. This indicates a success rate of 30 or more percent. This may seem small, but given that (1) a large majority of these new start ups are by beginners with no business experience, and (2) the enormous "opportunity" to make fatal mistakes, it is marvelous that even 30 percent survive and succeed. Here are some typical mistakes that prove fatal to the new, small businesses:

- ■ Failure to understand the meaning of profit. Many beginners in business think that everything left after paying the bills is profit, but they fail to count their own draw or salary as cost. (Your own salary is cost, not profit.)
- ■ Marketing by being the low bidder, underpricing everything and assuming that they will somehow manage to muddle through, since their main cost is their own labor.
- ■ Overpricing everything they bid on, so that they rarely win a job.
- ■ Failing to count as business costs and charge their enterprises for facilities they provide from personal possessions, such as use of their personal computer, automobile, telephone, office space at home, and other such resources, under the naive premise that they are going to own and pay for these anyway!

Independent consultants who operate this way do not necessarily fail to remain in practice; many go on for years eking out a meager living, but their practices are failures as business enterprises. Success should mean being able to earn personal income that is at least as much as you could earn on someone else's payroll and yet showing a reasonable profit—at least 5 to 10 percent after taxes—each year. Profit is necessary to build reserves for the future and to provide for necessary new investments.

SOME BASIC RULES

Here are some suggested basic rules to keep in mind:

- You must know and charge on your books each and every cost incurred in your practice.
- Your personal draw or salary is cost, not profit.
- Anything you supply in kind, such as office space in your home or a personal computer you already own, must be evaluated and charged at fair value. Pro-rate the cost or sell the property to your practice, as appropriate. Pro-rate costs for space that you furnish the business: The IRS allows such charges for space dedicated to the business.
- All costs must be recovered by the practice. Price work to recover all costs and show some profit.
- Despite this, you must be competitive in price. That means you must keep close control over your costs.

BASIC COST CENTERS AND COST DEFINITIONS

I will not try to teach you accounting, nor am I qualified to do so. But finding success in any venture is difficult enough, and failure to understand and recognize costs can be fatal. Years of experience in delivering seminars and consulting services to the owners of small businesses revealed clearly the need for this kind of information.

In a formal course in accounting, you would find yourself learning many technical terms to communicate complicated ideas about accounts recorded in ledgers and financial reports. But here we consider only basic concepts about costs so that you will gain a general appreciation and know enough to ask the right questions when you do not understand something.

You should become familiar with these terms to understand costs and the language accountants use, but recognize that these special terms designating and defining costs are themselves management information. You need to know exactly *which* costs are out of control when costs get out of control, as they sometimes do. You need to know for what you are paying too high a price or buying to excess. And you need to know what expenditures are bringing adequate returns—represent good investments—and which are a waste of money.

First, consider a basic truism that often becomes lost in the jargon and complexity of accounting systems and accounting language: There are only two kinds of dollars: those you take in and those you pay out. Don't allow jargon to cloud this fact. Every dollar posted in any accounting system is either income or outgo, no matter what the accountant calls it. (Dollars invested in plant, inventory, or other centers are not an exception to this; they are neither income nor outgo, but are simply dollars converted to some other form.)

Cost Centers

There are *profit centers* and *cost centers.* Every main category of cost is a cost center. For example, there are *fixed plant costs,* the cost to your practice of your physical facility, with its subcategories of heat, light, maintenance, and so forth. *Payroll* or *labor costs* is another cost center, as are *marketing* and *printing,* if you have appreciable quantities of these costs.

Cost center is an arbitrary term, which you may assign as you wish. Each enterprise has its own cost centers. For example, advertising is a cost center if you spend enough of your operating budget on it to justify monitoring it regularly. Otherwise, make it part of your marketing cost center. Do this for all other costs.

There are other ways to define or identify costs, again arbitrary identifiers, often with functional names. Certain costs, for example, are identified as *variable costs* because they vary from one accounting period to another. Telephone toll charges, travel expense, and printing costs may fall into this class, if they do vary a good bit. On the other hand, rent and Yellow Page advertising are *fixed costs,* at least for a given accounting period, usually a year at a time.

Other common categories are *overhead costs, material costs,* and *general and administrative costs* (G&A), a type of cost similar to that of overhead. This can get confusing if you do not remember that these are functional names, assigned to remind you of the nature of the costs and help you understand where the money is going. For example, advertising may be a fixed or variable cost, as well as an overhead cost, depending on where and how you choose to assign it. But it is always a cost. Regardless of terms and concepts, all *costs* are dollars going *out,* and no amount of argot or idiom changes that.

One major distinction in type of costs that is essential to make, however, is that of direct and indirect costs.

Direct and Indirect Costs

It costs money to operate any business venture. However, the ratio of direct to indirect costs varies for different enterprises, often inherent in the nature of the enterprise. In fact, what is direct cost in one kind of venture may be indirect costs in another venture, such as two independent consulting practices. The difference may be due to the nature of each field, a characteristic of a given accounting system, or a reflection of the owner's preferences.

For many enterprises, it is important to understand fully the nature of these two broad categories of cost. In some cases, such as most marketing to governments and their agencies, success in winning the contract may depend on this understanding, as reflected in your proposals.

These discussions focus on the small, independent consulting practice, but refer occasionally to other kinds of ventures in order to make certain concepts clear. But first some definitions to distinguish direct from indirect costs:

■ Any cost incurred specifically and exclusively for and assignable totally to a given project, task, assignment, or client is a *direct* cost.

■ Any cost incurred in general and not assignable to or identifiable as having been incurred specifically and exclusively for some project, task, assignment, or client is an *indirect* cost.

Consulting Is Labor Intensive

The term *labor intensive* refers to ventures or projects that consist primarily of services and do not normally require a significant investment in or operating cost of equipment and/or inventory. It applies to most industries and ventures where the client is billed primarily for the services rendered, with other items of cost usually only incidental.

Most consulting practices fit that description. As an independent consultant, you usually bill your client mainly for your services, based on the time you have devoted to the client.

Direct Costs. In most cases, the chief item of direct cost on your bill is for *direct labor,* which is probably your own labor, but might include that of associates or employees. However, you often have some other direct costs, even if they are not significant portions of the entire bill. For example, I often have travel costs and per diem living costs—lodging and meals—to bill clients for, but you might have some other costs that you have incurred for your client. Here are a few costs typically incurred in consulting and often representing enough dollars to justify listing on your invoice for reimbursement:

■ Travel (air, taxis, car rentals)
■ Per diem (food and lodging)
■ Telephone toll charges
■ Printing/copying
■ Express delivery
■ Messenger services
■ Secretarial/other support services

There are occasional exceptions. Some consultants must add charges to their bills for printing, materials, laboratory work, and costs other than their own time. Normal accounting practices accommodate this easily.

One exception is the result of individual systems or preferences. If your system provides no way of distinguishing those printing costs or telephone toll charges incurred for a given client from other such charges incurred for other clients or other purposes, you cannot bill your client directly for such charges. Still, you must recover those costs if you are merely to stay in business. That leaves you no alternative; you must call those costs *indirect* and recover them in your overhead charges.

It is usually not to your advantage to lump extraneous costs as overhead. That offers only the slight advantage of convenience by simplifying your record keeping to a small extent. But, treating these items as direct costs wherever possible offers distinct advantages, such as minimizing your overhead rate and making you more competitive in marketing.

If you make a number of toll calls in connection with a specific project, those calls should be charged to that client. To do so you must keep records of and ascertain the costs of those calls. The same thing applies to printing, messenger service, travel, and other expenses. They are other direct costs (other than direct labor, that is), and are normally included as such in cost estimates. If you do not take the trouble to keep track of such other direct costs and charge them to the proper contract and client, you inflate your overhead unnecessarily and thus inflict those costs on other clients, as well as add to your own burdens in marketing your services.

Indirect Costs. Most ventures have many indirect costs, a few of which have been cited earlier, and these fall into several broad categories, according to the choices made in setting up the system. Here is a more complete list of typical indirect costs.

- Rent (which may or may not include heat, light, and other utility expenses)
- Parking
- Insurance, all kinds required
- Taxes, various
- Licenses
- Depreciation (major equipment, furniture, other capital items)
- Stationery
- Advertising
- Telephone (that portion covering the general service, not assignable to specific projects)
- Travel (general, including auto expense, unless assignable to specific projects)
- Printing and copying (general, that portion not assignable)
- Contributions to charitable causes, political campaigns, etc.
- Subscriptions

- ■ Memberships
- ■ Marketing

Some of these costs or portions of them may appear as other direct costs in some projects. It is possible that a project will require you to travel, have printing done, or incur other costs as part of the project. Those then become direct costs.

Many people equate indirect cost with overhead, using the terms interchangeably. In some systems, where the accounting system is very rudimentary, the terms may be interchangeable. Generically, however, indirect cost is the broader term and *overhead* is one of several possible categories of indirect cost.

In some accounting systems, fringe benefits are accounted for and posted separately from the rest of the normal overhead, so *fringe benefits* becomes another category of indirect costs.

There is also the indirect cost known as G&A—general and administrative costs. The G&A expense pool includes certain special classes of expenses, but usually only for large organizations, and not for independent consultants.

Overhead is a *rate*. Overhead and G&A are dollars, of course. However, for estimating purposes (to be sure that you are recovering overhead costs), it is necessary to establish an overhead *rate*. That is the ratio of the overhead dollars to some other factor. In consulting, the something else is generally direct-labor. If you find at the end of a year that you have had direct-labor costs of $100,000 and your various overhead charges for the year total $65,000, the rate is 65,000/100,000 = 0.65 or 65 percent.

That is, to put this more clearly, for every dollar paid out for direct labor you had to pay out 65 cents for overhead expenses, so that your total *loaded* labor cost—direct plus indirect—was actually $165,000 for the year. To that must be added whatever other direct and indirect costs you may have incurred—perhaps you experienced another $14,000 worth of such costs—so that your total cost for the year was $179,000. If you had not separated out those other direct costs your overhead rate would have been somewhat higher—100,000/79,000 = 79 percent.

The first year you have no last-year's figures, so you have no basis for an historical overhead rate. You therefore make the best estimate you can. You should be able to accommodate an overhead rate of 65 to 85 percent in a typical independent consultancy if you keep track of all charges that should be recorded as direct costs and thus do not burden your overhead rate unfairly. That would be a reasonable expectation for an established consultancy, one in which you were able to bill a reasonable proportion of your time—say two-thirds. Unfortunately, that is often not the case in newly established practices. Time and money spent in marketing effort is likely to be a major overhead activity the first year, and may well occupy more than one-half your time.

That does not mean that you should shoot for a 100 or 150 percent overhead rate the first year. To do so is likely to make your marketing even more difficult, unless you compensate for the high rate with a modest direct rate for your time. Either way, you will have to be competitive, and you may have to subsidize your first-year operations extensively.

In today's consulting market, there are probably few capable consultants accepting a daily rate of less than $500, although that may vary somewhat with local conditions and individual policies. For example, $500 works out to $62.50 per hour on the basis of an 8-hour working day, but one $500/day consultant does not charge for overtime—10- or 12-hour days—while another does. Or one may charge a $50 hourly rate, but charge premiums for overtime, weekends, and holidays.

Let's take a hypothetical case in which you decide that you ought to pay yourself $25 an hour (a $52,000 salary), but you estimate that your first-year's overhead rate will be about 125 percent. That means that you must charge the client $25 + $31.25 = $56.25 per hour = $450 cost per day + $50 (pretax profit) = $500 a day. That is a competitive rate in today's market. (In fact, it is an overly modest rate in many localities today.) If you are doing billable work about one-third of the time you are billing at the rate of about $43,300 a year, not recovering your own salary, much less all the costs, which your estimate will have established as $114, 500 ($52,000 + 1.25 × $52,000).

Even if you raise your rate to $600 a day, you will have increased total income by only about $5,200. However, if you have succeeded in keeping overhead down to, say, 65 percent, while charging $500/day and paying yourself a more modest $15 an hour, the figures are quite different:

Total estimated costs for year:	
Salary	$31,200
Overhead	20,280
Total	$51,480
Total billing (income)	43,300 (approximately)
Gross profit (loss)	($8,180)

While still a loss figure, the latter is considerably more tolerable and a great deal closer to the point of breakeven. Only a few percentage points of billable days—an increase of about seven percent—would absorb the loss and put your practice on the brink of profit. On the other hand, increasing the number of billable days is not the only answer. While this illustrates the need to be especially conservative in generating and controlling costs, as well as in minimizing what you draw personally that first year, it illustrates two other cogent points:

1. You need to market aggressively and continuously. There is probably never a time when it is safe to relax in the quest for new clients.

2. You need to maximize the number and type of profit-potential activities in your practice, for there are many ways of providing your consulting services to clients.

Both of these are matters of prime concern. There are other profit potentials, but let us turn first to the important matter of insurance.

INSURANCE

To most of us, insurance is a mysterious field with the special jargon of the legal and accounting professions and heavy overtones of statistics. The complexity bewilder and intimidate most of us, causing us to surrender decision making to the experts, the sellers of insurance, often to our great cost.

Buy Only What You Need

You do need to be insured, but you do not need to be over-insured, as so many of us are. Many of us are victims of persuasive presentations by insurance professionals trading on our fears. So we play it safe, or so we think, paying heavily—buying $100,000 coverage of $50,000 worth of assets, for example.

Paying extra for insurance when renting an automobile is usually a waste of money: Most of us are covered by the insurance on our own automobiles. Insuring rental property, such as rented offices or equipment, is probably duplication of insurance already held by the property owner. Check on all such possibilities before buying insurance. Ask plenty of questions before you sign up. One basic problem is that the harried business executive either thinks that insurance policies are too complicated to be understood by ordinary humans or he or she is too busy to spend the time. The result is leaving the decision to the seller. "Just sign me up for what I need," are words uttered too often, an invitation for others to put their hands in your pocket and help themselves. If the seller cannot answer all your questions in such a way that you understand what you are buying, be alarmed immediately and refuse to buy until you do understand what you are getting. But there are some general guidelines:

- Buy insurance for protection of your business against disasters, such as fire, flood, and burglary.
- Buy some kind of medical or health insurance.
- You may need some kind of liability insurance guarding against the risk of someone being injured on your property or as a result of what you do.

These are obvious considerations, but other insurance matters are more specialized and require guidance from insurance experts. No matter how many questions you ask, there will always be questions you should have asked but did not know that you should have asked them. You need professional guidance. Where will you get it? From an insurance direct writer? The direct writer works for his company, the underwriter, not for you. It is in his or her interest to sell you as much insurance as you are willing to pay for, and he or she is locked into that single underwriter, although there is a possible advantage in having all or most of your insurance with one underwriter and possibly getting a slightly lower rate. A broker or agent? He or she usually represents more than one underwriter, can offer greater flexibility. A good broker is an honest broker and will give you honest advice, but you must be the final judge.

Insurance people, like lawyers, accountants, and other professionals use all sorts of legalistic terms that often do not mean what you think they mean or simply leave you completely baffled. Don't be afraid to ask questions.

Getting medical and health insurance is a major concern and problem for many self-employed individuals. Individual rates are much higher than group rates. The best solution may be to get group insurance via some association. Consider that when evaluating what associations to join, professional association or otherwise. You may join the AARP (American Association of Retired Persons) or any of many other associations that offer group insurance plans.

TAXES: AVOIDANCE IS LEGAL

Tax *evasion* is illegal. You can go to jail for it. Tax *avoidance* is perfectly legal and honorable. You are foolish if you fail to arrange your affairs, personal and business, in a way that incurs minimum tax obligations.

As a business owner, your tax situation is different from that of a typical wage earner, although you may be one of many consultants who derives part of your earnings from wages. That is, if you work part of the time via a labor broker as a W2 temporary, part of your income will be in the form of wages, from which taxes will have been deducted. For that part of your income that is 1099 income—1099 is the form clients must fill out and send to you and the IRS identifying payments to you—you will have to calculate what you owe and pay it to the IRS.

Unless you are yourself an accountant, you probably will retain an accountant or professional tax preparer, although it is not excessively difficult or complex to file a tax return for a simple, one-person proprietorship. If you are incorporated, that adds complications, and you must file both corporate and personal tax returns. You will probably find it useful then to turn to an accountant to handle your tax-calculation and reporting obligations. Nevertheless, you need to know the basics of what you can and cannot do under current tax laws. Since I am neither a lawyer nor an accountant, I cannot represent these suggestions to be technically irreproachable. They are based on my experience and what lawyers, accountants, and IRS officials have told me in the past. I have found that even advice given to me by IRS staff is not always dependable: I have acted on such advice and found it reversed by IRS when they reviewed my tax returns. The following advice is what I have found to be generally true, but it may pay you to check with the IRS or another authority—your accountant—when considering a specific application. The tax codes change, as new legislation is enacted, so what is true now may not be true when you read this. You must thus ascertain what is the law at the time.

Taking Deductions

Probably the most common question asked about taxes concerns deductions for offices in one's home. That is also one of the most misunderstood aspects of tax obligations and deductions. The position of the IRS is clear enough: Anything deducted as a business expense must be dedicated to—used solely for—that business. That means that you can make a deduction for a spare room or any space you have converted to office space and used exclusively for your business, but you cannot take a deduction for the use of your kitchen table to address envelopes or do your books. You cannot charge to your business more than the business takes in. If you are running a business, whether part or full-time, and are not yet profitable, the nominal charge for space and other deductions may be greater than the total income of the business, but you are limited to your total business income for deductions. That means, too, that if you have other income, losses from the business cannot be used to reduce your tax obligations arising out of the other income you receive.

The way to calculate the deduction for business space is to prorate the cost of the space. If you have 1,600 square feet in your home and it costs you $800 a month in rent, you may use a factor of 50 cents per square foot to calculate the monthly cost of the space you have dedicated to business use. Use the same principle to allocate deductible costs for your telephone, automobile, and other costs. If your business shares your personal telephone line, automobile, and other costs, you will have to either keep a log or make a reasonable estimate to calculate the allocations. Don't forget, when you do this, that your telephone costs mount up for other business uses than voice communication, if you have a fax of your own and use a computer for communications (via a modem, that is). Also consider the cost of your Internet use.

If you buy equipment for your business, it is totally deductible, and may be depreciated over five years or charged off the year it is bought if the cost is not more than $10,000, or you may charge off the first $10,000 of the cost the year it is bought if the total exceeds $10,000.

SPECIAL SITUATIONS

Occasionally, a special accounting problem arises in which you write off some cost to overhead as a normal business expense or as a loss. For example, travel, lodging, and meal costs for business purposes are normally wholly deductible if they are not reimbursed by your client. However, if you have charged off such costs as overhead expenses and the client later unexpectedly reimburses you for these costs, you must treat the reimbursement as income to make your books reflect the true picture. The same thing applies to uncollected bills that you saw no hope of collecting and so charged them off as losses. If you do later succeed in collecting them or some part of them, that must be treated as income.

Accounting is, then, a completely logical system, once you understand the principles and the jargon that might otherwise confuse you.

Marketing and Sales:
Finding Leads and Closing Them

There are several ways to judge the health of an enterprise, and a close study of the sales log is a good place to start the evaluation.

Herman Holtz

SUCCESS IN MARKETING IS ALWAYS A TONIC FOR AN AILING BUSINESS

One cause of small-business failure, according to experts such as executives of the U.S. Small Business Administration, is what they call undercapitalization or not enough money. But not enough money for what? Not enough to make a proper original investment? Not enough to advertise adequately? Not enough to market properly? Not enough to survive many months of negative cash flow? These experts rarely focus their diagnoses more closely than such broad generalizations.

Other causes cited frequently are inadequacies in management, accounting, inventory control, purchasing, and other general catch-alls.

The one cause of failure that seems to be the most rarely cited is the failure of marketing. And yet that is almost surely the most common cause of business failures. It is why even well-established businesses who do not have that dreaded disease of undercapitalization go from success to failure. It is why many vanish from view into bankruptcy, dissolution, or acquisition of their assets by more successful companies.

We can find many general causes for failures, such as the companies didn't keep up with the times. Organizations can have poor management, fail to meet competition, and have other shortcomings. Still, these are more rationalizations than explanations; they fail to explain what "keeping up with the times," "poor management," and other alleged faults really mean. Almost all business failures ultimately translate into failures in marketing. The sales volume declined or never grew to a necessary level. Yes, they fail to keep up with competition and the times—the inevitable changes in the marketplace, changes in popular merchandise, changes in methods of marketing, and many other changes. Perhaps they become overly complacent and fail to detect or choose to ignore the changes and the slippage taking place. Perhaps they smugly assure themselves that they have become household words, have built such secure niches that they simply cannot perish. But even mighty Chrysler would have perished as a result of declining sales without the intervention of the federal government, and a new and tough chief executive officer who did something about their lagging sales, as well as almost single-handedly persuading the federal government that the U.S. economy could not afford the failure of Chrysler, and—do not overlook this—an almost-too-good-to-believe recovery of the automobile market at the right time. In fact, Chrysler is probably the proof because once new Chrysler chief Lee Iacocca persuaded the government to furnish relief for the immediate problem of financial distress, he turned immediately to the marketing problem and personally led a massive and successful sales campaign.

It resolves ultimately into marketing—sales success. It resolves into being hungry and fighting vigorously for sales. Those failures just referred to were the failures of organizations who no longer felt hungry enough to fight for sales, who took their customers for granted.

All the most brilliant management, superb accounting systems, totally efficient inventory control, tough-minded and shrewd purchasing, and other signs of good management will not save the organization that does not have adequate sales. Nor will the normal deficiencies in all the important functions of management and administration bring about the collapse of an organization with great marketing success. A great many shortcomings of management can be found in every company and probably in every division of every company, but the company that is highly successful in the marketplace can and does survive these problems. It is actually difficult to fail when your marketing is producing enough sales. Conversely, it is impossible to succeed when your marketing success is marginal.

It is therefore no exaggeration to say that marketing is by far the single most important function of even the established organization, but far more so of the new venture, as far as survival and overall success are concerned, for neither is possible without successful marketing. Every other problem can be solved or overcome when the sales are producing the dynamicism and income that are the muscles and blood of the organization.

WHAT IS MARKETING?

There is a great deal of confusion about marketing, beginning with understanding—or, more exactly, *trying* to understand—just what marketing is. Many people believe that *marketing* and *sales* are synonymous. That is not so, and the difference is more than semantics.

Marketing is not confined to businesses or other organizations dedicated to earning profits; every organization, from the smallest to the largest, must market to survive. Churches and temples seek additions to their congregations and donations. Military organizations seek recruits. Associations seek members. Politicians seek voters and campaign contributors. Political parties seek volunteer workers. The Red Cross seeks blood donors and volunteers. Even the U.S. Postal Service and the Federal Supply Service have marketing organizations, and all government agencies lobby—market to—their legislatures, seeking supporters for various issues.

It's all marketing. Marketing is the pursuit of whatever or whomever it is that provides the sustenance for the organization—customers, clients, contracts, members, donors, contributors, volunteers, enlistees, or whatever represents successful accomplishment of the organization's mission.

That begins to sound very much like sales, and in many ways it is difficult to distinguish the two from each other, especially in terms of independent consulting. One way is to consider the sales function as part of marketing, the final act, where the earlier actions are preparation for the sales functions. Here are the major steps of the progression:

- Decide (define/identify) exactly what you want to market—what is to be your service.
- Decide (define/identify) your market—to whom you are going to sell. Who are the right prospects for your service.
- Determine how you will reach those prospects with your presentation.
- Define your specific offer.
- Design your sales campaign.
- Carry out your sales campaign.

Decide What You Want to Market

There is a built-in dilemma in deciding exactly what your service is to be. Making the service too narrow limits your market—the number of prospects. But making your service too broad dilutes and weakens your image as a consultant. This is the classic trade-off problem in consulting, and the answer has already been offered: Start with whatever appears to you to be the right answer—a compromise between the two extremes—and use your experience, as you go, to modify your services until you are satisfied you have found the right answer.

Decide What Your Market Is

As an independent consultant, you can't market effectively to the entire world. (Even supercorporations have difficulty trying to do this.) Having decided, at least tentatively, what services you will offer, identify the right prospects for those services—those most likely to need or want those services, hence most likely to become clients.

Determine How You Will Reach Those Prospects

To make use of that prospect list, you must be able to reach the prospects and present your offer. I tried to rent mailing lists of the kinds of prospects I wanted to reach—those who were most likely to need help in writing proposals—and found that I couldn't do so. Despite the enormous variety of mailing lists handled by the list brokers and despite the many ways in which they could have their computers manipulate, sort, merge, organize, and reorganize lists that made up their databases, they could not produce for me a specialized list of government contractors of the types that I wanted. It was not their fault; none of their names were coded so as to enable them to do that for me because few of their customers demand such lists.

I had to build my own mailing lists, finding or inventing the means for doing so. It does no good to identify the best prospects if you can't reach them with an offer, so creating the mailing lists was crucial.

Define Your Offer

In defining your specific offer, you draw much closer to the sales function, to devising a sales strategy. Here, too, is where we get to some fine points of definition about what the word *offer* means. Probably to most people, including many marketers, the offer is simply what they wish to sell. My offer, for example, would be along the lines of proposal writing services or marketing support. But that is not what the term *offer,* means or should mean, as I learned through patient experimentation—trial-and-error testing. I do help my clients develop proposals and train their staffs as a byproduct, but my offer is help in *winning contracts.* That is what my clients really want, regardless of how I do it.

The offer is therefore what you promise to do for the client, the benefit resulting from your services, and it must be based on whatever you believe is the client's goal, the end-result the client wants. That is the reason for retaining you and paying you: The client wants the result, not the means to it. Not all of those who attend aerobic exercise classes enjoy the exercises, and some may even hate them, but they submit to them in the hope of losing weight. Therefore, don't offer them aerobic exercises; offer them a better figure or greater sex appeal. To define your offer properly, you must understand the client's mind—to know what benefit he or she is seeking and hopes to achieve by retaining you.

Design Your Sales Campaign

Now that you know what you wish to sell, to whom you wish to sell it, how you will reach those prospects to present your offer, and what your offer is to be, you are ready to design your sales campaign.

You reach prospective clients in any or all ways—networking, direct calls, direct mail, becoming active in associations, lecturing, writing, getting your name on bidders lists, and registering with agents or brokers who help you win assignments or subcontract to you.

In this phase, you decide what ways you will use, prepare the sales materials you need, and plan the methods and schedules. The more carefully you design this campaign, the more successful it is likely to be. But design includes all those earlier marketing steps, so the effectiveness of your campaign depends on how well you did the marketing work earlier.

One desire I have heard from others in discussions is for greater coverage of networking as a marketing measure. There was general agreement that it helped to be active in associations, write articles, publish newsletters, and otherwise work at raising one's image and visibility, but no one seemed to recognize that *these are networking activities,* although informal. They are the means for word-of-mouth advertising and referrals that so many consultants report are their chief sources of business. Many people who have no direct experience with you or your work will recommend you to others because they have gained a favorable impression of you somehow, such as hearing you speak or reading something you have written. This is an informal and general way of networking, but it is productive.

There is also a formal, organized networking that some organizations sponsor, staging mixers—meetings of people in various trades and professions who get together for the express purposes of getting acquainted. At mixers, one may establish contacts, exchange business cards and brochures, and engage in conversation, during which some referrals and leads are passed out and the basis for future ones are established.

Networking versus Word-of-Mouth Marketing

Whether formal and organized or informal and spontaneous (such as meeting people during happy hour at a lounge in the business district), all of these activities are networking. Many consultants claim to get all their work from word-of-mouth referrals and recommendations from satisfied clients. That is a pleasant way to market: It costs you virtually nothing in time or money—at least for as long as it lasts. That kind of recommendation cannot happen until you have had the opportunities—projects—to satisfy clients and inspire such referrals. Left to chance, it can take years for word-of-mouth referrals to be an adequate source of new business, but you can accelerate the process by being active in all these things.

Not every satisfied client has occasion or inspiration to recommend you. There are some consulting activities—marketing support, for example—such that clients are not likely to recommend you to others because the others are their competitors. Don't depend on passive methods as a source for new business; take an aggressive role in marketing yourself.

Fortunately, today we have a new and important milieu for marketing: cyberspace. That is that imaginary place where we meet each other across the entire world via computers and telephone connections. Our principal highways, byways, and roadside stops are along the Internet—the maze of dial-up telephone connections among millions of computers everywhere, with the Web, newsgroups, and e-mail. The Web is where we erect our billboards, entertain prospects, make sales presentations, and take orders. Newsgroups are meeting halls where we discuss things with others, and e-mail is the chief means of cyberspace communication. We use e-mail to communicate, publish newsletters, hold group discussions, send out quotations, and carry on correspondence generally.

The Internet is thus an almost ideal medium for networking today, and as a consultant you should be making maximum use of it to elevate your visibility and your image. Get active in discussion groups, publish a newsletter, answer queries, and do all the related kinds of things that constitute networking. You can do it all without leaving your office, so you can make maximum use of your time.

DISCOVERING WHAT CLIENTS WISH TO BUY

Deciding what services to sell cannot be a unilateral decision—cannot be based, that is, on what *you* want, but must be based on what clients want. But how can you know what clients want?

Only in some cases can you anticipate or estimate clients' wants accurately. What do you do when you cannot do this? The answer is *ask them,* not literally, of course, but there are ways to ask prospective clients what they want or what it will take to persuade them to become your clients. Let's start with a few generalities we know to be true:

- Everyone has problems.
- Everyone wants to solve those problems.
- Everyone has at least one problem that is more worrisome than the others, more urgently in need of solution for some reason.
- Everyone has desires, things they want to gain.
- Everyone has fears, things they want to avoid.

These are the basis for all advertising and sales success. It is through taking advantage of these truths that all successful sales and marketing results are achieved. These are the motivators, the reasons people buy, why they say yes to sales offers. Sales and advertising success depends on choosing and using the most effective motivators.

Consider how insurance is sold. Probably a few people buy insurance as a means for saving money, but by far the majority of people who buy insurance do so out of fear, the fear of being defenseless in an emergency. They are motivated by the sense of insecurity most of us have, which insurance salespeople fully understand and use in reminding us of the need to have this hedge against disaster.

Basic Motivations

All marketing and sales efforts are necessarily based on some motivational factor. Fear or the desire to avoid some result is one basic motivation; desire to gain something is the other one. Most efforts to sell material items are based on that gain motivation. (More cynically, people are driven by fear and greed.) Every effective sales appeal conforms with this. Consider just a few possible consulting specialties and check off the motivational factor, fear or gain, you believe would be most likely to inspire prospects to become clients:

Plant/office/home security measures	_____ Fear	_____ Gain
Engineering	_____ Fear	_____ Gain
Financial advisor	_____ Fear	_____ Gain
Executive search	_____ Fear	_____ Gain
Convention planning	_____ Fear	_____ Gain
Hearing aid	_____ Fear	_____ Gain
Public relations	_____ Fear	_____ Gain
Safety	_____ Fear	_____ Gain
Training	_____ Fear	_____ Gain
Mergers and acquisitions	_____ Fear	_____ Gain
Receptions and party planning	_____ Fear	_____ Gain
Taxes	_____ Fear	_____ Gain
Industrial methods	_____ Fear	_____ Gain
Transportation	_____ Fear	_____ Gain
Office organization	_____ Fear	_____ Gain

In some of these cases, the optimal choice is obvious. The first one, services in behalf of physical security, is obviously a service to be sold via fear motivation for that is dictated by the nature of the service. On the other hand, anyone seeking executive search help wishes to gain something.

Did you check both Fear and Gain for any of the choices? You should. In most cases, the motivation could be either fear or gain. Even in selling plant security the motive could be gain. For example, a company has someone on staff charged with plant security who needs help in discharging that obligation. The reason for having the security function is fear, but the motive in retaining a consultant is gain—gaining help to do the job.

The same consideration applies to some other items and can be applied to marketing them, given certain circumstances and needs. The owner of the plant needs to make it secure, but the individual responsible for making it secure needs help. Either might retain a security consultant, but each has a different problem than the other, and that dictates the marketing strategy. You must understand the problem and the differences to make the most effective appeal, the right *offer.*

It is identifying the problem that is the key to developing the strategies of the marketing and sales campaign. It is a truism of marketing that every salesperson must be a consultant to be effective, because the salesperson should analyze the prospect's problem and offer a solution. That is the offer, an offer to solve the prospect's problem. But first it is necessary to determine what the problem is—what the prospect wants.

Pause now and go back to scan the list again, deciding which offers could be made to appeal to either or both motivations and the circumstances under which one or the other appeal would be used. This analysis leads directly to formulating the offer because it is based on identifying each prospect's need—what want must be satisfied.

What I hope you found in scanning the list again is that most of the services listed could conceivably be sold by either motivation or both. That does not mean that all sales appeals ought to be based on both motivations. In most cases, one is more powerful than the other and applicable to more situations. That makes it the natural solution, one most likely to appeal to the majority of prospects. Even in selling life insurance, gain motivation—gaining peace of mind—might be used with some effect, but the fear motivation is almost invariably far more effective.

Occasionally, someone finds a means for using both fear and greed as sales motivators in the same presentation. One example is the title of a best-selling book of a few years ago: *Wealth Without Risk*. The greed factor is exploited by the promise of wealth and the fear factor by the mention of risk. The title alone is a buying influence, since the title appeals to both the bulls and the bears, the bold plungers and the timidly cautious.

Motivation versus Prospect

The matter of *who* the prospect is may be the determining factor in choosing the motivation. In the plant-security example, the difference was in what the plant owner and the security manager wanted because each had a different want as a result of different responsibilities. Simply knowing the prospect's job responsibilities furnishes the major clue to best motivation. Suppose you were a security specialist and had decided that the prospects you would target were all individuals responsible for plant security. But you knew that these prospects were not themselves expert in the field of security, and they didn't have much time to research the subject because all were general administrators with many duties to perform. That would dictate your general strategy of offering your help and special expertise, perhaps in a "Don't go it alone; special, expert help is available" kind of offer. But even so you might find a fear motivation workable in the argument "Your plant is not as secure as you think it is; let an expert make a free inspection and show you the most modern methods."

It is essential to know who and what your prospect is and to have selected a target audience carefully and thoughtfully when devising your strategies.

It might be helpful to go back and scan that list of consulting specialties and motivations yet again, considering the different types of prospects you might target and how each choice would affect the motivator you would use and the general strategies on which to base your offer. It would dramatize the extreme importance of identifying the prospects for your services when planning your marketing.

Motivational Research Methods

Motivational research or learning what inspires people to buy is an entire field of activity in the advertising field for the general consumer market. In marketing your consulting services, the research you do is far different, and depends on how, as well as to whom, you propose to sell your services.

Most Basic Method

Marketing campaigns can be based on your own knowledge of your field and of the prospect your offer is addressed to, combined with a simple analysis of probabilities. That is sufficient in many cases. But there are other research methods, some far more specific and more focused.

Personal Interviews

If your marketing includes making personal calls, you have an opportunity to conduct a kind of research that leads to effective sales presentations. We have been discussing common problems, defined generally as they apply to many prospects. In personal discussions with prospects, you can discover and address specific problems of individual prospects, as well as learning over the course of many such calls and interviews what are the general and most common problems of your prospects.

Identifying problems should be the direct objective in such calls. I once called on an executive in the training office of the Occupational Safety and Health Administration (OSHA), an agency of the U.S. Labor Department. I introduced myself and asked what was the nature of the work in that office. I learned very quickly that the major focus of the moment was the installation of courses to train occupational safety and health technicians, and the immediate need was to develop a junior-college curriculum based on a new training program that a contractor had developed for the office.

The contractor had delivered a student manual and an instructor's manual, but no guidance in implementing these into a course of instruction. The manuals themselves were complete in their coverage, but the instructor's manual failed to lay out any guidelines for their use.

A simple letter proposal I offered to solve the problem won an immediate purchase order and, subsequently, a great deal more work from that office and others to which my services were later recommended by this satisfied client.

The key is to do far more listening than talking, especially in the early stages of the visit. Encourage the prospective client to talk and have and show a healthy and sincere interest in learning more. There is a pattern for this:

- Learn in advance—before the actual visit—as much as you can about the organization and the individual upon whom you are calling. The more advance information you have, the more productive your questioning (research into the client's wants) will be. (The Internet is an immediate resource for this.)

- Ask a few general questions, making it clear that you have done your homework and know something of the organization, but want to learn more. The typical client is pleased to know that you are somewhat familiar with his or her organization and equally unhappy to learn that you know absolutely nothing about it.

- Guide the conversation to learn about the problems generally—the routine, everyday problems of the organization, but particularly any special problem that urgently needs solution. Learning that can be the most important objective of your visit.

- Continue this to zero in on the most troublesome problem(s) of the moment (the chief worry item(s) or problems the prospect appears most eager to solve).

- Discuss possible solution approaches to plumb the prospect's interests. (See, too, if the client has some ideas of his or her own.)

- Offer specific services to test reaction, discover organization's normal methods for purchasing services, and getting clues for best follow-up.

- Propose specific follow-up: submittal of a proposal, a presentation, or other measure, as discussion has suggested. Never leave the matter hanging or with no understanding as to subsequent action. It is essential to have some specific follow-up agreed on, and that almost invariably means an action by *you,* not the client. You must retain the initiative if you are to have control, and control is essential if you are to close and win a contract.

Don't focus your call on getting an order. Focus it on learning the prospect's problems and wants, most desirable result, and needs for follow-up.

The call may be the follow-up of a lead gained earlier via some method or it may be a cold call. The purpose of such calls is to make sales, with research into the prospect's needs and problems the key to closing. In many cases, the call should close with the client's agreement to receive a brief proposal from you. A brief letter of a page or two may be adequate for that.

This approach may not be suitable for you. One individual who counts himself an independent consultant is a hypnotist who focuses his services on helping people overcome phobias. He makes special efforts to help individuals quit smoking, and he conducts both individual sessions and group sessions. For him, the personal call on prospective clients is not viable. The same consideration would apply to others who deal in services to individuals or groups and charge by the hour, by the visit, or by the series constituting a program, such as financial advisors, investment counselors, and resume consultants. You can call on prospects via telephone, mail, broadcast media, and now the Internet and e-mail. You may also be able to sell your services to organizations, many of which will sponsor seminars or classes to employees or members of the organization.

Surveys and Questionnaires

Surveys and questionnaires are traditional methods of gaining information from a large number of people. This may or may not be suitable for your purposes, depending on whether you have or can acquire a suitable mailing list and can devote the time and money to what is usually a tedious and expensive program. However, if your practice already includes a direct-mail element, such as a newsletter, you are already well equipped to conduct such a research program.

Using Inquiry Advertising for Motivational Research

There is a special way to use the survey/questionnaire research method to determine how to focus your offers. It has the enormous advantage of being a cost-free spinoff or fallout from normal marketing methods, from a lead-generation program.

Except for those special situations such as those sought by the hypnotist and the investment counselor, consulting assignments are normally fairly sizable, running to at least several hundred dollars and more often to thousands of dollars. This consideration alone dictates that the marketing of consulting services is not a one-call business. You rarely win a significantly large or long-term contract in a single call or sales appeal to a prospective client. Sizable contracts almost always requires a series of contacts, appeals, and presentations to acquire a new project or client, and often even to win a new contract with an old client.

This means that making sales of your consulting service normally involves and requires at least two distinct steps: (1) Prospect for and get sales leads, people, and situations that appear to be good prospects for contacts; and (2) follow up the leads to sell and close.

It is the first step, generating leads, that is the real heart of marketing; and it determines the ultimate sales success. It is no exaggeration to say that sales success is dependent on the quality of the marketing, on the quality of the leads. No one closes all leads, but if the prospecting is not done well, too many leads that result prove to be not really leads at all. It is thus the quality of the leads generally that is the chief factor determining what proportion of leads you can close.

There are many ways to prospect for leads. One basic, widely practiced method is inquiry advertising. It can be carried out through advertisements in periodicals, direct mail, e-mail, and other cybserspace activity.

Inquiry advertising is designed specifically to elicit responses. One method is to run advertisements offering something free or for a nominal cost—a newsletter, a special report, or whatever is likely to draw responses from only those who would be good prospects for you. You thus build a list of good prospects for mail, telephone, personal calls, or other follow-up.

Judicious mailings or advertisements of your own can provide you with the clues you need, while they also develop leads for you to follow up. By experimenting with what you offer as an inducement to respond, you can determine what the respondents' chief interests and concerns are. Suppose you are a security consultant with a mailing list you developed from association directories, advertising, the Yellow Pages, and other sources, and you decide to make a mailing to ask the prospects what they want.

You construct a simple sales letter in which you introduce yourself briefly and advise the reader that if his plant is using security devices and systems that are more than 10 years old they are woefully out of date and not at all effective in today's world. But if he or she will send you a request on a business letterhead or accompanied by a business card, you will send, free of charge, a special report explaining what it takes to be up-to-date in plant security today.

You construct a slight variation of that letter, too. The second version explains that plant security is not a part-time job; it requires frequent inspections. You'll be happy to send a free report explaining how to make such inspections if the respondent makes the request on a letterhead and/or with a business card.

A third variation says that there are at least a half-dozen common mistakes made in designing plant security systems as explained in a free report you have. Again, you make the offer of the helpful report free of charge to anyone who requests it on a business letterhead or with a proper business card enclosed.

You code each of these letters so you can tell which one each request responds to. (The report you are going to send is the same in each case and covers all the points made in all the letters.) You can do this by making variations in your name—J. F. Smith, John F. Smith, J. Frederick Smith—or by adding Dept 23, Drawer 46, or Security Specialties to your address—or by other such devices.

You print and mail an equal number of these to portions of your mailing list—perhaps 500 or 1,000 each—and wait for results. They tell you which was the most productive appeal—which produced the largest number of good leads to follow up.

You could offer to make a free plant inspection to anyone who requests it, but that may produce fewer responses because it may be taken by many as equivalent to "Yes, I am interested. Please send a salesperson to see me." Probably a better time to offer that free security inspection, if you wish to offer it (it is probably an excellent gambit), is in following up the first response, when you are trying to set up a personal call and interview.

Alternatives to Mailing

There are other ways to get that offer before prospects, if you do not have a mailing list, don't want to run advertisements, or want to supplement these. One is to put the letter (or those several letters) into a simple brochure and distribute these on literature tables at conventions, conferences, seminars, workshops, association meetings, and other such events and occasions.

You can often manage to run your simple print advertisement, offering your brochure or special report, as an editorial or news item in local newspapers, trade magazines, association journals, and newsletters. You can also make that offer by mailing news releases.

"I KNOW IT WHEN I SEE IT"

The foregoing discussion was based on the assumption that the client knows what he or she wants—recognizes not only the existence of a problem, but knows what the problem is and what is necessary to solve or eliminate it, what is referred to as a felt need. However, there are other kinds of needs or wants. One is that of the client who feels a need generally, but has not identified it precisely. It is this need that people refer to when they say, "I know it when I see it." In fact, the client probably observes certain symptoms but has not tried or been able to analyze those symptoms and decide what the problem or the remedy is. Often the situation is like the nail in your shoe; it's an annoying condition, but not intolerable, and you are too busy to take care of it right now. You'll get around to it one day, when you have the time. If you just happen to be standing in front of a shoe-repair shop while waiting for a bus, you might just pop in there and have the nail removed or pounded down because it is now convenient to do so. Many sales are made spontaneously because it has suddenly become convenient for the client to settle that troublesome problem without further delay.

That is the exceptional case. In most cases, this condition requires that you offer some aid to the client in perceiving that what you offer is what he or she needs. That means that your presentation ought to describe symptoms to help the client recognize the applicability of your services. Sheridan Cody, marketing a correspondence course in English some years ago, did this successfully for years by advertising, "Do you make these embarrassing mistakes in English?" But you need not be quite that blunt or that direct to help the prospect recognize the applicability of your offer to his or her own situation. Simply listing or describing the benefits in clear terms will accomplish the same purpose. For example, some of us who bought personal computers when the CP/M operating system dominated the scene had a substantial investment in software programs for those computers. That made us reluctant to buy the later computers using the PC/MS-DOS operating systems which soon came to dominate the market but which could not use the CP/M software. It would require us to scrap all that expensive software. But someone invented a chip that enabled those of us with CP/M software to run at least some of it on the newer DOS computers. The mere information that this was possible was enough. (I bought the new kind of computer with the chip that enabled me to continue using my old CP/M programs.)

You must bear this in mind as you help the "I know it when I see it" client make the connection between what you offer and the symptoms that trouble him or her. It is a mistake to assume that the client will see and understand spontaneously the value of what you offer. You must operate on the premise that the client knows what you tell him or her, but no more.

CREATING NEEDS

There is at least one other kind of prospective client to consider: There are prospective clients who are untroubled at the moment, and do not have any problems or worry items. Or, at least, they do not yet know that they have a problem. You can help them discover their problem and their need or want. That is a situation in which it is necessary to *create* the worry item.

Some marketers or advertising specialists speak of creating a need. Actually, you cannot literally create a need, and you cannot persuade anyone to want something they truly do not want. However, we sometimes speak of creating needs as though we actually can do so, recognizing that we are using an idiom.

There are two ways to create a need. One is by creating a new service or product. The mere fact of offering your consulting services as something new creates a need, especially if the services you offer are somehow unique and prospects decide to want them. Your client thus satisfies a need or a want that did not exist before—could not have existed before because the service did not exist before. No one wanted or needed a radio before it existed. Ergo, the availability of something new may create a need.

The other way to create a need is by educating the client—by giving him or her the problem and then the solution. An entire sales campaign of Warner Electric Clutch & Brake Company of Beloit, Wisconsin, was devoted to training salespeople to educate prospective customers in how obsolete their systems were and how Warner products could be used to modernize them efficiently.

FACE-TO-FACE CLOSING

Ultimately, in most sales situations, you must come face to face with the client to close. To many closing means getting the order, as in closing the sale. To the professional sales expert, closing has a second and more subtle meaning. It means *asking* for the order. And in the classic sales situation, especially when a big-tag item such as an automobile or large contract is involved, it is an accepted premise that the salesperson must close—ask for the order—many times before getting the desired signature on the order form. At some point you must consummate your presentation and try to complete the sale.

Even on modestly priced items this is often true. How many times did you get a solicitation for *Time* magazine or some other item sold via mail before you finally caved in and ordered it? The seller would be surprised if you responded to the first solicitation with an order, although a few prospects do. It is accepted in marketing that far more sales are closed on second, third, fourth, or even subsequent closes than on first ones. Perseverance and patience are keys to success here.

Selling consulting services may not appear to work quite that way. But it does, albeit on a more indirect, less obvious, and usually more protracted basis. You send out many brochures and letters, speak at numerous gatherings, chat with dozens of people at conventions, follow up with innumerable telephone calls and perhaps lunches, submit more than a few written bids and proposals, make frequent presentations, and ultimately you wind up with a few signed contracts or purchase orders from some of those activities. In most cases, you have made many closes before you won the prize. Even after you have won good leads, you have had to make several closes to most of those leads before you won a contract.

Are there exceptions to this? Of course there are. Once in a while you get lucky and get the lead, make the sale, and close the order all on one occasion. If you get that lucky on your first try—and that has happened, unfortunately, to some beginners—don't let it destroy your good judgment and cloud your vision. Such a stroke of fortune is a fluke that will probably happen only rarely, if ever again. You must recognize it for what it is.

Marketing is playing percentages. You do everything possible to stack the odds in your favor by trying to generate the best possible leads and every other means available. But in the end, your success is controlled by numbers, by probability. You cannot close every lead, but only a percentage of the leads. The more leads you generate, the higher the number of sales you will make, normally. That means that you must do something to reduce the time wasted on prospects you are most unlikely to sell—determine who the poor prospects are before you spend too much time on them.

There are some leads you cannot close for any of many reasons. You will run into prospects, especially in large organizations, who have nothing better to do than to chat with you, but who have no authority or perhaps no sincere desire to do business with you. (Don't be misled by impressive offices and what appears to be serious interest.) You may run into a prospect who is simply picking your brains so he or she can become a big hero/heroine in the organization, using information and ideas stolen from you. Or there is no budget available and the prospect is probing possibilities for a future project that is not likely to ever materialize. Sometimes an idle executive is desperately seeking to develop a project to protect his or her own job, but wasting your time in the process.

Because these kinds of things do happen, it is essential to qualify prospects.

Qualifying Prospects

Qualifying a prospect is a simple process that everyone who sells must learn. It means taking measures to assure yourself that the individual you are spending time with is a true prospect, one who *can* retain you and is serious about retaining a consultant.

Here are the kinds of qualifications the prospect must have to be a real prospect for you:

- A need appropriate to your specialty—one that you can satisfy.
- The money or authority to retain you or an effective link to such authority.
- The sincere intention of doing business with someone.

There is first that matter of making sure that you are not wasting your time discussing some vague need that may very well turn out to be outside your field. The only practical way you can address this is to probe until you are satisfied that you know what the client requires. Be aware, however, that frequently the client really does not know what the need or problem is, but can describe and list symptoms or complaints and may be rather vague about those. You must probe until you gather enough information to make an analysis and reach at least a preliminary conclusion. A word of caution here: Keep that conclusion to yourself, for now. You have not yet been retained nor paid for your time; disclosure here would be premature and might result in your analysis being passed on to other consultants as a definition of need.

The question of money to retain you has different practical interpretations. In some cases, the question might be literally whether the individual has the cash in hand. In others, as when dealing with organizations, rather than individuals, it is a question of whether the individual has both budget and authority or has access to and influence with someone else who has the spending authority.

That latter is an important consideration. In many cases, someone in an organization can recommend and help sell you to the right individual in the organization, although personally lacking the authority to retain you.

Finally, try to determine whether you are discussing a project that will come to pass for someone or wasting time on an imaginary project.

A suitable euphemism for asking about money tactfully is, "Are funds currently available for this project?" Another way to put it is, "Is this project budgeted yet?" Or, "Has this been funded yet?" Any question along these lines, delivered quietly and matter-of-factly, will usually be accepted as an objective, businesslike query, asked strictly for information and not as a challenge or intimation of mistrust.

All the questions you ask must be not only tactfully phrased, but asked in that same quiet, matter-of-fact tone. That's especially the case in asking a question or two to establish the authority—or lack of it—of the individual you are talking to. Among the questions you might ask in checking on this are such as these:

- Who will have to sign off on this?
- What's the decision-making (or approval) process on this?
- Will somebody besides you have to okay this?

If you find that you need to probe the matter of the client's intent, you may have to ask some rather direct questions. Here are a few leading questions that ought to steer the discussion in the right direction for you to make a sound judgment:

- Has an official decision been made yet to go ahead with this project?
- Is this exploratory, or is there definite commitment already to the project we are discussing here?
- How soon do you expect this project to begin?
- When would you need me to start on this?
- Has this project been budgeted yet?

From the answers you get to these latter kinds of questions, you can generally judge whether you are discussing a definitely planned project or wasting your time on a prospect's wish that is not likely to materialize, or even on being used cynically, for that happens occasionally too.

Releases, Brochures, and Other Materials

Miscellaneous tools for and routes to marketing successfully.

—*Herman Holtz*

MARKETING AND MESSAGES

Marketing of your independent consulting services means making general presentations to prospective clients, using many forms, routes, and media. You strive to build an image of competence, dependability, and integrity, and explain what it is that you do for your clients—the benefits you deliver.

Writing is an important part of this because we depend heavily on written presentations to broadcast our offers and sales arguments. The role of writing in marketing is a dual one: The presentation must be persuasive enough to carry out the mission of building your image and explaining the benefits you promise, but readers must be persuaded to read your message. That is itself a difficult job today, when so much competes for the prospect's attention—radio, television, newspapers, magazines, and the bedlam in cyberspace. Seizing and holding the reader's attention is no minor chore.

Is this familiar? It should be. It's the same set of principles we discussed in the previous chapter as the prerequisite of sales presentations: Capture and hold the subject's interest. Let's look first at developing press releases.

RELEASES AND NEWSWORTHINESS

Publishers and broadcasters recognize the releases you send out as requests for free advertising. They understand that you are using the publications or broadcast medium for advertising purposes. It is really a barter offer: You provide useful editorial matter and the editor buys it with print space or broadcast time, if it is *newsworthy*.

Newsworthiness is the key. I use that term loosely here, for the typical publicity release is not newsworthy in the sense of hard news, but if it is of interest to readers/listeners/viewers, that is what editors care about.

The broad lines of those interests are readily apparent. Subscribers to *Jones' Daily Investor's Report* do not want to read articles on inventory management, so don't send that inventory-management release to Jones. Send it to *Management Daily, Manager's Monthly,* and *Inventory Weekly.* It is their readers who will identify with that release and want to read it.

The physical format of a release may vary over a wide range of options (Figures 9.1, 9.2, and 9.3). Minimum requirements are that the piece must identify itself as a release and identify its source: Who issued it. There are other considerations, perhaps not musts because many violate these principles, but considerations that can make a considerable difference in whether you do or do not succeed in getting the publicity you are after. For example:

- Double-space the copy. The editor will want to edit your copy in most cases.
- Put a date on the release.
- Provide release information—"For immediate release," if it is not embargoed, a specific release date if it is embargoed.
- Provide a contact—someone to call for more details if the editor wants more information.
- Indicate where the copy ends with a standard notation, such as "End" or "30," (an old telegrapher's sign-off).
- Type on one side of the paper only.
- Use the journalist's style of summarizing all the key points of who, what, when, where, and why in the first sentence, if your release purports to be news—a new product or service offered an eager public or a startling new discovery in your field. If it is the feature type of piece, try for a novelty type of attention getter in the headline and follow it up immediately in the first sentence.
- Don't be cryptic and above all don't get cute or clever if you use a headline. (I recommend that you include a headline, although some counsel otherwise, for what I think are irrelevant reasons.) The headline should get attention and summarize the main point of the release so the editor can judge swiftly where/how it fits into the scheme of things. The easier you make it for the editor, the more likely you are to "sell" the piece.
- Don't get "literary." Use simple language and straightforward explanations. That is the best kind of writing.

It is always possible to find attention-getting and interesting items for releases. It is worth the effort, for the vast majority of releases are unimaginative, self-serving, and poorly written, earning firm discard quite swiftly. When I sought items for my own releases to publicize my services, I found

NEWS (W) WILEY

John Wiley & Sons, Inc.
605 Third Avenue New York, N.Y. 10158-0012 (212) 850-6000
New York ● Chichester ● Brisbane ● Toronto ● Singapore

FOR IMMEDIATE RELEASE   Contact: Julie Williams
(212) 850-6336

WRITERS: SICK OF LIVING IN POVERTY WHILE YOU WORK ON THE GREAT AMERICAN NOVEL?

How to Start and Run a Writing and Editing Business
proves you can earn good money with your writing skills.

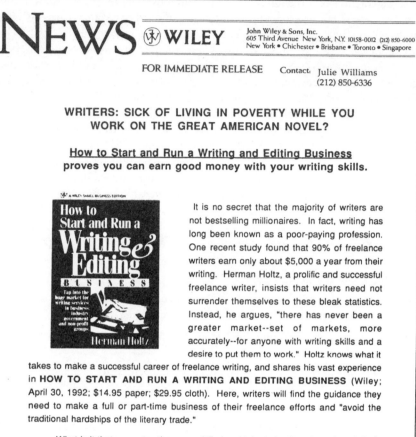

It is no secret that the majority of writers are not bestselling millionaires. In fact, writing has long been known as a poor-paying profession. One recent study found that 90% of freelance writers earn only about $5,000 a year from their writing. Herman Holtz, a prolific and successful freelance writer, insists that writers need not surrender themselves to these bleak statistics. Instead, he argues, "there has never been a greater market--set of markets, more accurately--for anyone with writing skills and a desire to put them to work." Holtz knows what it takes to make a successful career of freelance writing, and shares his vast experience in **HOW TO START AND RUN A WRITING AND EDITING BUSINESS** (Wiley; April 30, 1992; $14.95 paper; $29.95 cloth). Here, writers will find the guidance they need to make a full or part-time business of their freelance efforts and "avoid the traditional hardships of the literary trade."

What is it that separates the many skilled and talented writers from the relatively few who achieve economic success? Marketing. Even the most talented writers, according to Holtz, will not receive monetary rewards until they learn how to market themselves aggressively to the fields most in need of their services, namely: business, industry, and government. Holtz tells writers how to target unique markets and offers an introduction to essential business skills such as pricing and customer relations. He also covers related services, such as editing, proofreading, typemarking and designing publications.

This useful guide also includes practical advice about the writing process, including:

- how to acquire good writing habits
- how to choose the correct research and data-gathering methods
- how to overcome writer's block, and
- how to effectively organize disks and files.

--more--

Figure 9.1. Typical publicity release.

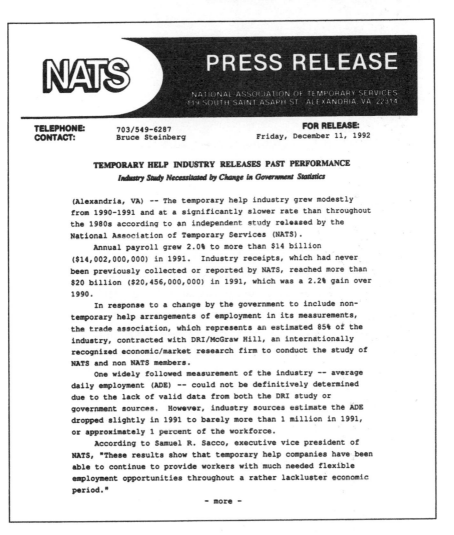

Figure 9.2. First page of news release.

opportunities among the government's procurements, so I could come up with headlines such as these:

- The government paid me $6,000 to answer their mail.
- Government contract issued for go-go dancing.
- Federal agency rents mules and handlers.

Of course, you won't always find material for headlines that is attention-getting, novel, amusing, or intriguing, nor should you use such headlines unless they are truly appropriate and accurate leads for your items. The clever headline won't help if it has nothing to do with the content of the release. But

News Release

GSA #9064 IRMS

September 22, 1992

GSA Awards $1.7 Million Contract to Washington D.C. Firm

A contract worth an estimated $1,700,000 has been awarded by the U.S. General Services Administration (GSA) to a small business firm, VMX, Inc., Washington, D.C., to provide voice messaging and call processing systems to federal agencies.

The contract is for one year, Oct. 1, 1992 through Sept. 30, 1993. It was awarded through the multiple award schedules procurement program under which GSA negotiates with vendors for goods and services required by federal agencies. The agencies then order directly from vendors at the GSA-negotiated price.

The estimated contract value is GSA's expectation of the purchases federal agencies will make from the firm during the contract year.

# # #

U.S. General Services Administration, Washington, DC 20405 (202) 501-1231

Figure 9.3. A federal agency news release.

it is not necessary to always have a blockbuster headline because you are usually addressing readers with special interests. Any appeal to those interests—to what is new and potentially profitable or otherwise useful—will do the job if the appeal is clear.

The headline may or may not be one the editor will like and use—editors have their own ideas about what their readers want to read about and how to best command their readers' attention—but the important point is to create a headline that explains why the editor ought to use your story. The headline is an announcement, "Hey! Look!" Remember, however, that unless the release is going to a specialized trade periodical, the editor will probably not understand special jargon or references that are peculiar to the field. That is, editors of *Personal Computing* would probably have no difficulty understanding the significance of TECHNOCOMP CORPORATION ANNOUNCES 444MHZ COMPUTER, but the lay person or the editor of the *Millersville Times* might have difficulty judging the newsworthiness (much less the attention-getting power) of that headline. You would do far better to use something such as NEW, SUPERFAST (440MHZ) COMPUTER ANNOUNCED BY TECHNOCOMP. That enables any editor to grasp the idea that this is a new and newsworthy development, whether or not he or she knows anything about computers. (Of course, the body of the release goes on to provide details and clarify the significance of the headline.)

Typical Items for Releases

Straight news in a release is practically never of the front-page-headline type. There are exceptions, such as news released by government offices and agencies, but news in a release tends to be of interest only to those within some kind of special-interest group, such as a given industry or profession. When releases are of interest to readers of a popular publication, such as a magazine or newspaper, they are most suitable for specialized sections of the periodical, such as the financial pages or food section. Following are a few examples of the kinds of news items found in releases:

- Information about people within the industry or sphere of interest: notices of newcomers, retirees, promotions, and obituaries, particularly of prominent figures in the industry.
- Announcements or advance notices of mergers, new starts, contract awards, divestitures, stock offerings, new constructions, expansions, and other such stories.
- Stories behind the story—inside or little-known information about developments such as mergers, divestitures, sell-offs, new products, and cutbacks.
- Technical details of new product, stock offering, merger, financial manipulation, or other development of interest.
- Government activities affecting the readers, such as new legislation, regulations, reports, and other such things.
- Announcements of relevant new books.
- Notices and/or reviews of new products and services.
- Announcements of special events, such as conventions, association meetings, and trade shows.
- Copies of speeches by individuals at special events, such as those just listed.
- Statements by individuals prominent in the field of interest.

What Is Interesting?

I happen to be interested in computers and electronics, subjects that bore some people. But I confess that most sports are of as little interest to me as they are of great interest to the vast majority of men. On the other hand, I am interested in remaining healthy, being successful, and enjoying life in general, as are most people. These subjects may even outweigh those reported by *Reader's Digest* many years ago as the most popular ones: They were Lincoln, mothers, medicine, and dogs.

Health, success, and happiness are subjects involving every individual's self-interest. You can almost always capture attention and sustain interest when you get into the subject of personal interest. Even this varies to some extent. Everyone needs to feel secure, for example, but security has different meanings for different individuals. To some, a job that appears to be steady and pays a decent wage represents security, but others require far more, such as substantial savings, a retirement account of their own, and perhaps a great deal of insurance.

Such motivations will inspire people to do things they might never do otherwise. How many would have thought to arise every morning before dawn, put on a special outfit for which they have paid a great deal of money, and run themselves to exhaustion before breakfast had they not been led to believe that this would assure them of better health?

The most basic drives are fear and greed discussed in Chapter 8. Appeals to these get attention and arouse interest. Fear drove many thousands of people to go deeply into debt to build and stock elaborate bomb shelters in the 1950s, and many things—insurance, alarms, and locks, for example—are sold principally through fear motivation.

Desire for gain also commands attention and interest. There is no apparent end to the appeal and the supply of books and newsletters purporting to guide people to success in the stock market and in other kinds of investments. The late Joe Karbo reportedly sold more than 600,000 copies (at $10 each) of a little paperback book he wrote and self-published titled *The Lazy Man's Way to Riches*.

Many other appeals are time-tested and apparently never wear out their welcome:

- Inside information or tips appeal to that human desire for information denied to most and is, perhaps, even a little illicit.
- FREE! How that word endures! It never wears out.
- SALE or BARGAIN. Like FREE, these words endure forever. Many successful businesses feature everything on special sale every day, and the public seems never to weary of it.
- How it works. Few can resist the desire to solve the mystery of how things work, whether about satellites or legislative horse-trading.

Humor helps, but it is double-edged. The ability to be humorous, especially in writing, is rare. Despite the fact that everyone—well, almost everyone—likes a laugh, humor that doesn't succeed is deadly. Best course: Report the facts without editorializing or trying to make the item humorous. No one will criticize you for straight reporting, if you are accurate. If humor is inherent in an item, it requires no embellishment.

A show-business cliché says there are no small parts but only small actors. There are also no dull subjects but only dull presentations. Every subject has interesting facets, which can be discovered and presented. Lancelot Hogben, an engineer in Great Britain, passed the time during a lengthy illness by writing *Mathematics for the Million,* a book on the history of mathematics. Published by W. W. Norton in 1937, it has remained in print in many editions since. Millions who find mathematics otherwise uninteresting loved Lancelot Hogben's accounts of the history of mathematical developments and disciplines.

You can find something interesting to report about any and every subject imaginable. Use the public library to do some research.

LINKAGES: KEEPING YOUR EYE ON THE BALL

Copywriters often get carried away with the challenge of writing effectively and forget what they set out to do—generate leads for future contracts, in this case. An excellent release that is widely published is not a success as a marketing effort if it fails to generate sales leads for you. To be successful, your release must do two things beyond getting published: It must somehow induce or provoke readers into responding directly to you in some manner, and it must be selective so that those who respond to you are qualified leads, individuals who are good prospects as clients for consulting services—for *your* consulting services.

Make it clear in the release that you are a consultant, and define at least the general area of your expertise and services. Provide the reader with a clue of what your services do for your clients—kinds of problems solved and/or benefits delivered.

One of the easiest and most direct ways to establish the correct linkage is to have your specialty incorporated into your business name or subtitle, such as:

- Accurate Real Estate Appraisers
- Government Marketing Consultants
- Convention Planners, Inc.
- Editorial Experts, Inc.
- Office Systems Designers, Ltd.

If you link that with the content of the release—if the connection is obvious—most readers will at least perceive where, how, and why your services can and should be of interest. And given that much, if your release is widely circulated, it will probably produce at least a few leads, in time. But you can improve the odds by doing something to stimulate the response.

The how-to success story is often effective, especially when it is the inside story. Promise to tell readers how so-and-so (e.g., the president of a prominent metalworking company) increased productivity 18 percent through a simple method available to everybody. That kind of thing almost always commands attention. Even better, promise to show readers how *you* helped that individual get those spectacular results. Of course, you can offer a set of several such reports and get even greater impact, especially if those reports show how your services can deliver the same benefits to different kinds of industries or clients.

That means offering to provide some kind of helpful brochure or report to any reader who requests it. You want requests from those interested in learning how to increase productivity. You send them your report (and it need not be elaborate; a report typed on regular paper and reproduced by some inexpensive means is perfectly suitable) and your sales literature, and follow up with telephone calls.

Powerful although this kind of response device (inducement to respond) is, it is not the only kind. Study the junk mail you receive and you will discover a great many ideas for response devices, including free appraisals, free estimates, samples, free newsletter, and many other ideas that you can borrow.

BROCHURES AS MARKETING TOOLS

Brochures are probably the most abundant of all instruments written for marketing. They are the basic marketing tools for many consultants and are found in every possible size, color, format, quality, and application. The word, *brochure,* is a general term with countless interpretations. It is possible to produce brochures that cost a fraction of a cent each, but you can also find brochures that cost many dollars each to produce. Some brochures are a single typewriter-sized sheet folded to fit into an ordinary business envelope, while others are dozens of pages long, formally bound, requiring a large envelope for their mailing.

Some situations call for and justify elaborate brochures, but it is rarely necessary to go to extremes. A brochure made up of a single sheet folded to fit into a number 10 business envelope is adequate if properly typeset and printed on a reasonably good grade of paper. Remember that the brochure is not intended to land a contract; even excessively elaborate and costly ones can't do that. Brochures help you generate marketing leads for follow-up. That is all they should be expected to do.

The $3 \times 8\frac{1}{2}$-inch size for a brochure offers advantages. It fits into a standard business size envelope and is convenient to carry in an inside pocket, purse, or briefcase, enabling you to carry a supply with you at all times.

That convenience extends to anyone to whom you hand such a brochure: The recipient is also not faced with trying to handle something awkwardly large, but may also slip your brochure into a pocket or purse easily. In fact, a $3 \times 8\frac{1}{2}$ brochure is often even more useful than a business card: It is not only of a convenient size, but it carries a message far beyond that possible for a business card.

You can use your brochure as you might a release, offering the same inducements to respond and using similar copy. That gives you total control over distribution of your brochures. You may do the actual physical distribution yourself via direct mail, at business and professional events (conventions, conferences, trade shows, and other meetings), or have marketing support services do it for you. In fact, it is wasteful to mail brochures alone; if you are going to go to the expense and labor of a direct-mail program, you should make up a complete direct-mail package, which includes such items as a salesletter, a brochure, and a return envelope, as a minimum.

You may also have a more elaborate brochure—an $8\frac{1}{2} \times 11$-inch format, stiff cover, and other such refinements. But that expensive brochure should be reserved for follow-up contacts and should be in addition to, not in place of, the smaller brochure.

OTHER SALES MATERIALS

There are many marketing applications in which writing can be your most productive and fruitful marketing activity. Use your pen to develop salesletters, bids and proposals, advertising copy, newsletters, books, and articles for periodicals.

Salesletters

The typical salesletter tends to be high-pressure, with bold type, capital letters, two- and three-color inks, circles, exclamation marks, handwritten notations, and other high-excitement symbols. This is as inappropriate for selling consulting services as huckstering on the streets. If a salesletter is to be of any use at all to you, it has to be quiet and dignified, while still observing all the valid principles of selling effectively. Figure 9.4 is an example of such a salesletter.

Published Articles

Articles published under your byline in periodicals can be an important marketing tool, and you should make every effort to write such articles and have them published. They do a great deal for your professional image. Potential clients are impressed by them, and they add to your authority in your field. Reprints of your articles are useful promotional material to insert in your mailing packages and appendices or exhibits of your proposals. Question and answer columns are excellent, if you can persuade some editor to allow you to do this on a more or less regular basis. The idea is to prove your capability and the worth of your services by offering a few samples through such devices, but the mere fact of being published is itself an impressive credential to many people and is a great help to you in marketing.

Use that same idea when you speak to groups: Invite questions and comments from or open discussion by the audience. That not only gives you a chance to display your wares, but it helps you understand prospective clients'

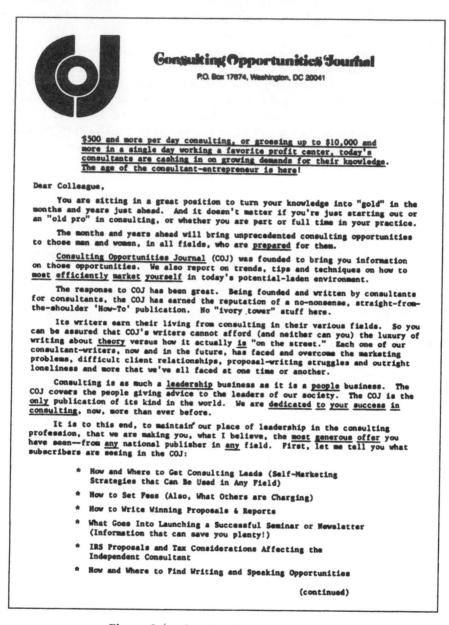

Figure 9.4. Sample of typical sales letter.

views, attitudes, problems, needs, biases, and other characteristics that should be aids in your marketing. Learn as much as you can about how your prospects think. Your main goal in every contact, especially face-to-face contacts, should be to learn about the prospective client. Do more listening than talking—much more.

* Consultant Networks, Consultant Brokerages: What They Are,
  How They Work and How to Work with Them (Are They the
  Ultimate Income Source?)

* How to Discover, Develop and Market Information Products
  and Other Profit Centers of Your Own

* Data Banks, Research Centers, Make Them Work For You or
  Your Client, Telephone Marketing and much, much more!

Along with covering scores of publications to bring you the happenings in the booming consulting industry, we have just acquired Consultant's Digest and merged it into COJ--at no extra cost to subscribers. There's even a Q & A column where you can get specific answers from specific questions from COJ's own consultant to consultant editor, Herman Holtz.

When you come right down to it, the COJ could be broken up into several newsletters--each with the same or higher subscription rates. There could be one on Self-Marketing Strategies, Consulting Contracts/Fee Negotiation, Direct Mail Marketing/Advertising Strategies for Consultants, Developing and Marketing Seminar and Newsletter Properties and others. But these are all included in your COJ subscription.

A year's subscription to COJ is only $24 for six full issues. And it's totally tax-deductible along with a money-back guarantee. Plus, there's no extra charge if we increase our publishing schedule during your subscription term. (Saves $6.00 over single copy)

Those watching the mushrooming consulting industry tell us that, within two short years, a weekly publishing schedule will be needed to touch all the bases. We don't know about weekly, but from the looks of things now, a monthly publishing schedule is not far off!

A 2-year subscription is just $39 (a savings of $21.00 off the single-copy price), and a 3-year term is only $57, a big $33.00 savings over single-copy!

Now, let's get back to my "most generous" offer I mentioned earlier. We've just made a special purchase of 7 top-selling titles of consulting guidebooks from The Consultant's Library, the nation's leading consulting book publisher (See the attached list).

As if all the foregoing benefits of a COJ subscription weren't enough, now you can get up to 3 (THREE) books FREE--up to an $80 value with your paid subscription! You simply select one book FREE for each year of your chosen subscription term.

This is a limited-time offer and may be withdrawn soon. To ensure your selections, order today on the special order form enclosed. Use the handy postage-paid envelope for additional speed and savings.

Isn't it time you discovered all the benefits to you and your family from your own consulting practice?

Yours for a successful consultancy,

J. Stephen Lanning
Publisher

Figure 9.4. *Continued.*

Books

Even more than articles in periodicals, books published under your byline help establish and confirm your technical/professional authority, and lend you added prestige. Many successful consultants are the authors of books about their own special fields. Among the best known of these is management consultant Peter Drucker. The late consultant's consultant, Howard Shenson, authored several books, as has Hubert Bermont, publisher of *The Consultant's Library* and Director of the American Consultant's League, and many other independent consultants. Consultant Jeffrey Lant chose to be his own publisher, and has written a number of books about consulting, marketing, and other business subjects. He markets them aggressively, partly through a column he self-syndicates in a number of opportunity or shopper periodicals, and has gained a great deal of prominence through these activities. (In recent years, he has become prominent as a marketer on Internet.)

In some ways it is easier to get a book published than to get an article accepted for publication, and many consultants have managed to do both. (Admittedly, you may not earn a great deal of money from your books, unless you publish and market them yourself, as Lant does, but you will reap benefits in publicity and image building to help you market your services.)

Advertising Copy and Writing Sales Materials Generally

We tend to think of advertising as the printed notices in periodicals, written by professional copywriters in the advertising industry. However, all those items we have been discussing are advertising copy, and the following principles apply to all of them.

The mark of the amateur writer and the kiss of death in advertising copy is overwriting, especially extravagant use of laudatory adjectives and adverbs, superlatives, and other excesses of hyperbole. The novice copywriter apparently reasons that readers will accept any claim that is outrageous enough and repeated often enough. We find brochures peppered with words and terms such as:

expert/expertise	renowned
highest standards	tremendous
remarkable	sensational
national authority	unmatched
adept	worldwide
leading	unique
superb	outstanding
peerless	incredible

Not one of these terms has an objective nuance to it. Without exception, they mirror opinions, claims, bias. They reflect self-appraisal, blatant Madison Avenue copy. Perhaps such words were effective once, in a less-sophisticated time, but they are an assault on one's senses and intelligence today. Today's reader hardly pauses over such words or pays them any heed. In fact, if today's reader thinks about it at all it is merely to snort in disbelief at such Madison-Avenuese. Such words are, in fact, virtually invisible to readers, the result of overuse and straining readers' tolerance for hot air; we speed-read our way past them at speeds exceeding that of light, which, Einsteinian physics assures us, makes them vanish from view!

The New Marketing

That extraordinary times call for extraordinary measures is as true in marketing as elsewhere. Greater marketing aggressiveness is one measure. New and better marketing ideas are better measures.

—Herman Holtz

A NOT UNCOMMON ECONOMIC PROBLEM

We are, at this writing, enjoying the healthiest economy in decades. Of course, we look for it to continue. However, the truth is that the economy is in constant cyclical motion, and you must be aware of this and act accordingly. Today's economic conditions are strange: Despite the prosperous economy, many corporations continue downsizing, laying off people, as modern technology inspires increased automation, and markets shift about unpredictably.

Even with a booming economy, the need to market regularly is as great as ever to sustain our business. We must still persuade prospects to place their trust in us and retain us to help them.

Despite the robust economy, many employers are reluctant to recruit new employees, even when workloads are increasing. That may be due to reservations about the prospects for the long-term, or it may reflect the increasing costs and problems in hiring and especially in laying off permanent employees. Whatever the reasons, many employers now see advantages in turning to temporaries and independent contractors to see them through peak loads or special projects. The availability of independent consultants and contractors represent labor pools that can be turned on and off on short notice with a minimum of start-up and downsizing costs. That also offers an advantage to those consultants willing to work on the client's premises.

WHAT'S WRONG WITH THE "OLD" MARKETING?

Mass production was the key to producing goods at prices that most of us could afford, and mass marketing was the way to sell those goods. It became the way to sell many services also. The advertising media for mass marketing were broadcast (radio and television), print (newspapers and magazines), and direct mail. It was effective, and it was cheap: A tiny return, often as little as a fraction of 1 percent of the prospects reached, produced enough sales to make the campaign profitable.

What has changed is the cost of mass marketing: Postage, printing, air time, and all the other costs involved in marketing have skyrocketed. It is increasingly difficult to make a marketing campaign successful with minuscule response rates. With today's costs, it is increasingly difficult to absorb the waste that has been an accepted condition of mass marketing.

IS MASS MARKETING DEAD?

Some enthusiasts of database marketing go so far as to pronounce mass marketing moribund, if not expired, pointing to need for more highly targeted marketing. That probably overstates the case. Mass marketing is not moribund, and it is not going to die, but it is going to change, and database marketing points the way. Where the targeting for classic mass marketing was broad—your name on a list of those who had bought golf balls or clubs was enough to ensure that you would start getting golf-oriented literature in your mail, whether you were a golfer or not. Mailers were flying blind, with limited knowledge of what a name on a list really said about the individual. The new mass marketing will put your name on the list only if you are known to be a golfer. In short, the mass in mass marketing will be a smaller mass because the individuals on the list will be much more highly qualified—the targeting will be far more precise. Database marketing uses much greater information about each individual to raise the response rate and reduce the waste.

BUT CONSULTING IS NOT SOLD VIA MASS MARKETING

Although consulting services cannot be sold effectively via conventional mass marketing, database marketing is still appropriate for most independent consultants. It is based on the idea of having enough information about each of our clients and prospective clients to target our offers more closely—to increase the quality of the leads. The possibilities are even more diverse and sophisticated than that. There are several aspects or possible outcomes, you can:

■ Tailor your presentations to the client—find common elements to create a presentation targeted to and having appeal for everyone in your database.

■ Select those in your database who represent the best prospects for what you offer and target those especially.

- Tailor your services/products to the interests of those in your database or tailor services/products to various subgroups in the database.

- Develop a profile of your ideal or best client, and thus profile your best prospect to strengthen your lead generation.

- Define one or more market segments or niche markets that are best suited to what you offer. That is one of the most important uses of database marketing.

THE MARKETING DATABASE

You cannot rent a marketing database as you would a mailing list. You must build your own. It will contain typical fields for name, address, and other data, but it must include many other fields—data useful for marketing. It should be a relational database, rather than a flat file type, to make use of other records you maintain. You may decide that your consulting practice is such that you ought to build and maintain more than one marketing database, but here we will assume that one marketing database will serve. It is the marketing database that is the heart of the strategy.

Clients versus Prospects

The original idea underlying database marketing was to build a database with detailed information about each individual vis-à-vis needs and wants. When you read what others say on the subject, you are likely to find all discussions cast in that mold of databases of existing customers.

That idea is of great use to those who sell a wide and diverse set of products or services, and whose success depends on repeat business with established customers. It has limited application to those who sell one-time items and need new prospects continuously. For that use, the marketing database should not be confined to clients only, but should include prospects, those who appear to be likely to become clients. I recommend building your marketing database to include both prospects and clients.

Kinds of Information

The information to be incorporated in the database is data related to marketing what you sell. If you sell computer services, for example, you are not interested in the individual's preferences in literature and education. That is why you must build your own marketing database: It must be tailored precisely to your own marketing needs. You want to know each prospect's probable interests, needs, likes and dislikes, motivations, and whatever else furnishes clues for your marketing.

Here are just a few of the kinds of information that would be typical for any marketing database, as they pertain to your market:

- Demographic data and lifestyle—age, occupation, income level, and so on
- Purchasing history—purchases from you or others, relevant to your own services
- Hobbies, outside interests
- Memberships

Sources of Information

There are many sources of information. You have some information on established clients because you have done business with them. You probably have invoice files and perhaps logs, copies of reports, and perhaps simple personal recall from casual or even formal conversations. You may very well have information about your clients in several different files (hopefully, all computer files). That is why a relational database is best: You then have no need to duplicate information in the marketing database, but can simply summon it up from those other files as needed.

The best source for information is the individual. Those who engage most actively in building extensive marketing databases take the initiative in encouraging information input from customers and prospects. They do so by asking customers and others for relevant information when sending for rebates, entering contests, joining clubs, requesting free goods offered, and whenever there is an opportunity for establishing a dialogue with customers and prospects.

If you have a newsletter, use it to help gather information for your marketing database. If you run a booth at a trade show, think up some device to gather at least starting data from each visitor. Think of other ways to elicit information for your marketing database. You can gather a lot of information passively through secondary sources, but the most valuable information comes directly from the individual. In effect, you are asking, "How can I do business with you?"

Market Segments and Niche Markets

As your marketing database grows, use it to discover market segments or niche markets. This capability alone justifies building a marketing database: It identifies the smaller and more efficient mass for marketing. Often, it identifies the market that has been there, undiscovered. You may discover, for example, that your best clients are always businesses of a certain size or of a certain nature. Focusing your marketing efforts on businesses matching that description may quadruple your marketing effectiveness, as it did for me when I discovered that small software-development firms were my best clients for proposal-writing and proposal-seminar services. The effectiveness of all business activity, especially marketing, is dependent on the quantity and quality of the information upon which decisions are based—the *available* information. Most of us never realize how much we base our judgments and actions on hunches, instead of real data. Database marketing allows us to base decisions on data instead of intuition, and the payoff is in discovering new and profitable markets.

NETWORKING FOR CLIENTS

The term *networking* is a fairly new one, although the concept is an old one and is used to refer to a method for marketing oneself via referrals. (See Chapters 3 and 8.) Many consultants report that their principal method of advertising and source of new business is word of mouth—recommendations from one client to another. What the stimulus is for such person-to-person recommendations is usually unknown to them. They like to think that they are being recommended because of the superior quality of what they do and sell, and perhaps because they are honest, fair, and honorable businesspeople. Probably there is no single cause: Superior performance and professional behavior are undoubtedly factors, but it is sometimes the result of being warm and friendly; many people are impressed by that, where they really have no basis for judging how good you are at what you do. But in a surprising number of cases, it is pure chance: Someone who needs help does not know where to turn and will eagerly welcome any recommendation from any source. I have been amazed at how often someone who does not know me, but has only heard of me from some source, will recommend me to someone else. In summary, it is usually pure serendipity and nothing more.

That is not to demean the beneficiaries of such serendipity; they are probably competent enough. But such marketing is marketing by chance, and its success depends on the state of the economy, the tenure of your practice, and the degree to which your name and reputation have become known, your visibility. It works, but it is hazardous to rely on chance, especially, if your practice is still new and not yet well established. The need is for more organized, more regimented, more controlled conditions.

Networking

Networking can be pursued via casual or directed means. Both work, although probably with different degrees of effectiveness. But you can use both. Here are a few things you can do:

- Belong to and be active in associations and local organizations—business clubs—where you meet and associate with prospective clients or with those who can recommend you to prospective clients.
- Attend conventions, symposiums, and other such gatherings to meet with prospective clients and with those who can recommend you to prospective clients.

- Be a guest speaker at seminars and other occasions where you can appear on the dais and make yourself known as a professional and consultant in your field.

- Be active in community affairs and become well known locally as the expert consultant in whatever you do.

- Produce an electronic newsletter and make yourself highly visible through that.

- Be active in the electronic discussion groups on the Internet, where discussions are carried on via e-mail.

- Organize you own message board or discussion group (called a mailing list on the Internet).

- Build your own Web site.

Seminars

As in the case of newsletters, seminar presentation is referred to in other chapters, and so this mention is merely to point out that seminar presentations are an excellent marketing tool for consulting services. Bear those possibilities in mind as you read the various discussions of seminars elsewhere in these chapters.

Booths and Exhibits

Engaging a booth and presenting an exhibit at annual conventions and other such occasions are workable marketing tools for many consultants. If you choose the right occasion, you will be able to do a great deal of prospecting for new clients by this means: You can hand out business cards, brochures, newsletters, and sundry other marketing and sales materials. You may also be able to gather a small crowd and do a kind of miniseminar, several times a day, while you gather names and addresses of prospects.

BROKERS, JOB SHOPS, SUBCONTRACTS, AND THE IRS

One way to win clients and contracts is via middlemen of various sorts—brokers, that is—and many independent consultants turn to that expedient because they prefer not to market personally or for other reasons. There are, however, problems bound up in this, too, problems that affect your status as an independent consultant. It is even bound up with that ancient problem of how one defines consulting and consultants.

The Many Faces of Eve

The word *consultant,* especially *independent consultant,* has several definitions: Independent consultants work under a wide variety of conditions. Some hire themselves out as technical and professional temporaries, working on the client's premises. Some undertake contracts and subcontracts, and work on either their own or the clients' premises, according to the conditions of the individual project. Some find these projects independently or for themselves, and some work through others who find the projects or assignments and make all the arrangements, taking a brokerage fee or profit of some sort for themselves. Some specialize in working under one or another of these methods, while others employ all the methods, as the opportunities and/or needs arise. Thus an independent consultant may be just that, a consultant, but he or she may also be a technical or professional temporary, an independent contractor or subcontractor, or perhaps some hybrid of these characterizations.

Even this does not explain the many elements that are responsible for the complexities. There arc certain legal questions, centering on questions of taxes and tax liabilities, that arise and have their own effects. They do not have an impact on consulting and contracting generally, but they do have a pronounced impact on independent consulting and independent contracting.

Four terms that are in common use in connection with the work we are discussing are *independent consultant, independent contractor, job shop,* and *broker.* These terms have been used here before and will be again, but they need clarification. Despite my own direct experience with all of the functions and positions referred to, I was confused for a time because these terms do not mean the same things to all people, in all situations, or in all places. Hence, the need to clarify them here. We will also introduce the term *Technical Services Firm* or TSF.

The subject of job shops and brokers is very much a part of the world of independent consultants and contractors. It is difficult to discriminate among the various terms. There will be some redundancies, but the need to be clear is great enough to tolerate those.

Job Shops and Brokers

The term *job shop* originally referred to small machine-tool shops who undertook small jobs—subcontracts—to manufacture or process small parts, such as to grind down or polish a rough casting. (One of my clients was a small job shop in the South Bronx, New York, who retained me to help them write a proposal in pursuit of a contract to manufacture tail fin assemblies for a small missile used by the Navy.) The term was later borrowed and is used to identify and refer to suppliers of technical/professional temporaries—engineers, programmers, designers, writers, and others, just as earlier there had been suppliers of clerks, typists, and other office temporaries. (Some suppliers, who don't like the term job shop, prefer to call themselves *labor contractors.*) The job shop recruits the help a client wants, puts them on the job shop's payroll, and assigns them to work on the client's premises, just as in the case of office temporaries. That is the mode of job shop operation: The consultant assigned to a project by a job shop is an employee of the job shop with limited hospitalization, leave, and other benefits, if any.

In some cases, suppliers of temporary specialists operate as brokers or prime contractors. Instead of hiring the specialists the client wants, the broker writes a prime contract with the client and subcontracts with each individual consultant specialist to work on the client's premises, ordinarily at some hourly rate, and usually with little defined beyond this. This makes the consultant an independent contractor who is responsible to take care of his own taxes, hospitalization, and other costs.

Generally speaking, the firms who provide consultants as independent subcontractors are called *brokers,* but they may be known also as job shops. In neither case is the shop responsible for producing a product, but are responsible only for producing bodies—specialists to work on-site for the client. That is a significant factor, for it makes of both what many refer to as *body shops.*

For the consultant, the consideration in turning to a broker or job shop is that of marketing. Using job shops and brokers means freedom from marketing for yourself, although it also means a lesser degree of independence. (Working for a job shop means even less independence than subcontracting to a broker.) For that reason, many independent consultants choose to shun brokers and job shops, unless they cannot avoid it. (Some consultants take pride in saying that they never use brokers or job shops, but always do their own marketing and find their own clients and projects.) Marketing is the most difficult task facing the independent consultants, which is what drives them into the arms of middlemen operators. That, however, is not the issue here: A much more important question of independence arises, as a result of IRS zealous enforcement of Section 1706 of the Tax Reform Act of 1986. It threatens the consultant's status as an independent operator.

In the meanwhile, the term itself, job shop or broker, is not significant; the contractual arrangement is. One makes the independent consultant an employee; the other makes him or her an independent contractor. As an independent contractor (IC), the consultant is legally entitled to have an overhead and deduct expenses for travel, tools, marketing, office expenses, equipment, and whatever else is a legitimate overhead item. As somebody's employee, however, whether temporary or permanent, none of these is deductible.

IRS AND SECTION 1706

The difficulty arises because the IRS resists recognizing consultants operating in this manner—working full time on the client's premises—as independent contractors or subcontractors entitled to take deductions for overhead. The IRS has disallowed IC status regularly for consultants in this kind of work situation, especially when the assignment, while technically temporary, is actually rather long-term—months and even years. The IRS regards such consultants as employees, temporary perhaps, but W2 employees nevertheless, who must have taxes deducted and who are not entitled to file tax returns in which they can deduct the normal overhead items of any business owner.

While a major disadvantage to the consultant is that he or she is denied the right to deduct a variety of business expenses, that is not the argument the IRS raised in lobbying for the passage of Section 1706 of the Tax Reform Act of 1986. The argument made by the IRS was that compliance would be greater if the consultants were recognized only as employees from whose salaries taxes had to be withheld. Their assumption was that independent contractors could not be relied upon to pay their taxes, and that the chief justification for 1706 was to ensure compliance.

The law permits IRS to apply 20 tests to determine the status of the consultant as an independent contractor or employee under the provisions of the Act. Some of the indications that the individual is an employee, rather than an IC, are that the individual is, has, or does the following:

- Has only one client
- Works entirely on the client's premises
- Is obligated only on the basis of hours to be available on the job (has no mission statement and deliverable item specified)
- May be terminated immediately and arbitrarily by the client
- Takes orders during the day from the client or client's staff

These and the remaining items are taken as indicators of employee status, and that conclusion does appear reasonable enough, at least superficially.

Indicators or arguments that the individual is truly an independent contractor are that the individual does, is, or has the following:

- Is incorporated as a business
- Has several sources of income—more than one client—from business operations
- Keeps formal time, expense, and income records
- Maintains a formal business office
- Is contracted to deliver a specified end-product
- Works at least part of the time in own facilities

Some consultants report that incorporating their practices has made it much easier to satisfy the IRS that they are, in fact, independent consultants and independent contractors. Others report that IRS does not accept that alone as prima facie evidence of independent status, but look for other supporting evidence. Some consultants have reported being required to fill out a 16-page document to prove their independent status. One consultant reported that the IRS was not satisfied even by the facts that he maintained offices in commercial space and employed several people.

As a result, both clients and brokers have become increasingly bearish in using technical/professional specialists on a contracting or subcontracting basis. Many brokers have turned to hiring the consultants as W2 employees, rather than as 1099 subcontractors, and many clients have become reluctant to contract with independents, for fear of being forced to wrangle with the IRS. To work as an independent consultant today is increasingly difficult.

Under the provisions of 1706, it does not matter whether you subcontract with a broker or contract directly with a client for your services. The Act treats both cases equally and requires the same bona fides in either case.

There appears to be some regional influence. In some areas of the country, many independent consultants are subcontracting via brokers and maintaining a 1099 status with no apparent difficulty, whereas in other areas—Phoenix, Arizona, for example—consultants report virtually all such work done as W2 employees only.

TECHNICAL SERVICES FIRMS

You may opt to be a Technical Services Firm or TSF. That is a firm that accepts project responsibility, contracting to produce a defined deliverable item. If you are a TSF or subcontract with one of these, you have a much stronger argument to prove independent consultant status, even if you work on the client's premises, for you have contracted to help produce some specific item, and you take your orders from the prime contractor and not from the client.

Marketing to the Public Sector: Federal, State, and Local Government

•

American governments are the biggest buyers in the world generally, but especially the biggest buyers of consulting services.

—*Herman Holtz*

A BRIEF GLIMPSE OF GOVERNMENT MARKETS

Despite cutbacks, federal agencies alone make over 15 million purchases and spend over $200 billion annually for purchases in the open market. Even that does not cover everything: Purchasing by government corporations whose procurement is off budget is not reported by the Office of Federal Procurement Policy. The Postal Service, employing over 700,000 people, is just one such agency spending many billions for goods and services every year. Federal procurement is thus in excess of that $200+ billion.

Even that number is dwarfed by the total of state and local government spending for goods and services. The federal government consists of 14 departments, some 60 independent agencies, and several dozen assorted bureaus, commissions, and other organizations. Each is divided further into subordinate agencies, so that the total approaches 2,000 such entities. Moreover, most of these have offices throughout the United States, most of whom buy independently. State and local governments present this even larger array of what the U.S. Census Bureau refers to as governmental units:

State governments	50
Counties	3,042

Municipalities	18,876
Townships	16,885
Local school districts	15,132
Special districts	25,988

Each of these government entities has its own complement of bureaus, agencies, and institutions, some rivaling the federal establishment in number and size. That makes it easier to understand why this array of government agencies together spends twice as much as the federal government. We are talking about more than $640 billion annually in government purchasing, a significant portion of that for various consulting services.

WHAT GOVERNMENTS BUY

The nature of public purchasing has changed. Governments once were markets for public works, primarily construction of streets, highways, bridges, dams, and public buildings, except in wartime, when needs changed drastically. Today, there are few goods or services that governments do not buy, even in peacetime, and for certain items, the governments are the only customers. Who else rents mules and handlers today or issues contracts for the supply of baggers in military commissaries?

Federal purchasing supports both military and civilian programs, and the procurement practices of state and local governments do not differ much from those of the federal government outside of the military procurement. Here are a few typical areas of purchasing:

- Research and Development (R&D) projects
- Insect and disease control
- Crime prevention
- Communications
- Education
- Housing
- Health services
- Social services
- ADP services
- Program evaluation
- Studies and surveys
- Technology transfer
- Operations research
- Public relations
- Training

HOW GOVERNMENTS BUY

Some agencies have permanent or semipermanent requirements and authorization for consultants, usually some specific number of slots. For example, one office in the Occupational Safety and Health Administration (OSHA), Department of Labor, for whom I did considerable work, had three consultant slots authorized and had three consultants devoting three days a week each to the office. I had won several small projects there, but the major project I was awarded was to occupy my full time for eight months, working on government premises. They furnished me office space, a typewriter, and secretarial services, a not unusual arrangement.

Government agencies may need consultants for almost any kind of work, including work of the type that most organizations carry out with their regular employees. However, governments are often motivated by political considerations more than by considerations of efficiency. To illustrate this, here are a few examples of work I have been involved in or which I have observed being assigned to consultants, despite the fact that the work is similar to that ordinarily handled by regular employees:

- Public information/PR services, sometimes running the public information office
- Developing work statements and other elements of requests for proposals
- Reviewing, evaluating, and scoring proposals received
- Answering government's mail and telephones
- Managing and administering government correspondence courses
- Operating government facilities, such as computer systems, laboratories, training establishments, and warehouses

THE PROCUREMENT SYSTEM

All bureaucracies are given to excesses. In ours, there is an overabundance of supply categories. The general supply groups number approximately 100, with many subcategories. As a consequence, the total government procurement of consulting services is obscured because most of the services are not called consulting, although the government is a major purchaser of technical and professional services. The decision of which category is most suitable for listing a given requirement is often arbitrary and may or may not be the most appropriate place to list it. Study the *Commerce Business Daily*, the federal government's daily announcement of the agencies' felt needs and contract opportunities, and you discover that consulting services are solicited under many categories, including:

- Experimental, Developmental, Test, and Research Work
- Expert and Consultant Services

- Technical Representative Services
- Architect-Engineer Services
- Photographic, Mapping, Printing, and Publication Services
- Training Services
- Miscellaneous

That is not all; many needs listed elsewhere call for consulting services. You may find opportunities for consulting contracts listed under these categories:

- Maintenance and Repair of Equipment
- Modification, Alteration, and Rebuilding of Equipment
- Operation and Maintenance of Government Owned Facility
- Installation of Equipment
- Funeral and Chaplain Services
- Salvage Services
- Medical Services
- Training Aids and Devices
- General Purpose Automated Data Processing (ADP) Equipment
- Software, Supplies, and Support Equipment

Basic Procurement Philosophy

One aim of public purchasing is free and open competition, a basic philosophy of free enterprise. This is theoretically the fairest way to afford everyone equal opportunity to share in government business, while it helps keep suppliers honest and assures the government of the best prices and quality. It is less than perfect but is on the whole a clean system that achieves its main objectives reasonably well, despite occasional procurement horrors reported in the press. Whatever scandals we do have concerning government procurement are much more scandals of bureaucratic inefficiency and stupidity, than of venality and corruption.

Procurement officials would prefer to make all purchasing price-competitive, with sealed bids and awards to lowest bidders. Unfortunately, this is simply not practicable in a growing number of procurements: The humorist observes wryly that no one wants to fly in a plane built by the lowest bidder. But wry or not, it sums up the situation: Price is only one consideration in these times of ever-more complex and sophisticated systems and is a secondary consideration where there are other important factors such as safety, performance, durability, reliability, maintainability, viability of plan, ability to perform, and other items that must be evaluated in making awards. Nor is it only the military, with their general and special weapons and equipment who must be concerned with these other factors in making their purchases. The concern for technical/quality factors applies everywhere, since governments buy food, medical supplies, computers, and other items where factors other than price are critically important. It applies also to the procurement of services.

The ability-to-perform qualification is especially important. Too often, even with all safeguards in place, government agencies have found their contractors lacking in capability. They therefore scrutinize proposals most carefully for evidence of the proposer's ability to perform. That evidence is most important in your proposals and sometimes the key to success.

Specifications

Many believe that the biggest problem in doing business with the government is the difficulty of meeting government specifications. The fact is that both military and commercial specifications are far less onerous today than they once were. Ironically enough, in many negotiated procurements, the lack of specifications is a problem. It is when the government cannot furnish detailed specifications that the contract must be negotiated, rather than awarded to the lowest bidder. The government asks you to propose specifications in proposing a project to satisfy the need. If the government could furnish detailed and measurable specifications, it would be practicable and more efficient all around to invite sealed bids, rather than proposals.

Sometimes this inability to furnish specifications is inherent in the nature of the requirement, as when the need is for an R&D project or for pure research and fact-finding. But it may also be a reflection of the lack of suitably specialized knowledge or skills on the part of the client. But in many cases, the client knows how the job can be or is usually done, but wants to examine and consider as many new and possibly innovative ideas as possible.

This results in two kinds of competition: There is the typical and classic price competition of the familiar sealed bid; but there is also the quality or technical competition and technical evaluation to select the best proposal. There are some variants—hybrids—but all are based on these two competitive parameters, with technical factors increasingly reflected in the criteria for evaluation and selection. Hence, the importance of proposals: For clients, it is the role of proposals in helping to select capable consultants. For consultants, it is the importance of knowledge and skills necessary to the writing of successful proposals. More and more procurements by clients in private and public sectors require studies and recommendations: The competition is growing. Consequently, of the two ways governments buy most goods and services—via sealed bids and via proposals—you will most often and probably with only rare exception find it necessary to write proposals to win contracts. In recognition of this truth, an entire chapter of this book—Chapter 12—is dedicated to the subject of proposals.

Special Cases

There are some special cases, such as small purchases—up to $25,000 each in the federal system, somewhat less at state and local levels—for which there are special, simplified procedures. There are also provisions for emergencies, when the agency's need is urgent and there is simply not enough time for competitive procurement processes. Too, some procurements are set aside for small businesses, meaning that only those qualifying as small business (as defined by the Small Business Administration) are permitted to compete. These and other aspects of public purchasing are covered by regulations.

Procurement Regulations

The procurement regulations for all purchasing by the federal government are today a single set, the Federal Acquisition Regulations or FAR. The abundance of regulations tends to nullify control and order: With so many regulations to resort to and choose from, it is usually possible for a determined procurement official to discover regulations that authorize or appear to authorize almost anything he or she wants to do, even if it means stretching the law a bit! However, although there are exceptions, there are a few basic principles embodied in the federal regulations, which are generally reflected also in the procurement regulations of state and local governments. First the principle provisions of regulations covering sealed bids (also known as *advertised* or *formally advertised* procurements):

- Bids must be delivered to the place specified by the time specified. Late bids must be rejected.
- Sealed bids are opened publicly. Anyone may attend and witness the bids being opened and read aloud.
- Awards are made to the lowest qualified bidder in each case.

Compare this with the basics of what the government now officially calls procurement by competitive proposals, formerly referred to officially as negotiated procurement:

- Proposals must be delivered as specified by the time specified. Late proposals must be rejected.
- Cost information must be provided in a separate proposal and may not be given in the main (technical) proposal.
- Technical evaluation must be made of each proposal by some objective rating scheme, which must be described to the proposers, along with the impact of cost figures in evaluation, as part of the information in the solicitation.
- The government is free to negotiate with proposers after proposal evaluation, and may require supplements, presentations, or other additional inputs before reaching a decision.

Government representatives may opt to visit your premises to verify that you have the facilities and resources to perform. This can also be extended to include a pre-award audit to confirm the acceptability of your accounting system and/or your financial stability.

Appeals and Protests

You are always free to appeal or protest an award decision or any step in the procurement process. It is usually of little use to do so in the case of a sealed-bid procurement, since the rules are so simple and clear, unless you wish to argue that the low bid should have been disqualified or you have had your own bid disqualified. (It is usually quite difficult to disqualify a sealed bid unless the bidder has failed to sign the bid or made some other gross error.) On the other hand, protests of award decisions based on competitive proposals are quite common and are sometimes successful.

The procedure is simple because it is an administrative appeal, not an action at law. It requires simply a letter to the contracting official or, in the case of the federal government, to the Comptroller General of the United States, who is also head of the General Accounting Office (GAO), an office of the legislative division of our government (Congress). The letter may be informal and set forth the basis of your complaint. This action, regardless of how it turns out, in no way compromises you or your further actions. You can even go ahead and sue in the courts, if you wish to. (Some large organizations protest quite routinely and sue occasionally.)

There is a great deal more to the many pages that document government procurement policies, procedures, and controls, but it is not necessary to become a guardhouse lawyer to do business with government. You should, however, know the general policies and procedures.

Types of Contracts

Government contracts are usually one of two basic types, fixed price and cost reimbursement, although there are many variants and hybrids of these. Contracting officials prefer sealed-bid purchasing whenever possible, and they also usually prefer fixed-price contracts. However, that is not always possible because of the many uncertainties:

- *Indefinite quantities.* The government often does not know how many or how much of something will be needed. This is especially the case when someone is awarded an annual supply contract for goods or services. The contract fixes the rate(s) and the period for which they are to apply, but leaves the total open.
- *Research and development.* R&D is almost impossible to predict or estimate with any certainty.
- *Surveys and studies.* The rationale is the same as for R&D.
- *Phased projects.* Each phase is evaluated before deciding on the next one.

Cost-reimbursement contracts are generally of the cost-plus fee, time and material, basic ordering agreement, call, task order, and labor-hour types. These are all rather similar, as described in the item indefinite quantities.

The government also uses purchase orders, which are a specialized form of contract used for small purchases—not more than $25,000 in the federal system, and with lower ceilings in most state and local governments. Technically, a purchase order is a contract, too, and is a far simpler way of handling the paperwork of contracting.

Purchase orders may be used to contract for individual tasks, under the Small Purchases Act and the procurement regulations that apply to small purchases, but they may also be used to authorize each individual task under an annual contract with a consultant.

MARKET RESEARCH

It has been said that the biggest difficulty in selling to the government is finding the doors. Although the government market is highly competitive in general, there are many cases in which there is little or no competition. That is especially so for small purchases made with greatly simplified and expeditious procedures. For many small purchases, advertising of a procurement is limited, and for a large class of small purchases no advertising is required. There is also noncompetitive procurement when the client needs the job done yesterday and can't afford the time needed for formal contracting, or when what is required is available from only one source, usually a proprietary item.

Finding the doors means finding, bidding/negotiating, and winning contracts that have not yet been or won't be advertised. Old-fashioned leg work—knocking on doors—is still the best way to locate these opportunities.

Making a Start: Studying the Federal Marketplace

Most of us find those doors gradually, through experience in marketing to the government and becoming acquainted with government organizations and their staffs. It is possible to begin by the traditional knocking on doors or cold calls on nearby government offices. Probably the best initial research is done at your own desk studying the *Commerce Business Daily* (CBD), now readily available on the Internet. Most state and local governments tend to emulate it, so the federal procurement system is a useful model.

Studying the published synopses of current requirements, you can become familiar with what and where the federal agencies are and what they buy. You can send for many of the solicitation packages and study them. Study also the awards section, where you learn of contracts awarded, also valuable market intelligence.

You can order the paper copy of the CBD from the Government Printing Office (GPO), who prints it, or from the Department of Commerce, who is the publisher for whom GPO prints it. It is mailed to you daily, but it is expensive and seldom reaches you before it is from three to seven days old. Fortunately, there is an alternative, one that brings you the CBD on the day of its publication. The CBD is now available in various forms and in several places on the Internet.

Once you perceive which agencies are likely to be the best prospects, you can file copies of Standard Form 129, Application for Bidders List. You need to file a copy of this form with the contracting office of each agency with whom you wish to do business. This form tells the contracting officer what solicitations are likely to be of interest to and bring responses from you. You will then be listed on each agency's bidders list and receive many solicitations—invitations to bid or propose—without asking specifically for them. However, with the CBD and the solicitations available for reading on the Internet, the Form 129 is of greatly diminished usefulness.

You can also visit contracting offices and ask about current requirements. You will have the opportunity to examine file copies of current solicitations. The larger procurement offices often have a separate room, a bid room, with copies of current solicitations posted on a bulletin board. But, again, the Internet resources make this measure much less effective than in the past.

There are at least two other measures you can take to familiarize yourself with the federal system. The Small Business Administration (SBA) operates approximately 90 offices in the United States so it is likely that there is one near you. A visit will put you in conversation with someone who can help you. Even a telephone call will bring you some helpful literature.

Even more helpful is a visit to one of the 13 Business Service Centers operated by the General Services Administration (GSA) in Boston, New York, Philadelphia, Washington, Atlanta, Chicago, Kansas City (MO), Houston, Fort Worth, Denver, Los Angeles, San Francisco, and Seattle. These centers are operated expressly to aid businesspeople learn how to do business with the federal government.

With all these facilities and resources available, there is little reason to neglect the huge federal market for consulting services.

Following Up in State and Local Markets

State and local government markets, taken together, are about twice the size of the federal government market. Individually, however, each is relatively small. Hence, none do quite as elaborate a job in organizing their procurement systems and aiding prospective suppliers in learning how to participate. Still, most emulate the federal system.

State Governments

Each state government has, in its capital, a central purchasing and supply office. This may be an independent entity in the state government hierarchy or it may be an office within an organization, such as the state's finance office or administrative agency. In Georgia, for example, the Division of Purchasing and Supplies is in the Department of Administrative Services, as it is in Idaho, Indiana, Louisiana, and Montana, among others. The purchasing office is in the finance or accounting agency in Kentucky, Maine, and Mississippi, but it is a separate division in Massachusetts, New York, and Texas.

Despite these superficial differences, there are many commonalities existing among all or nearly all state purchasing and supply offices:

- All urge prospective suppliers to visit their offices and meet the buyers to learn the requirements, and the procedures.
- All have some form of required registration or bidders' list application, which prospective suppliers are urged to complete and submit.
- Many supply lists of all purchasing office personnel, including buyers and what each buys.
- Many have technical specialists for the approval or negotiation of contracts for computer equipment, supplies, and services.
- All award annual supply contracts for commodities—goods and services they buy regularly throughout the year.
- Most delegate to the various other agencies throughout the state that purchasing which is peculiar to the other agencies' needs, such as consulting services.
- Most permit local governments to utilize state supply contracts to buy goods/services the local government needs.
- All have some kind of provision for small purchases and noncompetitive purchases, as established by statute.
- Most will supply, by mail and upon request, a brochure, explaining their system and governing statutes, often accompanied by a listing of their supply groups and commodities they buy regularly in goods and services, with forms for you to complete to get on the state's bidder lists as approved suppliers.
- Some will also supply a lengthy list of state agencies—hospitals, mental institutions, prisons, museums, departments, administrations, commissions, and many others—often with the names of administrators who do independent purchasing for those organizations.
- Most advertise their requirements and bid opportunities in a local newspaper, generally in classified columns under the heading "Bids and Proposals." For major procurements they sometimes use display advertising in the financial/business pages of the newspaper, as in Figure 11.1.

Special Considerations

State governments have their own socioeconomic programs. These include, in some states, preferential treatment for in-state bidders. In practical terms, this usually means that an in-state bidder gets a 5-point edge in technical-proposal

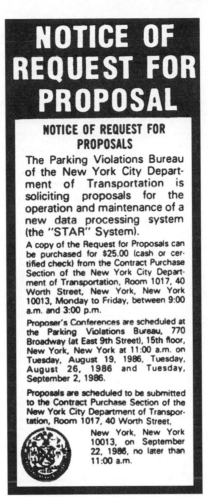

NOTICE OF REQUEST FOR PROPOSAL

NOTICE OF REQUEST FOR PROPOSALS

The Parking Violations Bureau of the New York City Department of Transportation is soliciting proposals for the operation and maintenance of a new data processing system (the "STAR" System).

A copy of the Request for Proposals can be purchased for $25.00 (cash or certified check) from the Contract Purchase Section of the New York City Department of Transportation, Room 1017, 40 Worth Street, New York, New York 10013, Monday to Friday, between 9:00 a.m. and 3:00 p.m.

Proposer's Conferences are scheduled at the Parking Violations Bureau, 770 Broadway (at East 9th Street), 15th floor, New York, New York at 11:00 a.m. on Tuesday, August 19, 1986, Tuesday, August 26, 1986 and Tuesday, September 2, 1986.

Proposals are scheduled to be submitted to the Contract Purchase Section of the New York City Department of Transportation, Room 1017, 40 Worth Street, New York, New York 10013, on September 22, 1986, no later than 11:00 a.m.

Figure 11.1. Solicitation advertised in newspaper.

evaluation or gets the award when he or she is tied technically or in cost with an out-of-state bidder. This may mean an edge for you when pursuing contracts in your own state.

Many states offer other aids such as loan and loan-guarantee programs, set-aside procurements for small businesses and for minority-owned firms, and counseling for small businesses.

Local Governments

We have, even at the local levels, a great deal more government than is readily apparent. Most of what has been said for state purchasing offices is equally true for the purchasing offices of local governments. A personal visit to the seat of government—county seat, town hall, or city hall—is always a good first step. The larger local governments often have purchasing organizations, descriptive literature, lists of supply groups, and procedures that rival those of the federal government and larger state governments, and they also often have an array of local agencies and institutions far more extensive than you may have dreamed. The list of local-government agencies in Washington, DC alone proved long, almost as long as the lengthy list of Massachusetts state agencies.

For your purposes, it is those many other agencies—that myriad of public institutions and government bureaus—who are most likely to become your clients. Here are just a few of the types of other agencies you are likely to encounter:

- Hospitals
- Halfway houses
- Transit authorities
- Equal opportunity offices
- Port authorities
- Offices of human rights
- Consumer protection agencies
- Environmental control offices
- Boards of education
- Library systems
- Departments of housing
- Child protective services
- Economic development administrations
- Health services
- Public roads bureaus
- Tax collection offices
- Prisons
- Special commissions of many kinds

These are the bureaus and agencies most likely to need consulting services. However, you usually must be registered with the government's central purchasing authority, before anyone in that government can do business with you. Purchasing authority can be delegated to other agencies, but in many cases, the other agency may select you for contract award but must have the central purchasing organization do the actual contracting with you. In such cases, you must market to those other agencies, but still handle all administrative and contracting matters with the central purchasing office.

SUBCONTRACTING AND OTHER SPECIAL
MARKETING APPROACHES

No contractor, not even the supercorporations, does everything. Most, especially the largest ones, subcontract a great deal of the work. A major procurement to a large corporation—General Motors, Boeing, IBM, GE—can easily result in 200 or 300 subcontracts. Thus, subcontracting to the winners of government contracts alone represents many opportunities, and is itself a multibillion dollar market.

One place to learn of contract awards and subcontracting opportunities is in the CBD. Most issues include an awards section, which lists the contracts awarded recently. Each of these notices offers a synopsis of the work contracted for, the size of the contract (in dollars), the agency for whom the work is to be done, and the winner of the contract, usually with an address included.

Occasionally the winner of a large prime contract will ask for and get permission from the government to advertise a need for subcontractors in the pages of the CBD. Be alert for such notices in the relevant categories.

Often the prime contractor who is seeking subcontractors will invite bids and request proposals, just as the government does. The terms of major contracts often clearly imply or even specify a requirement to do so when letting subcontracts. It is a good idea to prepare and circulate capability brochures, a presentation of your capabilities in general, to all organizations who appear likely to invite subcontracts for such services as you offer.

You may wish to offer your services to contenders for contracts before awards are made, even before you learn of the request for proposals! Many organizations pursue contracts for which they are not fully staffed—they lack some of the key personnel needed to conduct the proposed program. They need, therefore, to include in their proposals the resumes and promised services of experts who will act as consultants to support the program. You can thus be in a good position for a subcontract if the organization manages to win. (It is a good idea to have a written agreement with the other organization to that effect, in return for the use of your resume to strengthen their proposal.)

You may wish to permit more than one contender for a given contract to include your resume and promise of availability to support the program. This is not unethical if all parties are aware that your resume will appear in competing proposals and do not object to it.

As an alternative, you can co-bid with someone else, where the two of you are a far stronger contender for the contract than either of you alone. Usually this is still a prime contractor and subcontractor presentation, but in this case you both participate in writing the proposal. You must decide who should be the prime contractor and who is the subcontractor. This ought properly to be decided solely on the basis of which arrangement makes you the stronger contender.

Proposal Writing: A Vital Art

The best proposal writers win contracts because they appear to be the best qualified contenders. "Best," in "best proposal," however, does not refer to writing skill as much as it refers to other skills that are even more important.

—*Herman Holtz*

THE EVOLUTION OF MODERN PROPOSAL PRACTICE

A proposal was once little more than a brief description of what was offered, the prices, and the terms of sale. A printed brochure or two might be enclosed, and perhaps some boilerplate material—a standard form or two.

Technology and large government projects, with huge contracts and subcontracts, are a major cause of the evolution of the modern proposal. As the military began awarding contracts for the development of superweapons, multimillion dollar aircraft, missiles, radar, and computers, technical and management capabilities became more important than lowest costs. Even that is not the entire reason for using proposals to find the best contractor. Many government requirements are for research and development of basic concepts and systems that may or may not work out. The quest is often for contractors with new ideas. Even with the end of the Cold War, it is necessary for the United States to be on the leading edge of advanced technologies.

WHAT PROPOSALS CALL FOR

The following messages may be implicit in many requests for proposals:

- Here is our problem, with its symptoms and what we think is an accurate definition of the problem. This is everything we know about it. We want help in solving it. What do you suggest? Describe your understanding, analysis, and detailed plan.

■ Here is a concept that has appeared in the literature. Is it practicable? Can it be developed into a useful and practical methodology? How would you develop this? What kind of results would you predict?

■ Here is an idea for a new kind of weapon? How would you develop this concept into a working prototype?

■ Here is a need (to counter a new threat, new weapon by another power, new hazard of our own modern equipment, or other). Give us your best ideas for developing a counter or solution.

It is by such means that new, raw ideas, such as that of a laser, are developed into working models and practical devices that ultimately find applications in medicine and industry, as well as in military and space applications. Radar, computers, infrared devices, and others are similarly developed through contracted programs. But not only equipment is so developed. Many systems for improvements in safety, efficiency, training, and human betterment in industry, the professions, and society at large are born this way also.

The modern proposal is the primary medium for choosing the best qualified contractor or the contractor with the most attractive and persuasive ideas. It is a means by which we present our credentials and ideas, and by which the client evaluates those credentials and ideas and makes a choice.

The idea has spread rapidly. Not only governments select consultants and other contractors through proposals today; private-sector organizations have adopted the idea increasingly, and it has become commonplace to conduct proposal competitions in awarding contracts.

The following guideline in writing proposals is applicable and appropriate for responding to requests for proposals (RFPs) issued by the government, by private-sector organizations, and by foreign governments and foreign privately held organizations, who often refer to an RFP as a *tender*.

WHY PROPOSALS ARE REQUESTED

The RFPs are calls for help. The client does not know how to solve (or even define) the problem, needs additional resources, wants to study and evaluate different ideas and approaches before investing in one, and wants the benefits of competitive bidding. Also, the client needs something on which to evaluate the contenders for the contract and select one or more for negotiations. RFPs are signposts guiding you in writing proposals because they tell you what the client requires. They guide you to success if you read them carefully and accurately. They resolve into basics the merits of your plan or proposed program and your qualifications as a consultant/contractor. The following lists suggest some basic considerations and questions the client will be concerned with and seek in reading your proposal.

PROPOSED PLAN AND PROPOSER

- Is it what we want—what we are looking for?
- Is it practical?
- Does it appear workable?
- Is it likely to produce the results we want?
- Do you have the skills and resources to carry out the plan?
- Are you dependable—do you have a track record of making good and coming through in your projects?

Remember, it is the client's perception that is truth, and is (presumably) the consequence of your proposal: The client is influenced by your proposal and how convincing or persuasive you were in selling your plan and capabilities.

THE INGREDIENTS OF THE RFP

The typical RFP has four major elements:

1. An introductory letter with information on when proposals are due, where they are to be delivered, who to call with questions, what kind of contract is planned, and other general information, such as announcement of a pre-proposal conference.

2. Proposal instructions, including a specification of what information is to be in the proposal, how proposals are to be evaluated (if it is a government RFP), sometimes a dictated proposal format, sometimes forms to be used for cost estimates, and other such material.

3. Standard boilerplate information about the requesting organization, purchasing policies and regulations, contract terms, invoicing, and other administrative data.

4. A statement of work, describing the client's problem or need, symptoms, objectives, and other such orientation in the requirement. Theoretically, this is a specification, a complete and detailed description. In fact it is often far less than complete for any of many possible reasons. But it is what you must respond to and address.

Kinds of Information an RFP Asks For

To determine which consultant has the best ideas (proposes what appears to be the best program) and greatest qualifications, most RFPs ask you to provide these kinds of information:

- Analysis and discussion of the requirement, demonstrating full and complete understanding of the need and capability for designing and carrying out a responsive program.

- Preliminary program design or approach, with sufficient explanation to demonstrate the suitability of the design or approach proposed.

- Specific proposed program, with details of staffing, organization, schedules, end-products, interim products, procedures, management, quality control, schedules, and whatever else you deem important enough to merit discussion. Cost estimates must often be presented in great detail.

- Your qualifications to carry out the proposed program successfully. This includes knowledge, skills, facilities, and any resources normally required for such a program as you propose.

- Record of your verifiable experience in similar projects, naming other clients, proving your dependability as a contractor.

WHAT IS A PROPOSAL?

The answer to this question must be from the client's viewpoint, not from yours. First are questions of scope and size, questions of physical format of the proposals and amount of effort needed to produce them. Many consultants choose not to pursue government business because they consider the proposal requirements too onerous and proposal writing too expensive. Whether this is true or not depends on your personal view, especially on how you feel about writing and how badly you need business.

Depending on the size of the project, the proposal required may be large or small. Projects suitable for the independent consultant, roughly in the range of $5,000 to $75,000, usually require only simple, informal proposals, actually letters of several pages in which the proposal is embodied. These are often called letter proposals. But even formal proposals may be fairly small. For small to medium-sized projects, a formal proposal may be 25 to 50 pages, although many are far larger than this.

Before deciding that you will or will not write proposals to pursue contracts, you ought to consider these points:

- With only occasional exception, there is only one winner in a proposal competition. Second place is only slightly better than last place, although there may be advantages to being close.

- It is not enough to show that you can do a good job or as good a job as anyone. You must prove yourself and your plan better than all others.

- Clients won't perceive for themselves that your approach, plan, and qualifications are superior, and won't make an effort to do so. You must explain why and how they are superior, that is, *sell* yourself and the program you propose.

- Don't tell them that you will do the job; show them *how* you will do it.

The short answer to the question of what a proposal is from your viewpoint as the seller is this: A proposal is a *sales presentation*. It cannot succeed unless it sells.

This is why proposal writing—*successful* proposal writing—is not dependent on writing skills as much as on marketing skills. A proposal is a written presentation, but being well written is not enough; the writing must implement a winning marketing strategy.

PROPOSAL SCENARIOS

Here are some of the typical situations and causes that lead to proposal writing and influence the nature of your response:

■ A client has identified a need and seeks help from a specialist. Presumably, an award will go to the writer of the best proposal. This is a kind of self-fulfilling prophecy because the proposal that wins is therefore the best proposal! Still, there is at least one exception: When the need is not too pressing and none of the proposals submitted are very good, the procurement may be canceled. Don't count on being able to win by being the best of a bad lot.

■ Some RFPs are inspired unintentionally by consultants working with the client: The consultant suggests something intended to promote more work for himself or herself, but the client decides to solicit competitive proposals despite the fact that the original idea was yours.

■ In many cases there is the happier situation where you may suggest something to a client or prospective client that elicits an invitation to submit a proposal for a sole-source award. This may result because the client has complete faith in you and does not wish to consider anyone else or it may be the consequence of your offering a proprietary idea or product.

■ Finally, you may offer an unsolicited proposal as a result of some knowledge of a client's needs or as a normal follow-up of a sales lead, usually as a voluntary act, with or without advising the client that you are planning to do so.

WHO MUST YOU SELL?

You may have to sell to more than one person in the client organization. You may have sold the individual with whom you have had direct contact, but that individual may be required (or may prefer) to review the matter with others and get approval. In many cases, the individual wants to retain you or to select you as a contractor, but needs your help in selling the idea in his or her own organization.

In this situation, the proposal becomes all-important, even though you believe you are "in" already because the individual you spoke to was enthusiastic and assured you of his or her support and desire to retain you. But that individual may have limited power and may need your help in getting approval.

Always assume that there are others who must be sold when dealing with an organization. Even when there is not a formalized committee-type of proposal review, a number of people will review proposals and pass judgment on them. Those judgments will influence the buying decision.

I have often been asked for "something on paper" by executives in both private-sector and government organizations. Sometimes it is because the individual needs help and wants to present my arguments to his superiors. When the client writes a purchase request, he or she must write a purchase description or specification of some kind. Given that (a) many people have a great distaste for writing, (b) the client is not in nearly as good a position as you are to describe what the purchase is, (c) the client may be embarrassed to admit that he or she cannot write the description of what is needed without your help, and (d) it is always sound marketing strategy to make it as easy as possible to do business with you, you will find it a wise move to develop and document that purchase description in a proposal of some sort and be at pains to make it as easy as possible for the client to identify and transcribe the description or statement.

I have never found a sales situation in which a proposal was not a good tool to help make the sale. Nor have I ever found a situation in which the proposal should not have been a serious sales presentation. Verbal proposals are effective in selling situations where you might normally expect to close the sale on the spot, but it is only the opening shot in most selling situations. You need to follow up a verbal presentation with a written one, one that is a permanent record for clients to review, study, discuss, evaluate, and consider at length. But it is also a presentation, and a proposal offers you the opportunity to develop it at length, with careful study and consideration. That is one of its chief advantages: A written proposal allows you time to plan, draft, reconsider, edit, rewrite, and polish until you are satisfied that the presentation is everything you want it to be.

Remember always that you are in one of two selling situations, selling against competition to a client who has decided to buy but not from whom to buy, or against almost automatic reluctance of many kinds:

■ Reluctance to turn to outside sources for help.

■ Reluctance to break a pattern and do something differently.

■ Reluctance to do something finally about a familiar old problem.

■ Reluctance to battle internal resistance to contracting out.

■ Reluctance to admit that there is a problem.

■ Reluctance to spend the money.

PUBLIC- VERSUS PRIVATE-SECTOR PROPOSALS

The most significant difference between public- and private-sector procurement is that private-sector clients may do pretty much as they please, whereas public-sector clients are bound by public laws governing purchasing.

The consequence of this is not trivial. It affects what you must do in writing a proposal in many ways. Philosophically, when you respond to a government RFP you can often enjoy an advantage by being aware of the statutes and taking advantage of them. The objective is not to win recognition of your eloquence but to win the contract, and the award is for what you say, not how you say it—marketing strategy, not literary polish.

That is not the only difference between the two proposal situations. Another is that in the private sector you are generally accepted as whatever you say you are. Government clients, on the other hand, generally require that you provide information to prove your competence and your qualifications. This is at least partially a consequence of the legal requirement to evaluate each proposal objectively. But it also reflects the bad experience the government has had with contractors who were not competent and whose work had to be done over. So you may expect that RFPs issued by government agencies will require you to furnish evidence of your qualifications and capabilities, technical and otherwise, for performing successfully. It is a good idea to furnish such evidence, even when it is not required.

Governments tend to demand a complete cost/price analysis in all but small contracts, and that analysis requires you to reveal all your cost factors, direct and indirect. Reluctance to reveal such proprietary and confidential information is one reason some consultants do not pursue government contracts.

There is also the risk in revealing your program strategy. It is not unprecedented for unscrupulous individuals in the private sector to appropriate the plans and confidential information in a proposal and use this information for their own ends, victimizing proposers by what amounts to simple theft. This is a serious problem, and the risk should be taken into account in proposing to any organization, particularly in the private sector. (The risk of such treachery is much smaller when proposing to a government agency.)

By far the most significant difference between the two kinds of proposal situations, however, is the one referred to at the beginning of this discussion, that private-sector clients may do pretty much as they please in their purchasing, whereas government-sector clients usually have legal restraints that compel them to evaluate each proposal along a variety of significant parameters, and they are required to give you some intimation as to what those factors are.

THE EVALUATION SYSTEM

Federal procurement practice requires an objective rating system be used to evaluate and assign each technical proposal a figure of merit representing its respective technical quality. (Costs must usually be a separate proposal, to bar their influencing the technical evaluation.)

The resulting evaluation schemes vary widely in form and, especially, in level of detail. Following are two typical examples:

- *Example 1:* The following are the criteria on which technical proposals will be evaluated. Item (a) has twice the value of Item (b), which has one-half the value of Item (c).

  Item (a): Understanding and approach.

  Item (b): Qualifications of proposed staff.

  Item (c): Qualifications of the organization.

Award will be made to that proposer whose proposal is deemed to be in the best interests of the government, costs, and other factors considered.

- *Example 2:* Evaluation criteria are as follows:

(a) Understanding of the problem	0 to 5 points
(b) Practicality of approach	0 to 10 points
(c) Evidence of realistic anticipation of problems and planning for contingencies	0 to 10 points
(d) Proposed management and organization	0 to 10 points
(e) Qualifications of proposed staff	0 to 25 points
(f) Qualifications of organization	0 to 25 points
(g) Resources offered	0 to 15 points
Maximum possible score	100 points

In those cases in which greater detail is provided the several criteria listed (as in the second example) are further detailed by subordinate items reflecting the analysis of each.

The Cost Criterion

Note that little mention is made of costs in these examples, except that it will be considered. This leaves final decision entirely to the judgment of the officials making the procurement. There is, however, an appeal or protest process for seeking redress against unfair or illegal procurement practices.

There are other ways in which cost is taken into account. Cost may be simply one criterion item as a specific, weighted factor added to the technical score. Presumably the proposer with the lowest cost is awarded the maximum number of points allowed for cost, while the one with the highest cost earns zero points. But, as proposers we are not entitled to know exactly how the evaluation is made.

There is also a method that links cost with technical considerations, dividing the dollars by the technical points to arrive at a cost per technical point. Presumably this results in award to the proposer with the greatest value—lowest price per technical point. For this to be viable, the client must first screen all proposals and eliminate those technically unacceptable, regardless of price. Such an elimination of unacceptable proposals, regardless of other considerations, is a common practice, although there are a few exceptions (e.g., contracting officers who believe that every proposer is entitled to a chance to revise his or her proposal and make it acceptable).

The Inevitability of Comparative Evaluation

The listing of evaluation criteria with specific weights suggests that the proposals are to be measured against standards set for each criterion. This is virtually impossible to achieve. Take that 0 to 25 points listed for qualifications of the staff proposed. Would that mean that the perfect staff would merit an award of 25 points? That the client will attempt to judge how near to or far from perfect each proposed staff is? Or does it mean that the proposal with the staff adjudged *best* qualified earns the most points, perhaps the full 25?

The latter is unavoidably the method for choosing, and it means that the evaluation *must* be comparative. Your staff and all your other qualifications will go through two evaluations: One will be to screen it for general acceptability, and the second to rank it on each criterion. No evaluation scheme can be entirely objective; human judgment is inevitably involved. You must do all you can to influence that judgment in your favor by employing every element of sales and marketing strategy available to you. Do not lose sight of the fact that while the private-sector client can be as unfair as he or she wishes when selecting a proposer for award, government clients are well aware that you have appeals from unjust decisions, and so they are not always free to make awards on the basis of friendship or personal preference, but are often compelled to make awards they would prefer not to make. Your sparkling personality, friendships, and charisma may help a bit but are rarely decisive factors overall.

THE PROTEST PROCESS

Protests may be lodged with either the contacting official responsible for the procurement in question or with the Comptroller General of the United States, who is head of and has his office at the General Accounting Office (GAO), a branch of Congress. A staff of lawyers and others work there, assigned to resolving protests. But you do not require a lawyer to register a protest. A simple letter, setting forth the facts as you see them, is sufficient to start the ball rolling. If the protest involves computers, computer software, and related matters, the protest must normally be made to the Contract Board of Appeals of the General Services Administration, which has jurisdiction in those cases.

The protest is an administrative appeal, not a legal action, and so in no way substitutes for a lawsuit or compromises a future lawsuit. That is, you are not legally bound by the protest and decision, should you choose to sue the government, something major corporations and others do fairly often.

Probably most people who are not familiar with the process believe the protest is a measure to pursue after losing in the competition. Consequently the bulk of the protests made are made after an announcement of the award. That, unfortunately, is the worst possible time to lodge the protest. You may win, but it is likely that you will win nothing. Three possible consequences may snatch the victory from you even when you win:

1. The project is already well under way and even if the award was improper, it would cost the government too much money to cancel the contact and re-award it.

2. The decision is that the award was defective, but you have not demonstrated that it was you who should have won, and it would be prohibitive to re-compete the contract.

3. The agency decides to cancel the procurement entirely, possibly to re-compete it at some future time.

You may protest any element of and at any time in the procurement process if you believe that there is something improper. For example, a client of my own protested successfully that the requirement did not permit enough time to write a proper proposal, forcing the agency to extend the closing date. Another protested successfully that the evaluation scheme had built-in anomalies so that the award violated the scheme specified, forcing cancellation. And another, in quite a large procurement, protested successfully that the winning proposal had been delivered and accepted some minutes after the deadline, and managed to have the contract canceled and re-awarded to him.

There are a great many protests that do not succeed. Many of them fail because they offer specious and irrelevant arguments and should not have been made at all. A common argument is that the protester offered a lower price, rarely a valid argument. One protester who used that argument had submitted a proposal that had been rejected as technically unacceptable, and so could not have won anything in any case. Another complained that the winner's price was too low and he would lose money on the contract. The contracting official advised him that it was not against the law to lose money.

You may protest just about anything you believe improper about a procurement. The apparent impropriety may prove to be no impropriety at all, it may be the result of a simple mistake, or it may be an effort to "wire" the procurement for some favored consultant. That is, of course, illegal, and probably not as prevalent as many think it to be, but there is no denying that it does happen, and should be challenged whenever you come across it if it appears to deny you a fair opportunity to pursue government business.

Signs to Watch For

There are several ways in which a procurement can be rigged to give a favored consultant an advantage. These devices are usually rather transparent, so be alert for these signs as possible indicators of such effort:

- The closing date is so close to the date of announcement as to virtually preclude anyone not already prepared to respond to be able to get a decent proposal together in time.

- The specification of what is required as qualifying characteristics is tailored unreasonably vis-à-vis what is necessary to get the job done.

- The specification of what is to be done is excessively vague and thus is extremely difficult to respond to and easy to declare your proposal non-responsive and thus disqualify it.

- The statement of work or specification of what is required is excessively and unnecessarily tailored, preventing free and open competition.

Such practices are not commonplace but they do occur, although the system is basically fair and honest; it is. But circumstances lead to these situations, no matter how innocently, and you are entitled to relief from them via the protest process.

SOLE-SOURCE PROCUREMENT

Procurement regulations provide for sole-source procurement, generally under one of three conditions:

1. The need is urgent and for some reason (such as the typically late enactment of an appropriation bill by Congress or an unanticipated emergency), there is simply no time for the typical 3 to 6 month procurement process.

2. The requirement is for a proprietary product, service, or experience of some sort that is unique and unavailable elsewhere.

3. The procurement awards a contract resulting from an unsolicited proposal. (This is tantamount to contracting for a proprietary, since the idea is a proprietary one, and sometimes a proprietary product is involved as well.)

Unfortunately, not all sole-source procurements are justified. Many are announced in the CBD, (stating that the announcement is for information purposes only) with the stated justification that the favored consultant has some special qualification, such as that cited in the second or third of the preceding examples (most often the second one). This is alleged then to offer the government the benefits of a more efficient program than would be possible with another contractor. To add insult to injury, that special, unique experience was often acquired in a current or recently concluded contract with that same agency!

Again, this may be legitimately so, but there is evidence, often cited by the GAO in their reports, that many agencies make sole-source procurements that are not justified, often simply to speed up the process. (Sole-source procurement is a much simpler process than competitive procurement.)

You may protest to challenge such procurement intentions and demand the right to compete if you believe that you can refute those allegations—you can do the work and do it as efficiently as anyone else.

What Happens Next

Your protest results in a request by GAO for copies of all documents involved—the RFP, the winning proposal, your proposal, or whatever documents are relevant, along with a statement from the contracting official, responding to your complaint. While GAO studies these you can respond to the contracting official's statement and he or she to your response. GAO may then issue its decision, although the process may be iterative and progress through several cycles.

In most cases, that is the end of the process. However, you still have the right to sue in a federal court.

PROPOSAL FORMATS AND RATIONALES

Some RFPs mandate a specific format for the proposals requested, even specifying a format for resumes. Most list, describe, discuss, and even specify the information required, often in great detail, but do not specify a format, leaving that to you. A recommended four-section general format that has proved to be highly satisfactory for and readily adaptable to most proposal requirements is offered here, with appropriate rationales and explanations.

General Discussion/Rationale

Not surprisingly, the recommended proposal format is based on the general premises that (a) the client is asking for help with a problem, (b) you're writing a sales presentation and must use sound sales tactics, and (c)—perhaps most important of all—your proposal must have a single, major strategy that is its main thrust.

That latter consideration is all important. Bear in mind that a proposal saying, "Me, too: I can do the job as well as anyone," rarely wins. It is necessary to stand out, to be superior to other proposals in some decisive manner.

FORMAT AND GENERAL RATIONALE

The following format is one that has been successful in winning many millions of dollars worth of contracts. It consists of four main elements, with other elements included if and as necessary. It offers information in a logical flow, but still implements the promise-and-proof sales strategy. It also provides the seed bed for major technical/program strategy, discussed later. It is offered as a format for a formal, bound proposal, but the format is easily adapted to informal letter proposals.

The four main sections and ancillary elements (when needed) are:

1. Front matter (title page, abstract, table of contents, etc.)
2. Section/chapter I: Introduction
3. Section/chapter II: Discussion
4. Section/chapter III: Proposed program
5. Section/chapter IV: Experience and qualifications
6. Back matter (appendices, bibliography, notes, etc.)

The chapter titles are generic. Try to use more imaginative titles, specific to the RFP. That will make it clear that you created the proposal for the client and it is not boilerplate from your files. Another reason for devising specifically appropriate titles, rather than generic ones is that the proposal is a sales presentation and you should use it to sell at all opportunities: Each headline and caption is a special opportunity.

First Chapter: Introduction

The first chapter has two sections: "About the Offeror," an introduction to who and what you are, with a brief précis of your interest and qualifications, and "About the Requirement," an appreciation or preliminary analysis, validating your understanding of the requirement and laying the foundation for your approach, strategy, and whatever else is to follow.

Second Chapter: Discussion

"About the Requirement" was a prelude to this chapter and should have set the stage for it. Now you explore the client's problem in depth. Demonstrate full understanding of the requirement and all that it implies (possibly defining it even more accurately than the client does). Define the technical experience, knowledge, skill, and creative imagination required. Show that you have analyzed the problem thoroughly, identified all alternatives and possibilities, and identified the optimum approach, which you now present, with the rationale.

Here, make your technical sales arguments, implementing your strategy. You may have to educate the client, explaining your analyses, reasoning, conclusions, and plans for delivering all the benefits, especially those around which you have built your main strategy. Explain how you will meet the impossible schedule, reduce the costs, maximize the probability of success, eliminate the possibilities of failure, and bring to reality whatever it is you have promised or the client has demanded. Here, parade the benefits derived from your plan—especially the unique benefits that would not result from others' plans. Prove that here and in the chapters yet to come. But this one must end in a clear presentation of your approach, preparing the way for the next chapter. This chapter of your proposal is the promise. The next one is the proof.

Third Chapter: Proposed Program

This chapter is the proposal per se, the specifics of what, when, where, how, and how much you propose. Everything before has been prologue. Here you show exactly how you will implement the strategy and approach you promised in the chapter just concluded.

In this chapter, pull the curtain back and reveal the details. No theory or philosophy here; just the bare facts. What? (Program.) When? (Schedules.) Who? (Proposed staffing.) How much? (Quantification of effort and/or products, if any.) How? (Plans and procedures.)

You need a chart or two here. (Charts are generally far more effective than text and even more than tables, in many cases.) Include an organization chart, if there will be associates working with you; a functional flow chart showing phases of work and major functions; a milestone chart illustrating the schedule and a chart or table matching major phases and functions with labor hours required for them.

The second chapter made promises. This one must offer proofs. (A few more proofs appear in the final chapter.)

Fourth Chapter: Experience and Qualifications

It is my usual practice to include the staff resumes in the third chapter, although they can be fitted into this fourth chapter easily enough. But where the staff resumes provide evidence of the qualifications of the individuals proposed to staff the project, this chapter offers evidence of the organization's qualifications.

That can be tricky when you are operating as not only an independent consultant, but also as a one-person enterprise—that is, you bid for relatively small projects and you are the entire staff, except for possible clerical and administrative support. But in responding to an RFP with a proposal, you must comply and respond as though you were a larger organization. You offer your resume as an individual, covering formal education and all relevant experience, wherever it was gained, but you also offer your resume with accounts of your projects, as an independent consultant, experience in providing services to your own clients, rather than to an employer. Much of the information will be the same, but the orientation will be different in each case.

Also include an account of all facilities and resources that relate in some way to your consulting enterprise generally and/or with respect to the proposed program. That might include your offices and equipment (for example, computers, copying and reproduction machines, photographic equipment, laboratory facilities, a library, photo files, and/or access to any resources that are relevant).

Front Matter

Formal proposals include front matter—title page (Figure 12.1), table of contents (Figure 12.2), and executive summary. The latter is a kind of abstract, but used by most proposal writers to highlight the major selling points of the

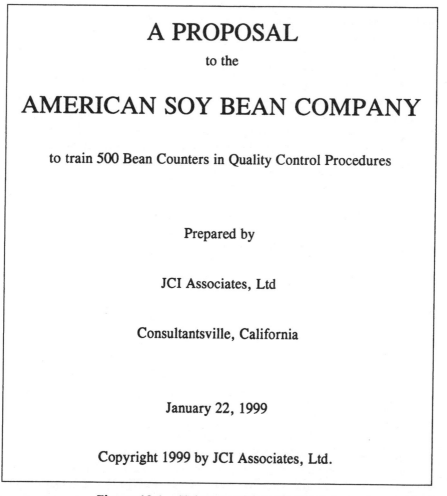

A PROPOSAL

to the

AMERICAN SOY BEAN COMPANY

to train 500 Bean Counters in Quality Control Procedures

Prepared by

JCI Associates, Ltd

Consultantsville, California

January 22, 1999

Copyright 1999 by JCI Associates, Ltd.

Figure 12.1. Title page of formal proposal.

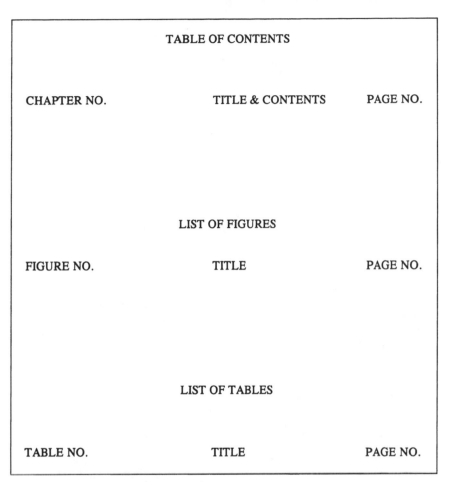

Figure 12.2. Format for table of contents.

proposal. However, an informal, letter proposal would not usually include front matter or an abstract (Figure 12.3). The effect of an abstract can be easily achieved in a normal letter format by using an inverted pyramid organization in which the entire story is summarized in the lead, with expansion into details following.

It is generally useful to incorporate into any table of contents a list of figures and a list of tables (Figure 12.2).

Back Matter

In some cases, it is necessary to include one or more appendices and sometimes an exhibit or two. An appendix is a proper resource when you have material to include that you believe will be of interest to some readers, but not to

HERMAN HOLTZ

P.O. Box 1731   Wheaton, MD 20915-1731

301 649-2499   Fax 301 649-5745

CompuServe 71640,563

June 29, 1999

John W. Herr
Vice-President
American Soy Bean Company
99881 Process Avenue
Soy Mash, Pa 17765   Ref: QC Training Proposal

Dear Mr. Herr:

    It gives me great pleasure to offer my assistance in helping you to reduce the number of rejects on your production lines while increasing customer satisfaction with your products. Our research, carried out since our recent meeting and discussion at the convention in New York City, bears out the correctness of your judgment: I agree completely that training in quality-control procedures is the proper avenue to improvement.

    I visited your plant, as you suggested, and interviewed several of your employees, using a structured interview that I developed some years ago in carrying out a preliminary task analysis for a similar program for the Acme Paintbrush Corporation. That program, I am proud to report, produced a 14-percent increase in net production, reducing line rejects by 11 percent. Subsequent reports reflected a 27-percent drop in returns.

    I am sure that we can do at least as well for you. Of course, while I will use the general approach that was so effective for Acme Paintbrush, I will develop a program designed especially for your company.

Full details are offered in the following pages for study by your staff and yourself.

(over please)

Figure 12.3.   First page of an informal, letter proposal.

all, such as the complete text of a document or drawing you refer to in your proposal. An exhibit, on the other hand, is often included when several copies of the proposal are called for, but only one copy of some supporting item—a set of slides or a sample of the product of some earlier project, for example—is available. When using such an exhibit, advise all readers that such an exhibit exists, although not an integral part of the proposal itself, so they are alerted to seek it out.

THE NECESSARY IMPACT

Any sales presentation, including a proposal, must have great impact if it is to do its job well. And if it is to have that hard-hitting quality, it must have a certain aura and deliver a clear sense of certain qualities. These are subtle emanations, but they allow you to leave the distinct impression that you are not only completely in charge of the situation, but know that you are. The client reading your proposal can sense these qualities:

- *Competence.* The reader must sense your power as a consultant who brings complete technical and professional competence to the job.
- *Dependability.* The reader must feel that you are completely reliable and will never fail to carry the job through to a successful conclusion.
- *Accuracy.* The proposal must convey the sense that you are careful to be absolutely precise and accurate in every action and in every step you take.

The keys to accomplishing this effect have already been provided, but to review briefly:

- *Specificity and detail.* Generalizations have little impact. A presentation that cites specific facts and details, particularly quantified data, is much more likely to impress a reader and be credible.
- *Startling statistics.* Study your facts and proposition quantitatively to see what impressive numbers you can develop—total person-hours of directly relevant experience, number of pages of training material you have written or directed writing of, or similar numbers that relate directly to what you can do for the client. (In my case, I am able to point to an impressive total dollar amount of contracts resulting from my proposals.) If the numbers are startling enough, see if you can work them into your introduction as an attention-getter.
- *Clear and unambiguous language.* Avoid euphemisms; you are not in the diplomatic corps. Use stark language, in good taste but words that are straight from the shoulder and can hardly be misunderstood or brushed aside.
- *Quiet confidence.* Hype is equal to protesting too much. It sounds defensive, as though you are trying to compensate for weakness. The absence of excessive adjectives and superlatives, the conspicuous lack of bombast, and the use of a plain-spoken and quiet reportorial tone conveys self-confidence and strength.
- *Take-charge attitude/approach.* Most clients want a take-charge type of consultant, one who will relieve them of worry and tedious, time-consuming involvement. Make it clear that you know exactly what to do—present highly detailed plans—and be sure that your explanations,

descriptions, and rationales reflect confidence in what you propose to do. *Caution:* Be careful; it is possible to overdo this. Make it clear that you will be responsive to the client's interests and wishes.

■ *Thorough response.* A consultant on annual contract in Arizona had been renewed year after year for four years. He got careless because he and the client knew each other so well. The contractor turned in a casual proposal for a fifth-year renewal and lost out to an aggressive competitor principally because of a lack of attention to detail in the incumbent's proposal.

STRATEGY AND ITS EVOLUTION

Over nearly 40 years of experience with proposals, I have become convinced that successful proposals are most often those based on specific, well-thought-out strategies. Again and again I have seen the dark-horse proposer, one that neither the client nor the competitors had ever heard of before, upset the cart and win because that proposer had an effective strategy that was implemented well. All marketing and sales effort ought to be based on some specific strategy, but proposals especially so because they are usually custom projects with only a single buyer. There are no percentages or probabilities to play with here; it's all or nothing in most cases. Even in the rare multiple awards procurement, the number of awards is limited, and you must still submit a first-class proposal to win anything.

Read the Client as Well as the RFP

You must read between the lines of the RFP, where the client is saying, "Yes, do explain your approach and program to me carefully, but don't stop there; sell to me, too; show me why I must select you as my consultant." Remember that the client is often not at all sure of what is needed and wants help in identifying the problem, as well as in solving it.

There is also the case of "Eureka!" in which the client reads a given proposal and reacts, "That's it! That's what I need!" That can happen when the client is able to describe only symptoms or unhappy results of some kind, and a consultant has been clever enough or, more likely, worked hard enough to infer the real problem. It is more likely, however, that the symptoms described point to a recognizable problem or the correct approach is to institute a two-phase program, in which the first phase is devoted to problem definition. There is an approach to devising strategies by first analyzing the initial situation, which is usually one of the following:

■ The client has a good and probably accurate understanding/definition of the problem/need.

- The client all but concedes that what is described are probably only symptoms, and the consultant will have to decide what the true problem or need is and respond to it.

- The client claims or professes to know what the problem or requirement is, but is probably mistaken; you must discriminate between what the client thinks is the problem and what it really is.

Understand What the Problem Really Is

Not every RFP calls for knowledge that the client lacks. In many cases, the client knows exactly how to solve the problem, but is looking for the best way to solve it or he may lack the wherewithal to do it. The client may therefore need supplemental staff for a short time, access to laboratory services, field workers, or other ancillary support. In such a case, best may mean least costly. But, depending on the client's orientation, it may also mean swiftest response to the need (often the client needs help yesterday); ability/willingness to respond under adverse conditions, such as an impossible schedule; most-qualified individuals to be supplied; most cooperative attitude; most dependable support; best understanding of the need; or some other factor not readily apparent.

The preliminary analysis necessary to develop a sensible and specific strategy should, then, consider these factors:

- What appears to be the best (fastest, most efficient, most dependable, least expensive, most risk-free) way to do the job?

- What prejudices/special concerns/worries does the client appear to have, if any, about how to do the job best?

- What appears to be most important to the client? (Cost? Schedule? Technical approach? Qualifications of staff? Qualifications of organization? Working relationship? Other?)

- Do these factors relate to each other? If so, how? (Incompatibilities? Can they be resolved? How? Or are they mutually supportive, lend each other strength? If so, how?)

The main strategic areas to consider are cost and program or technical matters. Even so, the two are often related, for if you offer lower cost you will be well advised to show how your proposed program makes cost savings possible, while meeting the clients' requirements. While there are secondary considerations that are not unimportant, the major strategic thrust is almost always in the proposed program plans and bear on factors such as these:

- Cost
- Schedule
- Reliability

- Risk of failure
- Staff qualifications/credentials
- Organization's qualifications/credentials

Evolution of the Strategic Base: Key Questions

The choice of factors on which to base your strategy is not a random one. It should be based on several considerations, the first and more important of which is usually the client's own perception of the need or problem, with which you may or may not agree. But that must be tempered by related considerations, represented by these questions among others:

- Is the client correct in his or her assumptions of problems and/or needs—that is, do you agree with the client's definition of the problem (and possibly of the solution)?
- Do you have a firm conviction about how to define the real problem or is it merely a suspicion that the client does not truly understand his or her problem—that work will be required to determine what the problem is before a reliable approach to its solution can be formulated?
- Has the client mandated in the RFP some defined set of services and method of operation to which he or she appears to be bound?
- If the client all but mandates (strongly recommends or even suggests) a method, service, or approach that is workable, is it the best one (most appropriate, most efficient, most likely to achieve the stated goals, etc.)?
- Is the client's definition so far off-base that it is impossible or would be risky to proceed without (a) an initial problem definition phase or (b) redefining the problem as you are sure it ought to be redefined?
- How firmly does the client appear to cling to his or her notion—would it be risky (to sales success) to confront the client directly about this in your proposal?
- Are there other problems the client fails to foresee (is possibly naive about the difficulties) or are there special problems of meeting requirements that are extraordinarily difficult, such as an impossible schedule?
- Does the client appear to be conscious of and/or especially concerned with some aspect of the problem such as meeting a schedule date, getting the job done at lowest possible cost, probability of eventual success, or other?

Making Lemonade

Eventually you come across most of these situations: each is both a problem and an opportunity. Some of the answers to these questions may pose a difficult sales problem: They may define whether or not you have an immediate problem of how to conceive and structure your approach without running head on into a client's bias or into a task that will be exceedingly difficult to complete. It is not at all unusual for a client to have a completely wrong idea about (a) what the problem is and (b) the best way to go about solving it. It is also largely true that you can't win an argument with a customer. It is essential that you recognize this common problem for several reasons, of which your professional integrity (and reputation) is the first one: You have an ethical obligation to be honest with the client. Aside from that, you can paint yourself into a corner if you go along with a false premise to win the contract. That may result in the problem of doing things entirely differently than you had originally proposed. You would then have to face the client and confess error. Such problems as these are, however, also seed beds for successful strategies. You can make lemonade out of these lemons!

There are strategies possible for all of these situations, but you must choose the right strategy for the occasion. There are clients who are willing to have you say plainly to them, "The approach you suggest is not the best one possible and will add unnecessary cost," or "The approach described is somewhat out of date today and is less efficient than the modern method." But even with those clients, it is better to put it, "There is an approach possible that will reduce your costs," or "A recently developed method promises greater efficiency."

Identifying the Worry Items

That is normal diplomacy, differing with the client without criticizing or challenging. But the possible strategic implication goes deeper: There is the matter of worry items. That refers to whatever appears to be of greatest concern to the client—cost, meeting the schedule, risk of failure, control of the project, the consultant's capability, the consultant's dependability, or other. Proposal success lies often in identifying that worry item accurately and focusing the proposal on that item.

For example, if an extraordinarily rapid turnaround time is required, you must focus on the schedule and how you propose to meet it. The promise is that you will meet it unfailingly—the client is assured of that—and the proof is your planned program and all the rationale you can develop to show why your plan must and most assuredly will produce the result you promise.

Build your program plan around a method for accommodating the client's chief worry item (and if there are several, decide which is the chief one and concentrate on it without neglecting the others), and be sure that the proposal dramatizes that suitably.

It is not always easy to identify the client's worry item. Sometimes you must read between the lines of what the client has written or said, or even resort to other methods for gathering marketing intelligence. You must decide what ought to be a major worry item, one that, in your judgment, the client will agree on, once it is pointed out. In short, help the client acquire a worry item!

Other Strategies

We have been discussing the master or *capture strategy.* That is the main strategy that is expected to sway the client and be a decisive factor in the award decision. We have operated on the premise that the proposed program design is the critical area around which the strategy should be built. Normally, this is true. But there are other strategic areas and supporting strategies to be considered. They are usually supporting areas, each requiring its own strategic approach, for none are unimportant. But any might become the main strategy in a given case, so they are never unimportant and do merit careful consideration.

There is the cost strategy, for one, which might become the major strategy. How will you organize and present your costs? How will you justify them? How will you demonstrate the value of what you are delivering?

There is also the competitive strategy. How will you position yourself vis-à-vis your competitors? How will you manage to outshine them, appear superior?

There is the presentation strategy. How will you present your proposal itself so that it has major impact and supports your master strategy well?

Here are a few suggestions:

Cost Strategy. Talk value, as well as cost, and be clear about value offered. Quantify and pro rate what you offer to do across the total budget to demonstrate the value. Provide as much detail as possible. That makes you more forthcoming and honest than competitors who are vague about what they will deliver for the dollars. That makes the costs you quote more palatable. It also subtly suggests to the client the possibility of negotiation and prepares the ground for negotiations by listing all the items that might be negotiable.

There is a special case you may run into: Some RFPs are so vague that it appears to be impossible to price the proposal. The client has furnished virtually no basis for you to estimate either the time or material required to do the job. In this situation, there is an almost automatic tendency to go back to the client and ask for clarification. That is usually a mistake for several reasons: Many clients think they have given you ample information, no matter how unclear their RFPs actually are. And you are throwing away an excellent opportunity to steer things your way, to develop a winning strategy.

This is a case where the client has failed to provide proper specifications. Instead, the client has clearly implied, if not explicitly stated, that your recommendation is solicited. Provide that recommendation. Decide what is probably necessary to get the job done and meet the goals, and draw up the specifications—the quantification, as well as the qualification, of what you propose. That is what you price.

This gives you several advantages, in addition to solving the problem: (1) It is a highly credible presentation because you are supplying the specifications: You are the true expert. (2) You are in control: You are telling the client just what ought to be done. (3) On both counts you are way out ahead of competitors. (4) This puts you in control of costs to a large degree. There is no special risk as long as you do quantify everything carefully.

There is still one other advantage you can gain here: You can offer the client options, and that is often a most powerful strategy.

Competitive Strategy. Don't refer to competitors directly at any time. However, it is perfectly legitimate and in good taste when you know that you are in a competitive situation to address this problem indirectly. One way is to include a discussion of what is needed to do this job effectively and meet all goals, schedules, and so on. In this discussion, list whatever is appropriate—experience, physical facilities, access to other specialists, willingness to burn the midnight oil, and other factors. This is a subtle way of providing the model to use in evaluating competitors.

Stress heavily anything you can offer that is unique or unusual and be sure to point that out. That also scores for you and against your competitors in the client's mind. (Is marketing a mind game? It certainly is!)

Presentation Strategy. Your proposal is a presentation and should be prepared carefully, even if it is an informal, letter proposal, to reflect professionalism and unblushing desire to make a good impression.

With today's office equipment, you can add sizzle where it is appropriate, as in drawings and charts, and you can use a variety of typefaces. You can thus present a proposal that is highly professional in appearance. But you can easily overdo this. Do not go to extremes in your creativity. Your proposal should still be a highly businesslike presentation. Here are some suggestions:

- Print your proposal neatly and cleanly on standard-sized white or near-white bond paper. You can use your regular letterhead if it is white, light cream color, or near that. Don't use dark papers; they are hard to read.

- Do use black ink, primarily, and colored inks sparingly and only as truly appropriate.

- Preferably use 12-point type and leave generous margins to make your proposal easy to read.

- Use illustrations—simple line drawings, charts, and photographs, as appropriate.

- Be careful about spelling, grammar, and other such details. Professionals should not be careless with the language.

- Use a good, up-to-date word processor and laser or ink jet printer so you can add a few appropriate flourishes, such as oversize captions and headlines. You may also find your desktop computer convenient for generating a few simple graphic illustrations—charts and graphs—to lend impact to your proposal.

Don't ask questions. Although many RFPs are sketchy and inspire more questions than answers, it is risky to ask the client to clarify or elaborate on a proposal request. You are likely to inspire the client to send out additional information to your competitors. Or the client may withdraw the request entirely and cancel the procurement. You are usually far better off to decide for yourself what the answers should be and bid on that basis (e.g., proposing the specifications), observing the precautions counseled earlier.

Don't be vague. Some consultants believe that if the RFP was vague, it is okay for the proposals to be vague. The result is disaster. Be specific, following the guides provided here. Many veteran proposal writers far prefer the vague RFP because it affords a much better chance of winning than does the crystal-clear one for several reasons:

- Reduced competition. Many others will drop out when the RFP is vague and appears difficult.
- It is an opportunity to outshine your competitors by being clear and specific, where they are vague and rambling.
- You are able to propose a project on your own terms.

Don't start writing too soon. The rush to paper—starting to write before reaching a complete understanding of the client's need and before formulating a clear strategy—is a common mistake that leads to poor proposals. Time is usually limited in proposal writing projects, and while it is almost an absolute rule that good writing results only from rewriting, the more preparation you make, the less rewriting you will need.

Do rewrite as much as possible. Although the compressed schedules in proposal writing usually make it impossible to do a complete rewrite, at the least do a thorough edit to ensure correct spelling and correct usage, and to polish the presentation as much as possible.

FUNCTIONAL FLOWCHARTS

People outside the technological fields appear to have difficulty with functional flowcharts. Yet, they are among the simplest ways to present and understand a process in which successive steps are required.

Such a chart, at least one depicting a relatively simple process, may be considered to be a graphic version of a written procedure. Consider, for example, a cook book explanation of how to make a plain omelet. The instructions might be written:

1. Heat butter in pan
2. Beat two eggs in a bowl
3. Pour eggs into pan

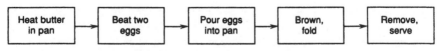

Figure 12.4. Simple flowchart.

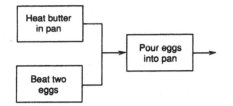

Figure 12.5. Flowchart showing phase relationships.

4. Brown and fold omelet

5. Remove when done and serve

Graphically, as a simple and straightforward flowchart, the process would be as shown in Figure 12.4.

The instructions might have directed the reader to beat the eggs while the butter was warming in the pan. Graphically, that would be shown as in Figure 12.5. That presentation shows a phase or time relationship between the first two component functions, to point out that they are or can be concurrent, which is often important in demonstrating how you plan to conduct the project and, especially, how you might organize the project to meet a difficult schedule.

As processes become more complex, it becomes increasingly difficult to explain them in words alone, and graphic aids grow more and more useful. On the other hand it is sometimes more expedient to show only the major steps, as in Figure 12.6, when the intervening steps are obvious. You have to be the judge of the right level at which to present and explain your plan.

These figures were highly simplified. In practice the processes are rarely that simple and straightforward. In fact, the processes are often iterative, as shown in Figure 12.7. This figure illustrates a most useful idea in proposal writing: Develop a functional flow chart that is based entirely on the RFP, as a first step, and then refine it before you begin to write at all. This is an idea and methodology that is particularly effective in developing successful proposals for large projects. If you do a thorough and accurate job of translating the RFP into a flow chart—usually a preliminary, rough-draft flow chart— you have accomplished a great deal:

1. You have your project design before you in a graphic form, one that enables you to study it effectively, perceive interrelationships among the functions, uncover anomalies, and perceive potential problems.

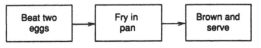

Figure 12.6. Simplified flowchart.

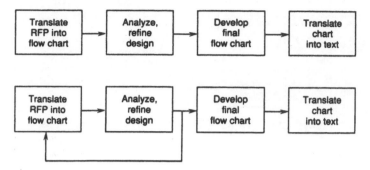

Figure 12.7. Proposal process showing iteration.

2. You have an almost ideal presentation tool. Clients value graphic presentations because it is much easier to grasp the logic of the project in a flow chart. Moreover, less text means less reading, a boon to busy executives.

3. The ability to envision the project in this manner says a great deal about your ability to handle the project. It demonstrates your understanding quite effectively, while it helps the reader understand your logic. The milestone chart (see Figure 12.8) is another aid to this.

4. Many of your writing problems are solved, since you now write to the flow chart. It's your road map and greatly reduces the volume of words you need.

The Logic of the Flow Chart

Flow charts have a definite logic to them, and the logic is itself one of the keys to creating flow charts (Figure 12.9). If you ask *Why?* to the notations in each

PROJECT SCHEDULE

Time in Months	0	1	2	3	4	5	6	7	8	9	10
Task Analysis . . .	▅▅▅	"	"	"	"	"	"	"	"	"	"
Preliminary Plan	▅▅	"	"	"	"	"	"	"	"	"	"
Review	. ▅	"	"	"	"	"	"	"	"	"	"
Revision	. ▅	"	"	"	"	"	"	"	"	"	"
Field research	. ▅		"	"	"	"	"	"	"	"	"
Interviews	. ▅		"	"	"	"	"	"	"	"	"
Draft lesson plans	. ▅▅▅			"	"	"	"	"	"	"	"
Tryouts	. ▅▅▅				"	"	"	"	"	"	"
Analysis of tryout results	▅▅					"	"	"	"	"	"
Final revisions and turnover	▅▅						"	"	"	"	"

Figure 12.8. Example of milestone chart.

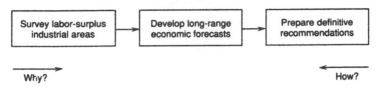

Figure 12.9. Logic of the flowchart.

box, the next box to your right ought to furnish an answer. Going in the opposite direction, you may ask *How?,* and the box to the left ought to answer that. In the illustration, you survey labor-surplus industrial areas to develop long-range economic forecasts, and you do that to prepare definitive recommendations, the objective of the project.

This helps you develop the chart and enables you to check its validity. Sometimes you can translate the client's statement of work directly into a chart, but often the RFP is not that definitive. Then you may have little to go on other than the required result. If, as hypothesized in Figure 12.9, the RFP asks you to develop a set of economic recommendations vis-à-vis the unemployment problem in labor-surplus industrial areas but gives you hardly a clue as to how you are to proceed, you might ask yourself, How? That is, you might inscribe "prepare definitive recommendations" in a box on the right-hand edge of a blank sheet and ask yourself what should go into a box to its immediate left. That is the beginning of the process in many cases, and it is where you can outshine your competitors.

A FEW ODDS AND ENDS TO CONSIDER

There are a few consultants who groan, inwardly at least, when they must write a proposal. Some groan because they hate to write; others for other reasons: They are sure that it is a waste of time, they fear that the client is simply trying to pick their brains without paying for the privilege, they have the belief that only those who have "fixed things" in advance win proposal contests, and they often actually resent being asked to write a proposal, which they consider an unreasonable demand and an imposition.

This is a short-sighted attitude. The RFP ought to be considered an invitation to bid, and a privilege, for it is an opportunity to present your ideas, rather than your personality. It doesn't matter here whether you are a six-foot elegant dresser with a winning smile and overpowering personal charisma or five-foot-six with thick eyeglasses. Your ideas and presentation speak for you here, not your persona.

In fact, it is wise to grasp every opportunity possible to submit proposals, even when they are not requested. Always put your offer on paper. Give the prospect something to study and digest, something to remember you by even if you don't close this one. In the end it will pay off.

The Initial Meeting

The key to successful consulting is understanding the problem—that means listening, as well as thinking. But you must also be businesslike, while being professional.
                                               —Herman Holtz

RULE NUMBER 1: HAVE A CLEAR UNDERSTANDING AT AND FROM THE BEGINNING

It's easy to have misunderstandings with others, especially clients. Many problems with clients are really misunderstandings. Probably many sales you thought you had, are lost due to misunderstanding, or, more accurately, the lack of clear understanding.

The problem can arise early in the process, even in the first meeting, when the prospect and you are sizing each other up, exercising caution to avoid anything that may have a negative effect.

Assume that this is a first meeting with a prospective new client. There are many circumstances under which your first meeting with a prospective new client might take place. Probably the other party is sizing you up as a source of needed help, as you are trying to assess the possibility for new business.

The meeting may have originated as a casual introduction at some convention or business club luncheon. But now you are seeking to ascertain the prospect's needs and the possibility of a sale. You ask questions, trying to get a solid fix on the possibilities, while the other makes conversation, possibly to pick your brains.

When Do You Start Charging for Your Time?

Most consulting sales, except minor ones, are made only after an initial meeting and follow-up. It is in the nature of consulting that it is a guidance, counseling, advisory, and doing service. Even in the extended meaning of consulting as a professional-temporary support service, face-to-face sales presentations and negotiations are common preliminaries to a contract. The question often arises, if this is a more or less formal meeting to discuss the client's need and how you view it, are you now providing consulting service for which you should bill the client? But is that other party now a client or still only a prospect? Are you still marketing and therefore charging your own overhead account? It helps to establish a clear understanding as early as possible.

There are no easy answers to this question of who is paying for your time in this initial session. You either have a fixed policy or you must judge each case individually. I get frequent letters and telephone calls from people who want to buy my lunch while they explore what lies under the increasingly sparse cover on my head. Most have no intention of paying for my time, information, and counsel; they haven't even considered it, and they think a good lunch is an ample fee for permitting them to pick my brains for an hour or two.

Once, I indulged such outrageous presumptions, in the hope of eventual assignments. I found it to be a losing game. Several thousand dollars worth of free time might produce one thousand dollars worth of paid time—perhaps. Too often, lunch was the only fee I ever earned from these encounters, although occasionally one of those lunches resulted in a worthwhile assignment and new client.

Not everyone is insensitive to the issue: Occasionally a prospect who invites me to lunch makes it clear, before I can respond, that he or she is not trying to get something for nothing, but is willing to pay for my time, information, and advice, as well as for the lunch.

Many authors and lecturers on the subject of consulting promise to teach you how to avoid giving away free information, suggesting that you lock your tongue up as though it guarded Fort Knox. I find that extreme. Face the facts: It is not possible to avoid giving away at least a few samples of our skills and knowledge. Few people will retain you without having had some first-hand evidence of what you have to offer. This does not mean that everyone is entitled to pick your brains and get free services or intends to do that. Quite the contrary, the questions are usually quite innocent, and the other party is not trying to victimize you. But that does not change the picture: You can't afford free consulting, but you must distinguish between free consulting and necessary marketing. Be ruled primarily by your judgment of each case, and decide whether you are willing to invest your time as a marketing expenditure or will require the prospect to accept billing for your time spent in conversation over a luncheon table.

Assess the gamble, the possibilities of work resulting from the meeting: Is the prospect a substantial organization with many needs that match the services you offer or someone who is unlikely to be able to offer any but a small commitment? Estimate the possible reward in deciding how much to gamble on the possibility.

You may fear that if you insist on charging for your time, despite the invitation to lunch, you will lose a potential contract. That is a false fear. Anyone who is offended by this businesslike charge (assuming that you have advised the prospect of your charges tactfully) is a poor prospect for business. You will almost surely lose nothing by turning such prospects away. To the best of my

184 of The Initial Meeting

knowledge and belief I have never lost a client or a contract by being businesslike and expecting my clients to be equally businesslike. Quite the contrary, this tends to inspire the prospect's trust and confidence. It establishes the business relationship on a much sounder basis than would be the case if you were completely pliable and allowed yourself to be used. To place your practice on a sound footing, you must inspire respect for yourself as a businessperson, as well as a professional expert and consultant.

My own inclination is to regard first calls and initial discussions as a marketing expense. Here is my own policy in this regard:

- I will give anyone a few minutes on the telephone. If the caller asks pointed questions, obviously with no intention to retain me, I will answer the questions as best I can, pointing out that I can't qualify my answers very well under the circumstances, and ending the conversation within a reasonable time—a few minutes. If I sense that the caller is a serious prospect, I will mention that I am available on a regular consulting basis.

- I may agree to lunch if the caller assures me that he plans to retain someone, that is, if I may regard the occasion as a proper sales call or presentation.

- I normally make no charge for a sales call/presentation/initial discussion if it is local and I think there is a serious prospect for business.

- I charge for my time and expenses for a first call/discussion if I must travel a distance and use up a day or most of the day in the process. I do make that clear, but I also make it clear that I will earn my fee by providing the guidance the client seeks, even if he or she does not pursue the relationship beyond that first day.

- I politely decline most lunch invitations.

RULE NUMBER 2: BE A DIGNIFIED
PROFESSIONAL ALWAYS

It is commonly said you are selling your time. Not so. Time is not the commodity you sell; time is a measure used to scale the effort and determine your fee. You may think that you sell information, and you do, but that is incidental. The client wants and pays for a result. But you have not yet produced a result when you make the sale; you have only promised a result, so inevitably that is what you sell, a promise. You sell what you will do for the client.

You ask a client for trust, and that is not given to you, a stranger, easily or automatically. It is your image that does or does not inspire trust. So it is in a much deeper sense that you sell your image as a competent and expert advisor, a professional who can and will make good on the promise. This is the image you must induce clients to perceive. Molding the client's perception of you (positioning, in advertising parlance) has a great effect on your success in closing sales. Still, striking a proper balance between extremes is essential. It is necessary to establish and maintain an air of dignity, if you are to be taken seriously, but taken too far this can make you appear cold, imperious, a stuffed shirt, or a pompous ass, all equally deadly.

Professional dignity, image, decorum, stature—all pertinent terms—are not easy to define, let alone prescribe. You must not be aloof and cold; you can be jovial, congenial, amiable, and even amusing, without losing dignity. It is not necessary to be somber or even a sobersides. You can even be laid back. Others should find it easy to talk to you and relax in discussion with you. It is helpful in many ways to be able to put others at ease. Clients and prospective clients are more receptive when they are relaxed than when they are tense.

Despite the difficulties in defining the professional image and the impossibility of prescribing a formula for creating it, it is possible to offer a few guidelines to help in achieving it:

- *Dress conservatively.* One consultant I knew in the past was referred to jeeringly by his associates and contemporaries as "Gypsy Jim," more for his typically green jacket, yellow slacks, and red shoes kind of wardrobe than for his itinerant working style. (As a result he was not taken very seriously even by his associates, let alone by his clients.) You need not go to the extreme of what was once the traditional IBM uniform—dark suit, dark tie, black shoes, and white shirt—but do dress quietly and in good contemporary taste.

- *Don't try to be the comedian,* but if you must be a humorist, do not relate ethnic, chauvinistic, or racy jokes. If someone must be the butt of your humor, make it yourself. But do smile easily and frequently, and be witty only at your own expense.

- *Keep an open mind.* If you are dogmatic by nature, work at overcoming that; it is essential to have an open mind, demonstrating that while you are knowledgeable, you are also always ready to consider dissenting views.

- *Keep calm and modulate your voice.* Carrying on conversation in a loud voice, getting highly excited, appearing anxious, trying too hard, bragging, showing signs of temper, or otherwise appearing other than cool and confident is taboo. Don't be self-deprecating or excessively modest; you should accept credit for what you are and can do, for the quality of what you offer, but without obvious "hype."

RULE NUMBER 3: SELL WITHOUT HYPE

Marketing is the most important thing you do. Without marketing success you don't have a practice. And selling—getting the contract—is the final act of marketing. It is far easier to win contracts when you have done proper marketing preparation: The main goals of marketing include getting good leads and positioning yourself to sell effectively.

Positioning yourself and selling are objectives of this chapter, and the subject of the right tone to adopt in selling is an important one. A few significant reminders are offered here. First, three simple don'ts:

1. Don't use such hyperbole as these examples: "millions" of cases, when you really are referring to several dozen or even to several hundred cases; "unprecedented," when that is not literally true; nor "magnificent" and other such verbal, Madison-Avenue and Hollywood-type hand grenades. They do not fit a professional image.

2. Don't use superlatives such as most, greatest, largest, latest, or other such terms, unless you can support them with evidence. Far better to quantify and be accurate in doing so.

3. Don't rely on adjectives and adverbs at all (with such exceptions as those noted). As Bertrand Russell remarked in one of his writings, "faith is what we turn to when we have no evidence," and extravagant modifiers and hype are what we turn to when we have no facts.

The do's are even more important than the don'ts. Here are a few of those:

1. Do stick to unadorned nouns and verbs, purveyors of fact, as much as possible.

2. Do make offers (what you do for clients), not announcements.

3. Do make reports, not claims. Sticking to nouns and verbs ensures this.

4. Do quantify as much as possible, especially when you have some impressive numbers to offer. (I refer to these as "startling statistics," great attention getters.)

THE DIFFERENCE BETWEEN BRAGGING AND REPORTING

One injunction given was to make reports, not claims. The difference is not a subtle one, but the difference in impact is enormous. Here are two hypothetical statements you might make, whether verbally or in writing:

When I design your systems and write your programs, Mrs. Murray, you can be sure that they will be many, many times more efficient than anything you now have, and will save you lots of time and money.

Mrs. Murray, Charley Sugrue, the comptroller of Western Lumber Products, said that I reduced the run time of their accounting and inventory programs by more than 12 percent and saved them over thirty-two thousand dollars last year in computer time alone. I have his letter saying this, if you would like to see it.

The difference between the two examples is, of course, quite obvious. The first statement is a brag, a claim of something. Will the prospect buy it? Maybe. It's a promise, but no evidence is offered. Anyone can make such a vague and general claim; it doesn't cost a thing. But the prospect is probably not so naive as to fail to perceive it as a claim with no supporting evidence or proof. (In fact, the clear implication is that of the deadliest two words in the language: "Trust me.")

The second statement is also a claim, in a sense, but is not a brag because it is specific, quantified, and factual. It names a client, reports facts, and offers to present the absolute proof. The prospect can call Charley Sugrue for verification, but almost surely will not because the client knows that you would not make that claim and name the individual if you could not back it up.

That alone makes your statement a report, rather than a claim. A claim may make what purports to be a recital of fact, but the lack of evidence and the sweeping generalizations, with their inevitable hype, give it away. A report has no need for hype because it has the strength resulting from stating facts. And the facts are whatever the client accepts as facts. So the client's reactions to your statement result not only from your citation of a client and the client's statement, but from the fact that you supplied figures and did not round them off. Had you said "almost 15 percent" and/or "over $30,000," the numbers would have been less authentic-sounding and, hence, less persuasive and convincing.

In the final analysis, it is a report because the client will accept it as a factual report. For practical purposes that is all that is necessary. For credible presentations, have the facts at hand and cite them in such a way that their truth appears indisputable. The truth is not automatically accepted, but must be presented in such a manner, with evidence and details, that it is perceived as truth.

SELLING IS CONSULTING

Selling is itself consulting. Don't sell consulting services; sell help, such as the solution to a client's problem, whether that is a sticky technical matter that the client does not understand, or some uncomplicated matter, such as a staff shortage. The mental set that produces sales is one focused on helping the prospect solve a problem and satisfy a need. Show the prospect how to get what he or she wants through what you sell. I sold successfully when I probed to uncover the worry items—what troubled the prospect most—that my services could respond to effectively. It worked for me even when I went knocking on government doors in Washington, DC.

For example, I called on OSHA offering my services as a writer-consultant. After chatting with people in several offices, I met a gentleman responsible for training people in subjects related to occupational health. After a pleasant exchange, I began probing into the problems this executive was having. I soon learned that he was charged with developing a syllabus and curriculum to be handed over to various institutions who would train occupational health technicians. This gentleman did not know how to implement this project. He had a student manual and instructor's guide that a large company had produced for him under contract, but he had no idea of how to use these. We talked about the problem, and I suggested, in general terms, what had to be done to put these manuals to work. I offered to furnish a detailed plan in an informal proposal. He invited me to do just that, and I went home to my office and wrote a simple letter proposal of a few pages. I submitted it to him and within less than three weeks, I had a government purchase order.

Every contract I won was the result of identifying the client's problem or need and offering what the client agreed was the best solution. All marketing can be explained as consisting of those two steps. Find out what the client wants (sometimes the client does not know it until he sees it) and furnish a solution the client accepts as the best one.

The Significant Difference

The difference between consulting in the sales function and consulting for a fee is this: In the sales function you learn of and analyze the prospect's problem to demonstrate how your services will solve that problem; in fee-paid consulting, you solve the problem. For example, when a company solicits my help in training their people in proposal writing, I study the kind of work the company does, the kinds of people (skills and jobs) in the company who are to be trained, the client's experience in proposal writing, and what, if any, are their specific worry items and perceived needs. Then I prepare and offer a sales presentation, such as an outline of proposed coverage and other details, with my rationales for what I propose as a direct and effective solution to their problem.

The Notion of Selling Benefits

You can't study selling very long before you discover the conventional wisdom of selling benefits, as in selling sex appeal, rather than lipstick, and security, rather than insurance. To sell products and services in vast quantities is a much different marketing problem than selling consulting services. The benefits promised in mass marketing must be generalized so as to fit everyone's hopes and aspirations—to be beautiful, loved, successful, and secure. But consulting is a custom service. To sell it, you must customize the benefits promise in terms of the prospect's individual need, showing the linkage.

This means that you are always a consultant. You must understand and analyze the client's need to make an effective offer. Every good salesperson is thus a consultant: It's integral in selling.

The Consulting Steps in Selling

You cannot afford to make an exhaustive and detailed analysis in a free marketing consultation, as you would in a fee-paid consultation. This is a consultation for which you are paying, as an overhead marketing expense. This is therefore a general, preliminary consultation, one in which you do enough to understand the prospect's need and win the sale, but no more. The scale of this consultation is different, but the steps and goals are not essentially different than they are in your normal consulting role. They address the same objectives:

- Identify the prospect's overall goal, desires, perception of problem(s), and apparent symptoms.
- Make a reasoned analysis of these factors to define the problem properly.
- Synthesize a broad approach to solution through your services.
- Formulate a sales presentation to implement your solution and explain it—sell it—to the prospective client.

The idea is to do enough analysis to synthesize and make a targeted presentation. You need details, whether for oral or written presentation, to make an impact. Anyone can generalize, but details are the evidence of true competence. They are what makes your presentation convincing and persuasive.

This idea of supplying detail to audiences almost always provokes questions reflecting a fear of giving one's expertise away free of charge. When I point out that everyone in every business finds it necessary to give out samples occasionally, the next question is almost always: "How much should I give away?"

A sensible answer is, "Just enough to close the sale." But how much is that? Alas! There is no way to measure this. Some client-prospects need only the mere suggestion of an approach, and they can take it from there and solve their own problems (at your expense!). There are others who can be led to the very brink of solution and still not be able to handle the problem without retaining you at your regular rates.

This means that you must size the prospect up, as he or she is sizing you up, to decide how much is necessary to sell the job without giving the store away. Generally speaking, it is far better to err on the side of giving a bit more than necessary than of giving too little to win the contract. A specific example may help illustrate this.

In helping clients develop proposals, I may be asked to help analyze the requirement and suggest a basic strategy, participate in writing the proposal, lead the client's proposal team, or even write the entire proposal myself. But in the discussion with the prospective client, before I am actually hired and on billable time, the client may be probing my thoughts to get ideas. To avoid giving away what I have to sell, while still keeping the prospective client interested, I might find it necessary to say something to my prospective client along these lines:

> It appears to me that your customer here is greatly concerned with costs, yet fearful that the contractor might sacrifice quality for economy. I believe that I can work out a strategy for you to keep your costs low while ensuring that quality will not suffer. I believe that I would need (some estimate of hours or days, as appropriate) to develop this strategy for you.

If the prospect tries to push me beyond this observation, which might itself be an indication that this prospect is trying to use me and get something for nothing, I would be deliberately vague and general, explaining that I need more time to work out the detailed answers. I thus make it clear to the prospect, as tactfully as I can, that I will offer nothing more unless I am retained. In the meanwhile I now concentrate on closing the sale.

This is not necessarily a typical case. If your own services are more highly specialized than mine are—if you are a specialist in some exotic field, for example—you may be able to give away quite a bit more that will still be of little value to the prospect without your specific services. Only you can make that judgment. But you should consider the probe and the alternatives. (Review discussions on closing in Chapter 8.)

PRICING PROBLEMS

At some point the subject of price will arise. Often, the way the question of price is handled becomes a critical point in the presentation. It can become the make-or-break point. But there are many indications of what is happening and what the prospect is thinking that are revealed in connection with pricing.

It is usually a grave mistake to volunteer the price when making a sales presentation. It is wiser to wait until the prospect asks the price. The advantage in doing this is not only psychological but is a practical indication of the prospect's serious interest. It says that the prospect has found you and what you propose acceptable, and so is ready to move on to the subject of price.

Sales wisdom therefore suggests that it is a mistake to quote a price, even when the prospect asks for it, before you are ready to quote. You must have the prospect sold on the proposition before you throw the cold water of price on it. A premature quote or an evasion not handled properly here can easily be the death knell of the sale.

Some prospects ask price almost immediately, even before having more than the briefest discussion of their needs and what you can do to satisfy them. Such prospects are generally price shopping. This means that they have a clear idea of what they want and are simply seeking the cheapest service available. Or it may mean a tight budget so that the prospect does not want to spend time in serious discussion before learning if you are affordable. (In fact, sometimes these are prospects who cannot afford consulting services but are desperately seeking someone who might want the job enough to work for a microscopic fee.)

Some prospects appear to be not seriously interested in the details of what you propose or they may have lost interest somewhere along the way but are tolerating you and your presentation out of courtesy. You are probably wasting your time here unless you can find a way to strike a nerve.

Serious prospects hear you out, ask pointed questions about what you propose, and then ask the price. That is the indication of serious interest and that is often the point at which you win or lose the contract.

The Significance of the Pricing Problem

The problem of the salesperson who talks too much is well-known: there are many stories of sellers who unsold prospects after they had sold them because they didn't know when to stop talking. More literally, the salesperson did not sense that it was time to stop selling and close.

It is not always easy to sense that moment to close. Some of the greatest salespeople have an instinct for sensing that moment, or perhaps they have simply trained themselves to estimate it almost unconsciously. However, it is possible to sense that moment by relying on specific indicators that the prospect is about ready to accept your offer. (Your presentation should be an offer, not a plea.) One of those indicators is the query as to price. Only a seriously interested prospect is going to ask you how much, normally (with a few exceptions, as noted). When this happens, you are at a critical juncture: You may make or break the sale by how you respond. When a prospect asks you to quote a price, ask yourself if you are ready to quote the price yet. Is it too soon? If it is too soon, how do you delay quoting a price without offending the prospect by avoiding an answer?

You should not close (normally) until you have completed your basic sales presentation, explaining your promise and presenting the necessary evidence to back it up and/or until you have some sound reason to believe that the prospect is about ready to agree to the contract you propose. There are occasional exceptions to this, such as when a prospect is pre-sold on you by virtue of earlier experience or personal recommendation or otherwise gives good evidence of a readiness to sign up with you without further discussion. Far more common is the case of the prospect asking the price before you have finished your presentation and before you are ready to close.

In the normal face-to-face situation, your presentation is not a lengthy monologue. It is delivered piecemeal, between questions and comments as you and the prospect ask each other questions and respond to those questions. This itself furnishes the best basis for tactfully avoiding a premature response to the "how much?" question without alienating the prospect in so doing. Here are some imaginary dialogues that suggest some of these tactful methods:

Prospect: Tell me, how much will all this cost me?

Consultant: Frankly, I don't know yet, and it would be unfair to you for me to make a guess at this point. I need to discuss this with you just a bit more before I can make a reliable estimate. But I will give you that estimate as soon as possible.

Alternative 1: I can make a rough guess now, if you want me to, but it would probably be on the high side because I need to gather some more information. If we can postpone that for a few minutes I can give you a more sensible answer to your question.

Alternative 2: There are several options possible, and we need to discuss these before I can give you a sensible estimate.

Alternative 3: I can price this on a total, fixed-price basis or open-ended on a day or hourly rate. If I can put off answering your question for a little while longer I'll be able to suggest the pricing base most favorable to you.

Prospect: Well, can you tell me what your rates are?

Consultant: Certainly. When I give you an estimate, I will also explain the rates and how I arrive at the estimate.

Alternative 1: My assignments and contracts vary a great deal and affect my overhead differently. Therefore, my accountant has set up a whole rate structure for me, with different day rates for short-term or casual assignments than for long-term contracts, with a daily rate and an hourly rate, and with a base for estimating assignments on a fixed-price basis. I don't mind quoting and explaining these to you now, but I don't think that will be very helpful here because I don't know yet which would be suitable in this case.

Alternative 2: Sure, here are my basic rates (quoting them), but that doesn't really tell you anything because it is the final cost, not the rates, that matters.

Alternative 3: Sure. My rate is $XX a day. But you should know that I don't count the hours in a day, and the day rate applies to 12-hour days, as it does to 8-hour days. It also applies to weekends and holidays, when it is necessary to work on weekends and holidays. My accountant calculated the rate to cover all that without charging premiums and doing a lot of extra record-keeping and bookkeeping. In the long run, I cost you less because I don't have all that extra bookkeeping of hourly time records and you don't have to worry about overtime and other premium time. And, anyway, in the end it isn't the rate that counts but the total cost.

There are still other options possible. Some consultants believe that the quotation of an hourly rate—for example, $62.50 an hour—is more palatable to most prospects than a daily-rate such as $500 a day. Others prefer to charge a relatively low hourly rate, but charge substantial premiums for overtime, weekend, and holiday effort. And some prefer not to quote verbally at all, but promise a follow-up written proposal and quotation, using wording such as these imaginary dialogues. This latter course may be dictated by an actual need for more time to research or check everything, but many consultants follow this practice for psychological reasons. For any but jobs on which you obviously can't quote anything but an hourly or daily rate, it may help to dramatize the importance of the proposed program by asking for time to study the program carefully to work out the lowest cost way to handle the project.

There are several advantages in putting your offer in writing, submitting a written proposal, even a brief and informal one, and you should seek and welcome every opportunity to do so. You should even create such opportunities because they offer you advantages.

There are some consultants who have sliding scales or who invent rates, even varying overhead rates arbitrarily, for each prospective contract, as they think suitable or necessary to capture the contract. While I think this an un-wise practice generally, I once offered special, lower rates to minority-owned enterprises that were struggling to get established.

WHERE TO CONDUCT INITIAL MEETINGS

Although your first contact with a new prospect may be a casual one, the first serious meeting, one at which you will make a presentation and try to make a sale, must be planned. Theoretically, when you are trying to make a sale, you call on the prospect at his or her own office. However, prospects may suggest calling on you. You should normally assume that you will call on the prospect and plan to do so unless the prospect suggests some other arrangement. Such a suggestion often results when the prospect is from out of town and expects to be in your city on some near date.

If your office is in your home and you find it impracticable to conduct busi-ness meetings there, for whatever reason, there are alternatives. The most ob-vious of these is to meet for lunch. Many business relationships begin that way.

Two questions arise in this connection: (1) Is it proper to have a drink and/or smoke at lunch with a new prospective client whose standards and mores you do not know? (2) Who should pay for lunch?

So far I have never had a problem about having a drink at lunch. However, I do assess the situation, and I do not have a drink if my companion does not also have one. This is a wise way to resolve that issue, if there is a question in your mind about it.

There is another problem in connection with that question of a drink at lunch. It often leads to a second one, and perhaps even a third one, and even the first one may lead to loosening your tongue or, even worse, tangling it. Obviously, that is itself a serious hazard to consider.

Today the question about smoking is similar and equally important. The issue has become a highly charged one; many people become quite emotional about it. In general, it is best not to smoke in the presence of a nonsmoker, and not even to ask the other's permission to smoke with a "Do you mind?" query. If the person does mind, the query is unfair for it is difficult and embarrassing to object, and he or she may agree to your smoking but silently resent having been placed in the position of being all but forced to assent, however unwill-ingly. Unless the client lights a cigarette, you do well to simply avoid the sub-ject and the smoking.

The question of who pays for lunch is stickier, but the right course to follow is quite clear: The individual issuing the invitation for lunch normally expects to pay for it, regardless of the business relationship between the two of you. In any case, but especially if the prospect has invited you to lunch or suggests it, it is unwise to put up a lengthy struggle for the check. For one thing, some in-dividuals can become quite offended by your refusal to permit them to pay, es-pecially if they suggested lunch. For another, it suggests some lack of good taste or good grasp of proper protocol on your part. You should know how to accept the situation gracefully and with courteous thanks. Make the gesture, especially if it was you who extended the invitation, but don't get into an extended struggle over it. It should not be that big a deal, in any case, and you harm your image by making it appear that you think it is.

THINGS TO SETTLE AT THE INITIAL MEETING

One thing that causes much trouble later, after a contract has been signed and the project is underway, is the failure to have achieved a complete and specific understanding with your prospect and soon-to-be new client. Distressingly often, consultants undertake assignments with only a vague understanding of what they are to achieve (and sometimes not even clear on what the price is to be), confident that they will somehow muddle through.

Clients are equally guilty in agreeing to projects with less than perfect understanding of the agreement made. And even having a written contract or letter of agreement is of little help if it does not include a clear specification or statement of work.

The problem is usually due to the normal difficulty in developing a highly specific statement of work. The client may have difficulty in even defining the problem, while the consultant, eager for the contract, is reluctant to press the client too hard for details of what he or she (the consultant) must do. And although this is quite often a problem even when formal proposals must be drawn up and submitted, it is even more commonly a problem when the agreement and negotiations leading to a contract are informal and based entirely on verbal understandings and agreements.

FOLLOW-UP

Some first meetings wind up in commitments or agreements, but many others turn out to be exploratory and inconclusive, the "let's have lunch sometime" type. Unless you do something specific and positive to prevent that dead end, you will have simply wasted your time and energy. The first meeting should never be permitted to end without preparation and planning of the next step. A definitely planned follow-up step is essential to prevent that first meeting from being a total waste of time. That next step may be a written proposal, a firm commitment to and date set for a meeting, a formal presentation (a dog-and-pony show), or other definite commitment to move the action forward—progress toward making a sale. But it is up to you to plan and prepare for a follow-up. Otherwise it is almost a foregone conclusion that nothing will result from the first meeting.

Negotiations, Fees, and Contracts

Consulting is a business and must be conducted as such.
—Herman Holtz

FEE, COSTS, AND PROFITS

Should you have occasion to fill out one of the government's forms for estimating costs you may be puzzled by the next-to-last line, which says *fee or profit*. Obviously the government considers the two terms synonymous and interchangeable.

In business, fee and profit are not synonymous. The fee is what you charge for your services, usually by the hour or day, from which you hope to realize a profit. Fees are your principal income from consulting, normally. Your salary and other expenses must be paid out of this income before you can enjoy a profit. Although you charge and collect fees for your services, you do not always enjoy a profit, as sad experience will demonstrate occasionally.

An hourly or daily fee is the classic, most-used source of income in consulting. Consulting work is, however, not always so identified. Federal agencies, for example, contract for many studies, surveys, research and development, and other open-ended programs and award cost-reimbursement contracts that permit the government to audit the contractor's books, if the contract is a large one. The government usually requires a cost estimate that reveals all direct and indirect costs. Because of this requirement to open your books to the government, many consultants do not pursue government business.

This is not to say that the government never pays consultants on a fee basis. Government work is a major source of income for many consultants. Unfortunately, most agencies have an archaic and unrealistic view of what a competent consultant is worth today because they try to equate hourly or daily consulting rates with hourly or daily earnings of government employees, an unrealistic measurement. For example, the Region III office of an agency within the Commerce Department hired me to conduct a half-day seminar for their contractors in Wilmington, Delaware. My letter proposal quoted $300 plus expenses. The agency agreed, I conducted the seminar, and I was duly paid. End of the story? Not quite.

Some three months later, the headquarters office of that agency asked me to present that same half-day seminar to their staff in Washington. Again I wrote a letter proposal describing the seminar and quoting $300. (No expenses involved this time, since my offices were then in Washington.) This office balked, objecting that their maximum daily rate for consulting was $150. (However, in their generosity, they offered to pay me that full daily rate for my half-day presentation!)

My response was that I would amend my proposal to accommodate their problem, and I did so. I made a rather minor change to the proposal. I modified the cost presentation to read as follows:

Preparation for seminar presentation:	$150
Presentation of seminar:	150
Total cost:	$300

The agency had no problem at all with this. They accepted it immediately and I presented the seminar and was paid $300.

How you present a proposition may be more important than what you propose. Understand the other's problem and solve it. In the case of that agency, the problem was their unrealistic standard, not the cost of my services. When I solved their problem, I solved my own.

Selling to any bureaucracy may mean encountering such apparently inflexible rules. Be a consultant here, as in all selling: Help yourself by helping the client solve the problem.

STANDARD RATES

There are no standard rates for consultants, but there are typical rates. One day a stranger dropped into my office unannounced and introduced himself. He represented a well-known company in Atlanta. He was seeking a consultant to help his company pursue a government contract. He had barely finished sitting down and identifying himself when he demanded to know what my daily rate was.

The message was clear. When a prospect wants to know the price before discussing his or her need, you are almost surely wasting your time in further conversation. Such clients are almost always impossible to deal with. Well aware of this from experience, I wanted to end the interview immediately and get back to my work. I quietly quoted him $500 per day plus expenses. His response was prompt: "You fellows must have a union. Everybody charges $500 a day in this town."

It wouldn't have mattered if I had quoted $300 or $5,000. I did not expect or want to hear from this gentleman again, nor did I. There is no profit and certainly no future in being the cheapest guy in town. I was unaware of what others were charging, but obviously I was middle-road with my daily rate. In fact, most able consultants at that time reported charging daily fees close to that figure, according to a poll reported by the late Howard L. Shenson, a trainer of consultants.

Today, the average daily rate is considerably more. Probably $1,000 or more per day is typical, although there are still many consultants charging fees on a more modest scale.

Unless your circumstances are unusual or you are just starting your practice and want to get yourself established by charging modest rates in the beginning, you will probably be well advised to make that your minimum. And a bit of analysis will show why that is a realistic bottom rate. Let's look at some figures.

As a specialized expert in your field is you are probably entitled, in today's economy, to earn at least $75,000 a year, and that is probably a modest figure for these times. But let's use it for these illustrations.

That works out to roughly $6,250 a month, $1,443 a week, $288 a day, or $36 an hour. That's a first expense, a direct cost. But you are an employee of your own business, even if you are the only employee. That means that the $288-a-day-cost goes on every day, whether you are working on a project or not. When you are working on a project, you can bill that $288 (plus other costs) to the client. Those are direct costs because they are incurred for a given, identifiable contract and should be defrayed by income from that contract. But when you are not on "billable time," and are marketing or planning, your enterprise must go on paying that $288 every day. That is indirect cost because your business must absorb it somehow.

Other indirect costs include rent, heat, advertising, travel expense, entertainment, printing, secretarial services, telephone calls, taxes, insurance, and miscellaneous expenses. They are indirect costs because they cannot be attributed to or incurred by any specific project and not charged to any client. They must be recovered indirectly as overhead.

This is usually done by levying a kind of tax on all clients and projects, called *overhead*. If your record keeping reveals that for every dollar you paid out to employees (even yourself) working on billable time you had to spend another dollar and a quarter for those indirect costs, you have a burden rate of 125 percent. That means that you must charge the client $288 + 240 burden rate) or $648 to break even. Add a modest 15-percent profit and you now have a daily billing rate of $744. And, as an individual who must manage, market, and administer, as well as consult, you will be a busy individual indeed.

CALCULATING OVERHEAD

Unless you are your own accountant, you need not calculate your overhead or other burden rates. However, you should understand what these are, what they mean, and where they come from.

You have had a basic introduction to the difference between direct and indirect costs. In consulting and other labor-intensive enterprises where labor is the major direct cost item, overhead is calculated as a percentage of direct labor. That is, if at the end of a year you find that you have paid out $75,000 in direct labor and $37,500 in all indirect costs, your overhead rate has been 50 percent ($37,500/75,000 \times 100$). You must charge a client $1.50 for every $1.00 of direct labor to recover your costs alone—to pay operating expenses, including your own salary for the unbilled time you spend doing such things as marketing and administrative chores, taking time off for illness, personal leave, and holidays, and whatever other costs go into your overhead pool. But that does not include profit, and every enterprise must turn a profit to establish some kind of reserve and to grow.

The overhead rate is therefore what you must add to your direct-labor costs to cover the indirect expenses. Your estimate might look like this:

Direct labor: 10 days @ $300/day	$3,000
Overhead: $0.50 \times 3,000$	1,500

Those are usually the two major cost items, but there are often others. There is also the matter of profit. So a more complete cost estimate might be along the following lines:

Direct labor: 10 days @ $300/day	$3,000
Overhead: $0.50 \times 3,000$	1,500
Other direct costs:	
Printing	$350
Travel	700
Express charges	100
Total ODC	$1,150
Total costs	$5,650.00
Profit: 15%	847.50
Total price	$6,497.50

Even that does not take into account an indirect expense pool many companies use called G&A, for general and administrative expenses that are not normally included as overhead costs. (These are normally incurred in larger, multidivisional organizations, rather than in independent practices.) It does illustrate, however, why you must charge approximately $750 a day, as a minimum, to pay yourself a $75,000 salary.

WHAT SHOULD YOUR OVERHEAD RATE BE?

You can see from this that although you might pay yourself only $2,000 in salary for a given project, the client must pay your consulting business more than twice that amount. And that is at the modest overhead rate of 50 percent, which is almost surely a lower overhead rate than you will actually experience. Your real overhead rate is likely to be more on the order of 75 percent if you are careful and manage your practice well, and can easily soar to 150 percent if you get a bit careless in exercising control and restraint. But look at the consequences of these figures: A 75-percent rate runs the bottom line up to $7,360 while a 150-percent rate would send it to $9,948. You would thus have to persuade the client to pay you $995 a day to cover all your costs and provide a profit. The effect of an increase in the overhead rate is not linear; it snowballs. Each dollar you pay yourself at 50-percent overhead (in the example used here) is billed to the client at $2.23, whereas at 150 percent overhead each dollar you pay yourself results in $3.38 on the bottom line.

This presents a dual problem. On the one hand your escalating costs compel you to ask for larger fees, and on the other hand they restrict your earnings. It is thus important in every enterprise to *control and minimize* overhead.

High overhead is a serious problem when dealing with government agencies, too, especially when you are required to supply detailed cost analyses (Figure 14.1). This is a government form, and it follows the general format of the example given here, although it is more detailed, providing for a G&A figure and consulting-fees as a separate item of direct cost. (Should you bid with someone else as a potential subcontractor, an estimate of the cost of your services would appear here.) The reverse side if the figure provides space to add explanatory detail. Because the government agencies buy so much from the private sector, government procurement officials are usually well aware of typical overhead rates in various industries and are quite sensitive to any they consider to be unduly high. They often consider that a high overhead rate suggests an inefficient contractor.

Provisional Overhead

The overhead rate given here was based on the premise that you had a full year's figures to study in determining what overhead rate you had experienced. This is an historical overhead. However, you will not have an historical overhead rate if you have not yet had a full year's experience and records to review, or you may have reason to believe that your current rate is or your future rate will be different than your historical rate. In that case, you resort to an estimated or provisional overhead rate. Overhead rates vary, and on large government contracts, the government may exercise a right to verify your overhead rate through an audit.

PRIVATE-SECTOR PARALLELS

That huge market represented by federal, state, and local government procurement has a profound effect on the economy generally and even on the purchasing practices of private business. Almost all large government contracts result in many subcontracts. Subcontracts became so important to small business

CONTRACT PRICING PROPOSAL
(RESEARCH AND DEVELOPMENT)

Office of Management and Budget
Approval No. 29–RO184

This form is for use when (i) submission of cost or pricing data (see FPR 1–3.807–3) is required and (ii) substitution for the Optional Form 59 is authorized by the contracting officer.

PAGE NO. | NO. OF PAGES

NAME OF OFFEROR

SUPPLIES AND/OR SERVICES TO BE FURNISHED

HOME OFFICE ADDRESS

DIVISION(S) AND LOCATION(S) WHERE WORK IS TO BE PERFORMED

TOTAL AMOUNT OF PROPOSAL
$

GOV'T SOLICITATION NO.

DETAIL DESCRIPTION OF COST ELEMENTS

	EST COST ($)	TOTAL EST COST[1]	REFER- ENCE[2]
1. DIRECT MATERIAL (Itemize on Exhibit A)			
a. PURCHASED PARTS			
b. SUBCONTRACTED ITEMS			
c. OTHER—(1) RAW MATERIAL			
(2) YOUR STANDARD COMMERCIAL ITEMS			
(3) INTERDIVISIONAL TRANSFERS (At other than cost)			
TOTAL DIRECT MATERIAL			
2. MATERIAL OVERHEAD[3] (Rate %X$ base =)			

3. DIRECT LABOR (Specify)	ESTIMATED HOURS	RATE/ HOUR	EST COST ($)		
TOTAL DIRECT LABOR					

4. LABOR OVERHEAD (Specify Department or Cost Center)[3]	O.H. RATE	X BASE =	EST COST ($)		
TOTAL LABOR OVERHEAD					

5. SPECIAL TESTING (Including field work at Government installations)	EST COST ($)		
TOTAL SPECIAL TESTING			
6. SPECIAL EQUIPMENT (If direct charge) (Itemize on Exhibit A)			
7. TRAVEL (If direct charge) (Give details on attached Schedule)	EST COST ($)		
a. TRANSPORTATION			
b. PER DIEM OR SUBSISTENCE			
TOTAL TRAVEL			
8. CONSULTANTS (Identify—purpose—rate)	EST COST ($)		
TOTAL CONSULTANTS			
9. OTHER DIRECT COSTS (Itemize on Exhibit A)			
10. TOTAL DIRECT COST AND OVERHEAD			
11. GENERAL AND ADMINISTRATIVE EXPENSE (Rate % of cost element Nos.)[3]			
12. ROYALTIES[4]			
13. TOTAL ESTIMATED COST			
14. FEE OR PROFIT			
15. TOTAL ESTIMATED COST AND FEE OR PROFIT			

Figure 14.1. Standard Form 60, government cost form.

that the federal government established special offices to aid small business in winning subcontracts. The big business represented by government markets today affected the shaping of procurement methods of private-sector corporations as they emulated government procurement practices.

This is not entirely a matter of choice. Government clients are well aware that their prime contractors will have to subcontract portions of the work so

This proposal is submitted for use in connection with and in response to *(Describe RFP, etc.)*

and reflects our best estimates as of this date, in accordance with the Instructions to Offerors and the Footnotes which follow.

TYPED NAME AND TITLE	SIGNATURE	
NAME OF FIRM		DATE OF SUBMISSION

EXHIBIT A—SUPPORTING SCHEDULE *(Specify. If more space is needed, use reverse)*

COST EL NO.	ITEM DESCRIPTION *(See footnote 5)*	EST COST ($)

I. HAS ANY EXECUTIVE AGENCY OF THE UNITED STATES GOVERNMENT PERFORMED ANY REVIEW OF YOUR ACCOUNTS OR RECORDS IN CONNECTION WITH ANY OTHER GOVERNMENT PRIME CONTRACT OR SUBCONTRACT WITHIN THE PAST TWELVE MONTHS?

☐ YES ☐ NO *(If yes, identify below.)*

NAME AND ADDRESS OF REVIEWING OFFICE AND INDIVIDUAL	TELEPHONE NUMBER/EXTENSION

II. WILL YOU REQUIRE THE USE OF ANY GOVERNMENT PROPERTY IN THE PERFORMANCE OF THIS PROPOSED CONTRACT?

☐ YES ☐ NO *(If yes, identify on reverse or separate page)*

III. DO YOU REQUIRE GOVERNMENT CONTRACT FINANCING TO PERFORM THIS PROPOSED CONTRACT?

☐ YES ☐ NO *(If yes, identify.):* ☐ ADVANCE PAYMENTS ☐ PROGRESS PAYMENTS OR ☐ GUARANTEED LOANS

IV. DO YOU NOW HOLD ANY CONTRACT *(Or, do you have any independently financed (IR&D) projects)* FOR THE SAME OR SIMILAR WORK CALLED FOR BY THIS PROPOSED CONTRACT?

☐ YES ☐ NO *(If yes, identify.):*

V. DOES THIS COST SUMMARY CONFORM WITH THE COST PRINCIPLES SET FORTH IN AGENCY REGULATIONS?

☐ YES ☐ NO *(If no, explain on reverse or separate page)*

Figure 14.1. *Continued.*

that in effect the prime contractor is acting as surrogate for the government, spending government dollars in subcontracts to carry out government programs. The government often extends the principles of open competition and equal opportunity to share in government business by providing in prime contracts a requirement to award subcontracts competitively. The private sector therefore tends to simply emulate the government systems as the simplest way to comply with such contractual requirements. As a result, bids and proposals have become typical procurement methods in the private sector, even when government contracts are not involved in any way. Even if you never pursue government business as a prime contractor or subcontractor, you may find yourself facing similar requirements for competing. The written proposal has

proved itself an effective marketing tool, even when the client has not specifically called for it; thus the ability to develop a good proposal should be on
your "must" list in any case.

GOVERNMENT CONTRACT NEGOTIATION

The federal Standard Form 33 is itself a contract when signed by the two parties, you and the client's authorized official, although it usually includes other
documents—work statements, item descriptions, bids, and/or proposals—by
reference. For contracts based on sealed bids, there is no further action or
follow-up, normally, because the award is made to the lowest bidder. Negotiations are reserved to competitive proposals, which are the instruments for negotiated procurement. However, even in that case, often there are no follow-up
actions after proposal openings and evaluations, other than simple signing of
the form by the procurement official, accepting your proposal as submitted,
and establishing a contract on that basis. Even when there is a follow-up, in
the case of a small contract, it will usually be nothing more formal than a telephone call from the contracting officer to verify your readiness to proceed and
accept a contract based on your proposal.

There are exceptions to simple acceptance and award. In some cases, even
when the contract is a relatively small one, the contracting officer will call,
write, or wire, inviting you to submit a best and final offer. This is an effort to
elicit a best price from you, and presumably (but not necessarily) is asked of
each proposer deemed equally qualified to be awarded the contract. The contract is subsequently awarded, presumably (but again not necessarily) to the
lowest bidder among those invited to submit a best and final offer.

For small contracts, this is usually the extent of the negotiation, if it is done
at all. But in the case of larger contracts, the request for best and final offers
is almost automatic, and even that is not necessarily the extent of the negotiation. There may be discussions with the client's staff and procurement officials around the table, and these may become quite extensive in some cases,
concerned with technical details of performance and programs, as well as
costs.

PRIVATE-SECTOR CONTRACT FORMS

I have had ample corroboration by other independent consultants of the hazard
in presenting a client an excessively legalistic contract form for a relatively
small contract. They corroborate the opinion I formed as a result of my own
disastrous experience: It involved a $26,000 contract with the American Red
Cross. After submitting a proposal, discussing it with the client's executive responsible for the award and reaching agreement verbally, we were invited to
meet and negotiate the contract. Alas, our corporation's marketing director,
for reasons that were a mystery to the rest of us, decided that he had to have

our corporate attorney present. The client became alarmed immediately that we were so distrustful as to feel a need for legal representation to conclude what were to be little more than formalities to agree on a relatively small con tract, and terminated our relationship at once. Nevertheless, failing to learn from this experience, our marketing director proceeded to draw up a state- ment of standard contract terms that would be boilerplate copy for all con- tracts. These were so legalistic as to scuttle many other contract negotiations and present us with a problem in negotiating all future contracts until we abandoned the new form.

Hubert Bermont, a successful independent consultant and author of many years experience, agrees. He believes that asking any client to sign a formal contract for a small consulting assignment is risky because it usually alarms the client. Today most of us are conscious of the exhortation to sign nothing without reading it carefully. We are also suspicious and mistrustful of the mysterious and often arcane phraseology of lawyers and legal forms—torts, habeas corpus, flagrante delicto, and so on. Even when we read a contract with great care, we are usually not sure what it says! (Many courts and tri- als have demonstrated that even the lawyers, as well as the rest of us, are often totally wrong in what they/we think the contract says.) So it is not sur- prising to understand why clients become alarmed by lengthy, multipage, Latin-laden contracts for small and simple programs. Even the U.S. govern- ment has forsaken those wherefores, whereases, and party-of-the-second- part terms in contracts and now executes contracts in simple, everyday English.

There should be a distinct understanding between you and your client, and the understanding should be recorded in some manner, but not as a thick doc- ument with numerous signatures. In most cases of small projects, a simple let- ter agreement or purchase order is adequate. Most of my own assignments are on such a basis.

I try to keep the terms as straightforward and as simple as possible. I make it clear that although I charge a substantial daily rate, but I do not charge over- time or premium time rates. I recommend what I believe to be the best courses of action, but I do whatever my client decides to have me do. I do those things to the best of my ability. I urge whatever I think is best for my client, but I rec- ognize the client's right to decide and act contrary to my counsel. I cannot guarantee any particular outcome, of course; I can guarantee only my best ef- forts. Therefore, the only things to reach specific agreement on are costs— fees and expenses—and length of commitment or estimate of time required to achieve the desired result. I may furnish a not-to-exceed estimate or guarantee completion within some specific time frame, in some cases. In that case, that information must be in the agreement too.

Your own terms and stipulations are likely to be different than mine, and they ought to be whatever you believe to be fair and proper for you and your clients. Whatever they are—if, for example, you charge premium overtime— draw them up as standard terms, stated as simply and as clearly as possible, and include them in any agreement you sign with a client or in a response to a request for quotation. At most you will normally require only a simple letter of agreement—probably a single page—and in many cases you will not require even that.

WHAT IS A CONTRACT?

The consultant accepting an assignment from a client has entered into a contract with that client as soon as the two of them reach agreement. A contract is not a piece of paper; it is an agreement. The piece of paper records the agreement for future reference. The agreement between the consultant and the client is a contract, even if the agreement is verbal.

Verbal contracts are valid and binding on the parties. However, human memories are faulty, especially if and when a dispute about what was agreed to arises. It is therefore wise to record the contract by specifying its terms on paper. It is also advantageous to record the contract in this manner because the act of writing the terms out compels the parties to think things out in advance, covering details that might easily have been overlooked, had the agreement been verbal only and reached only via informal conversation.

Potential Hazards

The principal hazard in failing to have a written contract is the possibility of disputes over the terms. There is no need to add the hazard of alarming a client with formal contract paper and rituals when the real contract is the understanding and agreement between you and the client. Unless that exists and is sincere, a contract that each of you intends to honor fully, the most elaborate and formal document will not be effective. Unless you are satisfied that the client understands the agreement and fully intends to carry out his or her end of it faithfully, go no further: The business relationship is most likely to be an unhappy and unsuccessful one. On the other hand, when there is mutual understanding and sincerity, a simple written agreement will serve as well as the most formal and elaborate one.

ALTERNATIVES TO FORMAL CONTRACT DOCUMENTS

This entire discussion is not in the context of the major, multimillion dollar project, where we would expect detailed specifications, letters, and multipage contracts. This discussion is entirely in the context of the small projects for which the independent consultant normally contracts.

The middle ground between the major project and the minor task is in documenting what is to be done in an informal agreement, and there are several ways to accomplish this: In some cases, the client issues a purchase order, which is itself an informal contract, even if you do not sign it, but accept it and begin work. This is normally evidence of acceptance. (Some clients do ask that you sign and return a copy of the purchase order to signify your acceptance of it.)

In other cases, the client issues a letter of intent or of acceptance of your written or verbal proposal. Often the client sends you two copies of such a letter, asking you to sign one copy and return it for the client's record.

Finally, if the client does not produce a purchase order or some other paper signifying a contractual obligation, you may produce your own informal contract.

THE INFORMAL CONTRACT OR LETTER OF AGREEMENT

It is probably best not to even use the word *contract* (that word itself can alarm a client), but call it a *letter of agreement* or, simply, *agreement*. One suggested agreement form is shown in Figure 14.2. It should be typed on your own letterhead, unless the client prefers to have it on his or her letterhead. In that case, simply hand over the letter, with the blanks filled in, and the client will have it typed up on his or her own letterhead.

In the interests of simplicity and informality, it is best to keep this to one page. If you think this agreement is too simple to furnish you full legal protection, bear in mind that no contract document, however detailed, however long, or however many seals, signatures, and other formal flourishes it contains, is worth the paper it is on if the parties have not executed it in good faith. The most elaborate contracts are violated and contested in the courts every day.

Most of the items in Figure 14.2 offered here are self-explanatory, but some need explanation. The form is generalized and suggests the major points such an agreement should specify. Modify it to suit any special needs or considerations of your own by deletions, additions, changes, or incorporation of your own boilerplate about your normal terms and conditions. Also, in the event the client prefers to have the agreement executed on his or her own letterhead, some of the items may require rewording to be entirely appropriate.

The item "No. _____" on the Fee line may be puzzling. It calls for the number of units upon which billing is based—hours, days, etc. That is followed by the rate of billing for each unit and the total fee. (If this is based on an estimate of the number of hours, days, etc. required, that should be indicated.)

Anticipated extra costs—travel, telephone tolls, printing—must be covered also, if applicable. They can be noted under the block provided for notes, remarks, or special provisions, if lengthy explanation is required.

Aside from that, you may wish to consider carefully the implications of some other blocks, especially the one suggesting an advance retainer. You may or may not consider this applicable in your own case. If your own practice is such that you are always paid in advance, the wording should reflect the receipt of the total fee. if you are retained by an individual or small organization of whom you know little, requiring an advance retainer (I suggest one-third of the estimated total cost) is a wise practice. It will almost surely prevent a

---

AGREEMENT

Client:
_____
     (Name & address)

*Client
contact*:_____
     (Name of individual)

Services to be provided or relevant specifications/proposal, if applicable:

_____

_____

_____

Reports/presentations:_____

On client's premises [ ]   *On consultant's premises* [ ]

Other or special arrangements:_____

Beginning date:_____ *Target completion date*:_____

Fees: \$_____ *per*_____ *No.*_____*Total est. fee/cost:* \$_____
   (hr/day/other)   (hr/day other)

Other costs: \$_____ (for:_____)

Advance retainer: \$_____ *Terms for balance*:_____

_____

Notes, remarks, special provisions, if any:_____

_____

_____

_____

For_____(consultant) For_____(client)
 (type/print)   (type/print)

_____ (signed) _____(signed)

_____ (date) _____(date)

Figure 14.2. Simple letter of agreement.

few problems. It is a good way to validate or qualify such a client, for one thing. But getting a substantial retainer and setting forth clearly defined terms for the balance due is good fiscal policy to ensure that you do not wait interminably for payment.

My normal practice has been to require a second one-third of the total at the approximate midpoint of the project, and the final payment on completion. However, where the project is long-term or of indefinite term, you may wish to set forth a system of progress payments on some regular basis, such as every two weeks, every thirty days, or at defined and identifiable milestones. You can add a second page, if it is necessary to describe the agreement in greater detail or if your client wishes more detail, but clients are usually more inclined to keep the agreement as simple as possible, and that has been a prime consideration in designing this model.

One further point: If the client has supplied a detailed work description (specification of what is to be done) and/or if you have supplied a detailed proposal of what you offer to do and the project is based on your mutual acceptance of either or both of these documents, the letter of agreement should cite and identify this/these document(s) and indicate that this/these constitute the details of the contract. In that case, the letter agreement need merely add any details not covered in those other documents and bear your mutual signatures. That incorporates the other document in the contract by reference and greatly simplifies the final contractual process.

ANNUAL RETAINERS

I have used the term *retainer* to mean advance payment or deposit made at the outset of a consulting contract. This I consider to be a must in most cases, and there is no harm is asking for it even in the case of large and well-known corporations. Surprisingly often, even the large corporation officials understand your cash-flow needs and will accommodate you in this.

The term *retainer* has another meaning, applied to an entirely different situation, although it is still an advance payment. There are cases where clients use consulting services frequently but irregularly—unpredictably, that is. To ensure that their chosen consultants will be available to them when needed, they sometimes place their consultants on a retainer basis, paying in advance for guaranteed availability and services if and as needed.

This is usually under an annual agreement in which the client pays the consultant some fixed monthly sum, in return for which the consultant guarantees his or her immediate availability when called. If services are not used in any given month, the payments accrue as a credit until the client does call for services, whereupon the client may use the equivalent in services, at regular rates, with normal billing for any services beyond the amount standing to the client's credit. If there is any credit left at the end of the year, it is wiped out and the agreement renewed with a fresh start. For example, if the client has paid the consultant $200 a month and used $3,500 worth of services, the client pays the additional $1,100. On the other hand, if the client has used only $1,000 during the year, the consultant keeps the $1,400 difference because the slate is wiped clean at the end of the contract year.

Should you enter into such an arrangement, key the monthly figure to whatever amount of time you expect the client to require of you each year. But you must also ask yourself what it is worth to you to guarantee your availability to a given client no matter when he or she calls on you. It is certainly a comfort to have some guaranteed income, but it may become burdensome if you do not think it out carefully.

NEGOTIATING TIPS, TACTICS, AND GAMBITS

In any negotiation, the other party is trying to psych you out, and you are trying to do the same to the other party. Each of you is trying to read the other's intent, willingness to yield on certain matters, and bottom lines. You want to determine the maximum price and other benefits you can win, while the client wants to know what is the best deal that can be struck with you.

As the seller, you probably believe that the other party, as the buyer, has a great advantage in the bargaining session. You are forced to compete with others, and it's all or nothing with you: you win or you lose. But the client can't lose because he or she has the capability of buying from someone else if your terms are not acceptable. And, presumably, the client already knows everybody's asking price, while you are playing a guessing game.

But you may be entirely wrong in that pessimistic assessment. The thing you need most here is information. It's easy to be a brilliant negotiator if you know that you are the low bidder or that the client is not seriously considering anyone else for the project. So you are asking questions and making conversational gambits in the hope that the client will let slip some precious clues to help you judge how close you are to the goal and how you compare in costs and quality with your competitors. You want to know how hard you can press and how stubbornly you can hold out for what you want without losing the contract.

The most reliable source of information on how the client feels and thinks about all the relevant matters is the client. I am constantly surprised at how many people resort to all sorts of devious means for getting information rather than first try simply asking direct questions. In trying to determine how the client really feels about the price or what importance he or she attaches to reducing the price, such questions as the following have often produced the information I needed:

> Mrs. Client, the project plan I have proposed is fairly elaborate and sophisticated, possibly beyond what you believe you need. Are there provisions in my plan that you feel you do not need so that we can cut them back and reduce costs or beef up other areas?

Even an evasive response to this question can be quite helpful, and sometimes the frankness with which the client answers tells you everything you need to know—how highly the client rates you and your plan, whether you need to find a way to reduce costs, or other valuable input. Moreover, the client who truly favors you as the prospective consultant will often actually hand you the information you need to win the contract.

If you have used the strategy of pricing a basic model and offering several options, the situation is tailormade for inviting the client to discuss quite openly the various options or to ask you questions about them.

An alternative approach is to invite the client to review the major features of your proposed plan, and ask questions as you go. I have known cases where the client has said something such as, "Mr. Consultant, I think your plan is fine and your personal reputation is excellent, but frankly I find your costs far too high."

The proper response to this is not an argument that your prices are right, but a question along these lines, "Mr. Prospective client, may I ask you on what basis you find my price high?"

Regardless of the answer you get to this, your objective is to get into a discussion of the value you are offering, and if the client tells you effectively that you are prescribing a limousine when a tin lizzie is what is needed, turn to the gambit mentioned earlier of reviewing your plan step by step to see what can be taken out.

You may find, as I have so often, that the client does not want to give up anything offered in your plan and convinces himself (or herself) that your plan is the right one and your price is right for that plan. It is truly amazing how often by asking the right questions, you can induce the client to do your final selling and closing for you!

On the other hand, if you do find it necessary to reduce your price, I believe it unwise to do so arbitrarily. Doing that suggests that you either priced the program higher than necessary in the first place or that you are desperate for the contract. It is advisable and adds to your general credibility to negotiate any price cuts by asking the client to give up something, no matter how small the sacrifice night be. Perhaps the client will chuckle inwardly at his or her shrewd bargaining powers in getting a significant price reduction in exchange for a minor sacrifice. That's fine; the client ought to be satisfied with the bargain he or she managed to achieve. What you employed here is a legitimate bargaining tactic, and it not only solves a problem but it encourages the client to believe he or she is making strides toward a favorable contract with you.

In one case where I was negotiating a contract for services to a small company, the client made what I refer to as "the usual proposition" because it has been offered me so often: My payment, the client proposed, would be some lucrative portion, a subcontract, of the contract I would help the client win. I politely but firmly made it clear that I do not work on speculation or contingency. (Bitter experiences resulting from my accepting such propositions at an earlier time are responsible for my making that a firm policy.) The client was evidently prepared for that response because he almost immediately proposed that I accept part of my fee in cash and part as a subcontract. I took time to appear to consider it, and then agreed reluctantly and proceeded to negotiate the cash payment and the size and nature of the subcontract. I managed to make the cash payment adequate to satisfy my normal fee requirements. Of course, the client was pleased with his competent negotiating strategy, and we concluded the agreement.

I was not disappointed: I never got the subcontract. (I did not expect it.) But we were both satisfied, so it was a fair bargain. A successful negotiation is one in which each party is satisfied, one in which each party believes that he or she got what he or she wanted. No contract and no negotiation is of any value if either party emerges feeling victimized.

The enemies of successful negotiation are greed, the intention to outwit and take advantage of the other party, and the ego-trip of believing yourself to be far more clever than the other party. The way to win at the negotiating table is to try earnestly to make a fair bargain, an agreement in which both you and the client get what you want in a fair exchange, and to respect the other's intelligence, a win-win strategy. This does not mean that you should not employ sound bargaining and negotiating tactics or that you should reveal your own hand. You may plant throwaway items in your technical proposal and/or proposed budget, items that you are prepared to bargain away. That's a common negotiating tactic, and you may expect the client to make some early demands that he or she is prepared to yield on eventually, as you approach agreement. Remember, however, that you may be bargaining against what your competitors have proposed, rather than against the client's notion of what the program should contain or cost. Using throwaway items is so commonly used, however, that it is effective only if you follow certain principles and practices in using them:

- Do not employ obviously useless or meaningless costs as your gambits. That is underestimating your client, even showing contempt for his or her judgment.
- Design your program full scale, the way you would prefer to see it done. Then study it to determine what could be cut out, if required, while still achieving the main objective.
- Determine the costs of those items to see how much you can reduce costs overall by eliminating them.

Those are proper bargaining chips. They are not trivial. They are useful to the design, but they can be eliminated without endangering the overall program in its main purpose.

When you feel that you must cut costs to win the job, use this information and negotiating strategy. Don't wait for the client to insist on cuts. Explain how costs can be cut with some predetermined sacrifices, admitting frankly that you analyzed and designed the program especially so that you could, finally, tailor it to the client's wishes, if cost cutting became necessary. This frank admission and the explanation of your farsightedness alone will help you greatly at the negotiating table. Be sure, as you do, that the client understands that you pledge three conditions:

1. A specific cost reduction.
2. Achievement of the main objective.
3. A sacrifice of some sort.

Consulting Processes
and Procedures

In this chapter, you will find three essential rules for success in building and conducting your independent practice. These are probably the most important ideas in this book.

—Herman Holtz

THE ART OF LISTENING

Listening must be a lost art, judging by the many training programs in listening offered today. We apparently hear less and less of what others say. Perhaps this is due to the growing cacophony: the blather of radio and TV, with loud commercials and ear-shattering rock music; the roar of traffic, and other sounds of modern civilization. We are besieged by sound. True quiet is rare!

We have learned how to filter the olio of sounds unconsciously and strain the unwanted out. Unfortunately, what we filter out is often what is very much in our interest to hear clearly.

We try to speed things up, to skim what others are saying, as we might skim a report or magazine article, trying to detect and draw out the essence, while rejecting the rest. So we often miss important details in our efforts to speed listen and leap to conclusions, usually wrong ones. We make preemptive judgments, deciding arbitrarily what to accept and what to reject of what reaches our ears—making summary judgments of what is valid and what is not valid.

Some of us go to the opposite extreme and decide that we haven't time to weigh things, and so we make judgments based on nothing more than impatience, the desire to get on to other things.

And finally, especially when trying to close a sale or win an argument, we spend listening time in thinking about what we want to say next to continue the exchange, and so we tend to miss almost entirely what the other is saying.

THE ART OF HEARING

Perhaps listening is not an accurate term, or perhaps it is only part of what we must do to grasp what others say to us. Many of us believe that we are listening, and perhaps we are, technically, but too often we are not hearing what is said; all we hear is sound and perhaps an occasional word that happens to penetrate the screen surrounding our consciousness at the moment. We must retrain ourselves to *hear*.

HEARING IS NOT A PASSIVE FUNCTION

In consulting, hearing must be neither passive nor unilateral. To truly hear what others say, you must assume an active role, prompting, asking questions, signifying understanding, indicating a need to repeat or elaborate on some word or phrase, and otherwise responding. Hearing is two-way, intercommunication. Your initial part in the exchange is quiet listening and hearing, but you can hardly expect the client to be able to judge what you need to know; you must guide the client in this with occasional questions and prompting.

Hearing Depends on Your Role

Hearing is not the same in all cases. It varies according to need. Hearing, when you are meeting and talking to a prospective client, is one thing; hearing, when you have won the contract and are listening to the client, is another thing. In the first instance, you listen for and try to hear that which will enable you to win the contract. You need to understand enough of the prospect's problem to suggest a program, and other information that will inspire the sales strategy to win the contract.

HEARING AS A SALESPERSON

Successful selling is consulting, counseling and guiding the prospect by showing how the product or service you offer will solve the prospect's problem and provide valuable benefits. Therefore selling ought to come naturally to professional consultants; you need only apply the consulting technique to the sales situation. It is almost unforgivable for a consultant to be a poor salesperson!

Hearing as a salesperson is hearing as a consultant, but as a consultant interested primarily in making a sale. This is not cynical. You cannot help the prospect until he or she is your client—until you have made the sale. You need to learn certain things to make this happen, so you must not only listen and hear; you must also respond and participate to elicit the information you need most.

As we mentioned in an earlier chapter, one of the most self-defeating actions of some salespeople is that of talking too long, talking when they ought to be closing. They fail to sense the prospect's readiness to buy (the signal for closing) and go on prattling until they unsell the prospect.

A second sin of selling is failing to listen, talking instead of listening. That is often an even worse sin: Not only does it tend to offend and even alienate prospects, but it blocks out information you need to close the sale. Be careful to always yield to a prospect who wants to say something. Ask the right questions, respond as necessary, but be brief and encourage the prospect to talk. The prospect will tell you how to sell him or her and win the contract if you listen carefully. You can learn while you are listening, but you learn nothing if you are talking instead of listening.

Listen and encourage the prospect to discuss these pieces of information that you need:

■ The essential problem or need, in as much detail as possible.

■ The prospect's own notions, if any, about how to approach the problem to effect a solution.

■ Whether the client's need calls for special problem-solving skills—application of special expertise—or simply services for professional and specialized work that is nevertheless more or less routine.

■ Any specific constraints or related requirements and problems, such as limitations of cost, time, or other factors.

■ Any special concerns or worries the client has in connection with the need.

■ The intent of the prospect, that is, whether firmly committed to retention of someone to help (and, if so, how soon), merely exploring to consider the possibility of retaining someone, or merely making conversation and trying, perhaps, to pick your brains with no intention of retaining you or anyone else.

■ Whether funds are available.

■ Whether the individual to whom you are speaking has the authority to retain you or, if not, who has, whose approval is needed, what the process is, and/or whatever else you can learn regarding approval and award requirements.

It is on the basis of answers to these and related questions that you can estimate or perhaps even determine whether you have a serious prospect for a contract or are wasting your time in idle conversation.

The Essential Problem or Need

There are consultants who offer solutions for which there are no known problems. They have a few favorite programs or processes, and they work energetically and enthusiastically in trying to force-fit every prospective client's problems to one of their off-the-shelf solutions. Some even believe invariably that the client's systems are hopelessly terrible and the need is to design and install a new one. There are also prospective clients who are no less biased and shortsighted in identifying and describing their needs. Some attempt their own diagnoses, despite having called you in as a consultant expert, and demand that you confirm their own diagnosis which is often far off the mark, making it clear that they consider you a charlatan if you fail to so confirm their findings. They appear to be embarrassed by being forced to call on a specialist for help and are apparently trying to get consensus or asking you to carry out orders mindlessly, perhaps to soothe their own egos or perhaps to try to be heroes in their own organizations. Often they will assure you that the only reason they called you in is because they simply don't have the time to solve the simple problem themselves, although they could do so easily enough.

From a sales viewpoint, the smart thing is to go along with this prospect's ploy; to embarrass him or her is to almost surely lose the sale. Even so, you need to know what the real need is if you are to respond intelligently. For example, a government General Services Administration client who was responsible for preparing public information to document changes in the forms and procedures to procure A&E (architect and engineer) services called on me for support and told me that he had already written the necessary brochure and manual. All he wanted me to do was to edit them and prepare them for the Government Printing Office, who would publish them. I agreed to do the job, but asked to see the manuscripts before I rendered an estimate. As I feared, they needed extensive rewriting and reorganization, rather than editing. However, rather than risk embarrassing and offending this executive, I agreed that the manuscripts needed a thorough edit to be made into truly first-class products, and I assumed that he wanted nothing less than first-class products as reflections of his work. Of course, there was no way he could object to that argument. I priced the job for rewriting, although the purchase order called for "editing," and we were both satisfied.

Another problem you may run into in identifying or defining the need is the tendency of some clients to surround the simple statement of the basic need with a jungle undergrowth of gratuitous remarks and speculations. (This may reflect the client's true misunderstanding of the problem, but it may be a case of the client trying to enhance his or her own importance.) The result is that it is not always easy to determine what the real problem is or, even then, to distinguish it from what are secondary and trivial problems you must respond to if you are to satisfy the client and win the contract. The following experience was an example of that.

The U.S Army Corps of Engineers at Fort Belvoir, Virginia, called for proposals to provide support of their night-vision laboratory projects in developing infrared (night-vision) equipment by supplying a number of engineering services. It appeared clear from the Corps' statement of work that the principal need perceived by the Corps was for value-engineering services, with some reverse-engineering services also required. (Value engineering would seek design and/or manufacturing improvements and cost reductions in products, while reverse engineering would update engineering drawings to reflect all changes made in equipment products.) It was thus necessary to write a proposal oriented primarily to and stressing capabilities in value engineering services, with reverse engineering services only incidental, and in fact it was on this basis that the proposal was evaluated. But in practice the project proved to be almost entirely one of reverse engineering services, with virtually no value engineering services required.

The Prospect's Own Notions

Even the client who openly admits the need to bring in a specialist as a consultant may stubbornly cling to his or her own prejudices about what needs doing and how it ought to be done. Some clients describe the requirement in such detail, even furnishing outlines and block diagrams, as to furnish a virtual blueprint. This directly contradicts the concept of competitive proposals as a quest for the best ideas. Too often, the client's bias denies him or her access to those best ideas, while it handicaps proposers seriously. It handicaps you in two ways: One, it tends to mislead you by directing your attention to the client's biased notions and diagnoses, instead of providing objective information and encouraging creative thinking; and two, it all but bludgeons you into agreeing with what may very well be a totally wrong concept and approach.

You must approach this kind of situation with great caution. Eyeball-to-eyeball confrontation with the client over what should be done or how it should be done will certainly not help much. But you can't agree to utilize a plan that will probably not produce the desired results or, at best, would be far less than the most effective or most efficient way to do the job.

A first step is to try to determine whether you have all the information you need to make a qualified judgment about the requirement. You must review critically the information supplied and make at least a preliminary judgment about that to judge the need for asking questions and probing for more details. However, you want also to know whether the client is truly biased about how the work is to be done or is merely trying to be helpful. That is, while avoiding a direct confrontation, you need to determine whether the client is open-minded and will consider approaches other than the one he or she has described and appears to mandate.

Both sides generally lose when a dispute arises. Positions become polarized, making each party feel compelled to save face by finding justification for his or her position, no matter how illogical the justification. The right approach, generally, is to suggest a possible difference of opinion in a non-threatening way, while carefully structuring the situation so as to avoid any necessity for immediate decision or immediate resolution. Give the other party a generous amount of time to ponder and adjust to the idea of possible change, without the stress of direct confrontation.

Be careful to avoid the appearance of attacking the client's plan. Drop the merest hint that you have not yet bought the client's plan, but are still open-minded by saying:

> Well, that seems to me to be an excellent way to go at this, but since we are in an early talking stage and I haven't yet had time to become familiar with the details why don't we discuss the specific approach later?

Even if the client wishes to pursue the matter at once, you can employ objective discussion, rational and unemotional arguments, and reactions conditioned to those of the client. That is, if the client appears to feel a need to defend his or her original position, your objective is still to avoid polarization and give the client ample time to think about and adjust to your ideas. Surprisingly often, the most determined opposition to your arguments or, for that matter, to any change melts away when the other party is given time to adjust to new ideas and allowed to save face. It is almost always a mistake to press for immediate decision when you and the client differ.

If this is a formal, written proposal situation, you won't usually have the opportunity to do this. You will usually be compelled to respond directly to a written request and statement of work. However, you are not entirely without recourse. You can always submit questions asking about the acceptability of exceptions and alternatives to the work statement or specifications. When properly posed, this question often leads to a written modification of the original statement of work or even to a preproposal conference where the entire proposed program can be discussed freely.

Often, an even better approach, one that avoids asking questions that may bring an amendment circulated to everyone, is the alternative proposal, offering an alternative approach, along with the responsive approach.

Expressed Need versus True Need

Presumably, the main function of a consultant is to use his or her knowledge, skills, and wisdom to troubleshoot, analyze, and solve difficult problems. The fact is that the majority of assignments do not require solving any but routine problems. The services required are mostly provision of skills and knowledge to conduct a survey, design a system, perform a study, write a report, plan a project, evaluate data, determine need, make a presentation, develop a program, and/or otherwise carry out missions that are more or less routine for the consultant, even when they are by nature creative services.

This is not to say that a specific problem to be solved is not the main objective of retaining the consultant. When the U.S. Postal Service found it necessary to update the rate data manual for using common carrier services in transporting mail, they discovered that the resident expert who had always done this work had retired and was not willing to come out of retirement even as a consultant to update the manual. They therefore retained a consultant to handle this task. It proved not a difficult task technically. It would have been pure routine for the former Postal Service employee, but it was a problem to be solved for the consultant.

The task required far less than the anticipated extensive overhaul and rewriting, as research demonstrated that rates had changed little since publication of the prior edition, and only a few pages required updating.

Clients err in both directions in their perceptions. Sometimes they grossly overestimate the difficulty of the task and the knowledge, skills, experience, or other resources needed to get the job done, while in others they fail to understand the true difficulties or the qualifications necessary for the assignment. But they also sometimes fail to understand what the need is, as in the case of the Fort Belvoir Corps of Engineers Night-Vision Laboratory and their confusion between their need for value engineering and that for reverse engineering services.

Partly because of this but also because they sometimes are unable to draw the proper conclusions from the symptoms and other indications, clients often fail to describe the true problem. In the case of the Postal Service and rate manual, the client thought that special knowledge of the common carrier systems and their rates was necessary to get the job done. The consultant, who was not an expert in common carrier systems or their rates but was experienced in research and data gathering, also thought that a great deal of research would be needed. It turned out that the data needed was readily available and could be gathered in only a couple of days. Learning this, the consultant was able to assess the need accurately and submit an appropriate bid for the task.

Clients have made gross errors such as calling for the development of written materials to give to people who are functionally illiterate, but usually it is not this easy to judge whether the stated problem is likely to be the true problem. It generally requires analysis to make the judgment, but it is essential to make that judgment before committing yourself.

There is one exception to this, especially in contracting with government agencies: If your proposal and contract make it clear that the detailed specifications to which you agree and commit yourself are those listed by the client in the proposal request and its statement of work, you are protected contractually. If it becomes necessary to make changes later because the original specifications or description of the requirement prove faulty, you can then make and support a claim for a change in scope or specifications and contract amendment to the price. It is exceedingly important that you make your proposed program clearly detailed and specified quantitatively, as well as qualitatively, in any written proposal or other documentation affecting your contractual obligations.

Specific Restraints and/or Related Requirements

Because of the inherent nature of consulting services and the arrangements under which consultants are so often retained—on an hourly or daily rate for indeterminate periods—you need to know whether there are any special constraints or requirements such as a cost ceiling or not-to-exceed figure established in advance. But there are other special constraints and requirements that you may encounter and should be alert for, such as:

- Requirements that the contract and work be reviewed and approved by higher authority, a list of individuals, or—even worse—a committee. Review committees, especially large ones, can be endless trouble unless they are under the firm control of a decisive leader. But a lengthy list of individual reviewers can be equally troublesome.

  Recommendation: Find out about this in advance, ask whether approval must be unanimous, ask what procedure is when there is serious disagreement or deadlock, and what is your protection against arbitrariness.

- Progress reports can slow you down considerably, especially when the requirement calls for formal review and approval of these reports, which often leads to special meetings, with the attendant demands on your time.

  Recommendation: Try to get as much information about this as possible in advance. If formal progress reports are required, factor estimated time for these into your schedule and price.

- Government-type cost analyses, cost revelations, and pre- and post-award audit requirements. Many people object to making such disclosures and therefore don't do business with government agencies or major government contractors who impose such requirements.

  Recommendation: If you feel this way, now is the time to find out if there are such requirements. These are not usually imposed on small contracts—those under $100,000—but check to be sure.

- Turnkey requirements require you to install the system you design, get it running smoothly, and then train the client's staff to run it before "turning over the key." Sometimes clients forget to mention that this is what is expected.

  Recommendation: Be absolutely sure that you know exactly what you are to deliver and protect yourself by documenting it accurately, as noted.

The Prospect's Intent

The question is whether the prospect truly intends to do business or is on a fishing trip, merely curious, or wasting your time for some other reason. This was referred to earlier (Chapter 8) in explaining that prospects must be qualified, which means assuring yourself that the prospect has serious intent and funding or the authority to negotiate and make a deal for your services, binding his or her organization. Investigate this as early in the game as possible by asking euphemistic questions such as whether "funds are currently available," whether the program "has been budgeted yet," who "must sign off" on the program, and other questions that do not appear to challenge the authority or the integrity of the prospect but yet elicit the information you need. If the prospect furnishes only clearly evasive answers or declines to respond at all, you should be alerted immediately.

This does not always mean abandoning a prospect whom, it turns out, has not the authority to contract or even to negotiate with you. Even such a prospect may be the key to business via some indirect means and should therefore sometimes be carefully cultivated, rather than written off. Such a prospect may be a rich source of information on the organization, its needs, its hierarchy, and other intelligence valuable for marketing purposes. Such a prospect may also be the conduit for meeting someone who does have the authority to buy and can be persuaded to do business with you. And, in some cases, even the prospect who does not have buying authority or any other true power in the organization can sell or help you sell your ideas to others in the organization. (I found this possibility to be significant in government agencies, but it is true for all organizations, especially the large, bureaucratic ones.)

LISTENING AS A HIRED CONSULTANT

You listened carefully, heard all you needed and closed the sale. Now it is time to listen as a consultant on chargeable time. Now you are listening for the information you need to carry out the contract successfully and efficiently. It's a different proposition with common points.

In the marketing phase, you must often discriminate between the problem stated and the true problem. You must now discriminate between the correct solution to the problem and the client's desired solution when these are not the same. In each case, recognize that you have two requirements to satisfy, and you must devise somehow to satisfy both.

One problem you often encounter in listening is that clients often cannot discriminate between problems and their symptoms. Those who are not trained problem solvers tend often to confuse the two. A client once told me that his problem was that he was not winning enough government contracts. I agreed that this was a serious problem for someone whose business was government contracting per se. But, I felt compelled to tell him, the lack of success in winning contracts was the problem only in his upper-management perspective; in my own in-the-trenches perspective, that was a symptom of some problem. But what problem(s)?

- Poor proposal writing?
- Poor estimating?
- Addressing the wrong market segment?
- Failing to keep in touch with requirements?
- Overreaching for markets in which he did not qualify?
- Poor track record (past performance)?
- Poor past contract administration?
- Overpricing?

Even this analysis is only a first step, for the initial problem identification itself yields to a similar analysis in which the problem identified must then be regarded as a symptom to be analyzed. For example, suppose the first analysis results in a judgment that the problem is poor proposal writing. What are the true possible causes or problems?

- Poor program design?
- Weak (poorly written) staff resumes?
- Weak (poorly written) organization credentials?
- Unpersuasive, unconvincing writing?
- Unimpressive/unimaginative presentations?
- Poor/lack of effective graphics?
- Poor/lack of strategies?

Each of these may be analyzed in similar fashion. Poor program design, for example, may be due to any of many factors, including:

- Unorganized proposal efforts.
- Inexperienced staff used to write.
- Poor technical (design) capabilities of staff.
- Cursory and imperfect analysis of client wants.
- Hasty and casual design efforts.

Each of the series consists of identifying the symptoms, some of which are obvious and others of which must be identified by troubleshooting methods, testing each as a hypothesis to decide whether it is a valid symptom or an irrelevant factor, and deciding for each symptom remaining as a relevant factor whether it is a cause or an effect.

Note that each series is more sharply focused on possible solutions. The series of analyses should continue until final solutions are suggested. The series ends only when you have isolated and properly identified the problem. Proper definition of the problem points to the possible solutions. The final step is to select that solution which is best suited to your own situation. The three ideas arrived at in this example are basic; in the actual situation you might opt for something slightly different, but it would embody one of these general ideas. (Of course, many problems have more than one practicable solution; you must decide which is most appropriate for your own case.)

In this case the next stage of analysis will be the critical one. All the possibilities listed begin to point to these choices:

- Create a proposal department or at least hire a proposal manager.
- Retain consultants to lead proposal efforts.
- Send someone (the marketing manager?) to proposal-writing training seminars.

The client will have to decide which of the alternative solutions is appropriate, but you might be asked to make recommendations. If so, you must conduct still another analysis to determine which is most efficient, most effective, most practical, and/or most acceptable to the client. The latter is a separate matter, which might involve other factors, such as company policies and goals. And in this case there is a special problem. How could a consultant recommend the hiring of consultants as a solution? It would be necessary to develop a complete set of pro and con facts for each alternative and ask the client to make the decision.

A BASIC APPROACH TO ALL ANALYSIS: FUNCTION

Analysis is the separation of something into its parts to determine what it is made of, how it is made, and how it all functions together (qualitative analysis). A quantitative analysis would determine the amounts of the various components and other data of size and proportion. Here, we are concerned primarily with qualitative analysis, although it is possible that we might have occasion to perform quantitative analysis, too. But in most of our work we are more likely to be conducting analysis not as an end in itself but as a means to an end: synthesis of a solution. We pursue analytical methods to uncover causes, so that we understand the problem and can develop a solution.

The key to analysis of most things, whether a physical device, an organization, a management system, or anything else is function. While the item being analyzed is subjected to an identification of all its component parts, each of these parts is identified also as a function. This functional analysis separates all the component functions of the item, whatever it is, and then sorts them out into their various functions, which must also be identified. This is the basis for that discipline known as *value management* (also known as *value analysis* and *value engineering*), and describes generally *systems analysis*. The basic methods can be a valuable asset to you in both your roles, as marketer and consultant because it is an orderly and systematic way of analyzing things, whether those are a client's requirements in the preparation of a proposal, development of a capture strategy, or analyzing systems, problems, needs, jobs, or other items as a consultant.

This discussion is not intended to be a definitive course in value analysis or its derivatives. That would go far beyond your needs. But it does borrow from that basic discipline and adapts what it borrows to your needs and interests as an independent consultant.

What It Does versus What It Is

The basis for the value method includes shedding our human tendency to consider only what something is—an object, practice, procedure, or system. To get a truer perspective of the worth and essential nature of anything, you must consider what it is only for purposes of identification, and focus on what it does—its function. Function is the essential item in value analysis from which all else stems.

The problem with answering "What is it?" by citing the item's name is that all too often the name does not tell us what a thing does but often misleads us. Take a wrist watch, for example, and ask what it is. The answer is, of course, a "watch." What does a watch do? The answer you get too often to this question is that it "tells time." But a watch does not "tell" time at all; people do that. A watch *indicates* time. The name does not even suggest what a watch does. The classic or conventional watch has a pair of hands that indicate the time. Many watches use digital readouts as indicators. Both types of watches indicate the time, but the digital watch has some advantages over the old style, often referred to as a dial or analog watch. For one thing, even the cheapest digital watches tend to be more accurate and far less prone to need service because they are entirely electronic and thus have no moving parts.

So, if they are superior in some ways, why do people spend more—much, much more—for analog watches in preference to digital watches?

They do so because a wrist watch is more than a device to indicate the time of day. That is its main function, a utilitarian function, but it has also a second function for some people as jewelry, with great esteem value. Analog watches offer more artistic opportunity to designers than do digital watches.

The value analyst would consider the primary function of a watch to be the practical or utilitarian one, defined as "indicates time," while its esteem value (if it is a watch that is also regarded as jewelry), is defined perhaps as "gives pleasure," is a secondary function.

A value analyst would go at the initial analysis in an organized fashion, to get answers to several questions:

1. What is it?
2. What does it do?
3. What else would do that?
4. What else does it do?
5. What else would do that?
6. What does it cost?

To ensure objectivity, clarity, and commitment, answers must be disciplined to appear only as verb and noun; modifiers of all kinds are banned. Hence, "indicates time," "gives pleasure," etc. "What else does it do?" forces you to look at other (secondary) functions, which may be of several kinds:

- Supportive of and necessary to accomplish the primary or main function.
- Supportive of but not necessary to the main function.
- Additional to and valuable or desirable function.
- Additional to but not particularly useful or valuable function.

I carry a tiny clasp knife on my key ring to open packages and assist in other such chores. It has also a screwdriver, nail file, and bottle opener attachment. I have no use for those extra gadgets; they add undesired weight, bulk, and cost to the item, and I would have preferred a small knife without these items, but I had no choice; it was the only such knife I could find. (Others might find those additional items useful and desirable, of course.) Inevitably the worth of secondary functions that are not essential to the primary function becomes a matter of subjective judgment, varying with individual interests.

Answering that question "What is it?" is usually easy; you need only name the item. Answering "What does it do?" is not always easy. In fact, it is sometimes rather difficult. Take that little key chain-sized pocket knife, for example: What does it do?

I am tempted to respond "opens packages," but that is wrong. I, not the knife, open packages. Moreover, someone else may use it for far different tasks than opening packages. We need to offer a simple but universally true definition, probably one that uses "cuts" as the verb—"cuts software," perhaps, since certainly it would not cut anything very hard.

Some people may use the knife for other things than cutting, but the definition ought to address the intended purpose of the item.

Without laboring the point, the idea is to identify function(s). By this, you can determine not only how well anything performs its function(s), but also how well the function or functions serve or contribute to the overall need.

Take the humble paper clip as an example. Undoubtedly a great invention as proved by the fact that has survived without significant change for so long and no other temporary binder of papers has become a serious rival. One secondary (support) function was added to some paper clips in the form of serration to add gripping power, but the idea has not really caught on because it has added nothing very significant to the function; by far the majority of paper clips are plain vanilla, as they have been since the beginning.

The reason for its greatness and its success is that it is simple, as most great ideas are. It has become an article of faith with me that any fool can find a complicated solution to any problem; genius lies in finding the simple solutions. It is almost a natural law that complicated systems die early deaths, replaced by simpler systems. Too often, we make a Swiss army knife of everything we do, burdening our products and systems with unnecessary additions that do not contribute to the main mission and even detract from its accomplishment. The simpler system is almost invariably the pure system, the one that single-mindedly pursues a clearly perceived and clearly defined main objective and permits no distractions to interfere. Early radios, for example, had several dials—as many as four to six—that had to be manipulated to tune each receiving circuit to the frequency of the desired station. But Edwin H. Armstrong put an end to all of that complication and difficulty with his invention, the superheterodyne, which simplified tuning by converting all desired signals to a single frequency for which all but the primary circuits were tuned in advance. Nor has anyone improved on the superheterodyne since; It is still the basic design of all radio and TV receiving equipment. And that is another hallmark of the right design or solution: It is difficult to improve upon.

The functional analysis is an organized, procedural discipline. It has rules. Here are the chief ones:

Rule 1: Verb-Noun Rule

The verb-noun rule has been mentioned earlier. It requires the use of a single verb and noun to define a function. No modifiers—adverbs and adjectives—are permitted, although sometimes a compound noun is necessary. The purpose is to enforce clear, unequivocal thinking and comment. You must decide what is/are the intended function(s) and/or needs or purposes without the hedging of adverbs and adjectives. In everyday life, we use euphemisms, hyperbole, and modifiers to dodge the issue, qualify our positions, avoid clear comment, and otherwise avoid taking a position. That won't work in problem solving. If you fail to define the problem clearly you are not likely to reach a solution, and you can't define the problem without having a good understanding of the need. You must learn to ask what and why and settle only for clear, unequivocal answers.

In one consulting organization, the manager was plagued by the frequent return of his invoices by customers, who asked that the invoices be corrected. Somehow in the accounting system error was creeping in almost inevitably.

Analyzing the system, in search of the problem—not the solution, for the problem was not yet identified—the manager found the system to be one in which raw figures were collected on a worksheet, from which they were transferred to the invoice. The manager asked the accountant what the function of the worksheet was. He was told that labor charges from employee time cards and other charges from suppliers' invoices were collected and posted on the worksheet before being transferred to the invoice.

"Why?" asked the manager.

"That's a standard system for this kind of operation," replied the accountant.

"What do you do with the figures on the worksheet?" asked the manager.

"Transfer them to the invoice," replied the accountant.

"But why do you need the worksheet?" asked the manager. "Why can't you post the numbers directly on the invoice?" (He had already discovered that the mistakes were being made in the final transfer of figures from the worksheet to the invoices.)

The accountant shrugged, while he looked somewhat incredulous at the question. "It's a standard system," he protested. "Everybody does it this way."

The manager eliminated the problem by eliminating the worksheet, which was clearly unnecessary in this case, since there was no processing or reorganization of the figures, but only a simple transfer. All the worksheet added to the system was a greater opportunity to make mistakes.

In this case, the worksheet had no truly useful function, and the slavish devotion to a traditional practice was a mindless burden and source of problems.

It was almost as mindless as the WW II British artillery soldier who stood to one side of the gun when it was fired. No one knew what his job was; it was merely traditional to stand there as the gun was fired.

Tedious research produced the answer: When artillery caissons had been drawn by horses, an artilleryman was required to stand to one side and hold the horses so that they wouldn't bolt at the sound when the gun was fired!

To define function accurately with a single, unequivocal verb and noun, you must identify the need or purpose first, as objective information. Take the case of analyzing the job and proper employment of a secretary: What is the need, the reason for using a secretary? In too many offices today secretaries are used as file clerks, typists, coffee makers, and personal servants. The traditional role of the secretary has all but disappeared, along with the office boy, who used to run all those errands, sharpen pencils, and otherwise perform the trivial duties that required no special skills. Unfortunately, relatively high-paid secretaries today spend much of their time performing the most menial of unskilled duties, and most of the rest of their time performing duties worth far less than their salaries justify.

The problem is that executives do not take the time to analyze the situation logically to discover that the truly traditional—and correct—verb-noun definition of what a secretary does (should do) is save time—the executive's time, that is. Even a relatively junior executive costs the organization much more per hour than a secretary does, but a secretary costs too much for filing and making coffee. Secretaries (properly) should open mail and answer telephones to save their boss's time, field routine matters, manage their bosses' schedule, fend off and redirect those who ought to be guided to someone else, and generally enable their bosses to maximize the time they have available to concentrate on important matters that require their attention.

Robert Townsend, former head of Avis, the car-rental firm, is one of a number of executives who refuse to have a secretary, instead calling someone from the typing pool when the executive needs filing or typing done. Some organizations increase efficiency by assigning a secretary to divide time among and support several executives. Both these approaches indicate some consciousness of the waste represented by the way secretaries are employed today, but they also reflect a complete lack of logical analysis. Why should the head of a large firm such as Avis spend his time making his own travel arrangements, keeping his appointment book, and answering routine mail? All of us, no matter rank, authority, wealth, birth, or privilege of any kind, have the same allotment of time every day, but our time is valued differently, especially in terms of what it costs the organization

I once had the good fortune to have a secretary who had been secretary to Harold L. Ickes, Franklin D. Roosevelt's Secretary of the Interior. It was soon apparent why she had gained and succeeded in a position serving a man who was not only a brilliant and most important official but was reputed to be a difficult man, a curmudgeon: It was rarely that I had to give her much in the way of instruction. When she heard me on the telephone discussing a trip (I customarily keep my office door open and I speak in boldface), she was almost immediately on a second line and ready to offer me the travel and hotel options available by the time I had hung up. When she brought the morning mail in she had pulled the files necessary for me to refer to in my responses and had already made notes for my approval or drafted responses on routine correspondence. In fact, she was far more than a secretary; she was an assistant, as all really good secretaries are or ought to be.

The same philosophy of analyzing needs and functions can be applied to many other things as well as to equipment and people—to forms, systems, procedures, and even to rules. The example of the error-ridden invoices and the unneeded worksheet is not an exception; it is typical. In another case a small print shop doing work for the Government Printing Office (which, despite its great size, contracts out about 70 percent of its work) was having a similar problem. The contract required furnishing rates for each element of each job— camera work to make negatives, plate making, make-readies (installing each new plate on the press and adjusting it), press washes (when different color inks are to be used), collating pages, stapling, cutting, trimming, packing, and shipping, among others. The print shop listed all these costs on an estimating sheet when bidding the job, used a similar form to record the actual count of pages, staples, and so on, and sent that latter form to the accounting department to be transferred to an invoice in all its detail, as required by contract. As in the other case, this double transfer of figures furnished excellent opportunities for mistakes. The cure was similar. The original estimating form was modified to provide a column for actual quantities alongside the column of estimated quantities, and a copy of the form was attached to the invoice, which listed only the bottom-line figure. The Government Printing Office found this quite acceptable.

Quite aside from eliminating the problems, consider the labor saved by the solutions to both problems. The increase in efficiency alone justifies the changes. And note again the simplicity of the solutions—that they simplify the systems, that is, by subtracting from them, rather than by adding to them. Bear that in mind as you study problems: Frequently the problem is the result of unnecessary element(s) in the system, and simple surgery is the most direct and best solution. Elements performing secondary functions that appear to be supportive of and necessary to the primary function are often really not only unnecessary but are actually harmful. So the questions "What is it?" and "What does it do?" often lead to "Do we need it?" and "Does it contribute?"

The opposite is also sometimes true. An engineering services firm employing thousands of people nationally in over 40 small offices ran the weekly payroll for all on a large mainframe computer in its New York City headquarters. Yet, when summer vacation time rolled around, the home office had to ask each branch office manager to determine how much earned vacation time each employee had. They had failed to arrange for the computer to keep track of this most basic element of a master payroll record.

The true cause of this is a common problem which many who have worked for large and bureaucratic organizations encounter: The home-office/corporate-offices staff are sure that only they are alert and aware and all others—especially those provincials out in the field offices—are naive boobs. The corporate sages therefore tend often to make decisions for the bucolic boobs without consulting them, with disastrous results.

These and many other irrational acts in organizations result from the failure to do reasoned analysis, especially the failure to identify the need and primary function required, and to do so in that simple and objective verb-noun discipline that forces commitment and clear thinking.

Rule 2: Agree on the Need

Sometimes we hear a dispute or failure blamed on a breakdown in communications. That's a partial truth in many cases: Two people didn't understand each other. But in a great many cases the misunderstanding is really a failure to reach agreement. The failure to reach agreement with a client in defining the need means that you are pursuing a goal that may be the right goal, in your opinion, but is probably the wrong goal, in the client's opinion. There are many reasons for such failures to reach agreement with a client on just what the need is, including at least these:

- The reluctance to dispute the client for fear of losing the contract; you hope you can muddle through somehow without having to confront the problem of a client who is grossly misguided as to what his or her true need is.
- A client who is less than clear in explaining his or her own ideas and thoughts so that you are not even aware that you are in disagreement.
- A client who has been totally non-committal and unresponsive to your proposal so that you mistakenly believe that you have persuaded the client to your view and that you are now in agreement.
- Your own failure to make your thoughts clear so that you mistakenly believe that the client understands and agrees with your diagnosis and proposed project.
- Your failure to think things out and express the need in that simple verb-noun definition.

It is not necessary to provoke a direct confrontation to reach agreement to ensure that you do understand each other. If you find yourself in disagreement with the client or, at least, have not yet reached agreement, working through the first few steps of the value analysis will often help persuade the client to your view. (If it does not, avoid confrontation and pursue the negotiating tactic advocated earlier of expressing arguments and proposing to shelve further discussion for a few days.)

The formal process in value analysis, then, is to pose and seek answers to these questions:

- What is it? (Descriptive, functional name)
- What does it do? (Main function)
- What else does it do? (Secondary functions)

- What does it cost?
- What else would do it? (The same main function with at least equal quality, reliability, and efficiency)
- What would that cost?

This series of questions compels you to organize your analysis and synthesis along unemotional, logical lines. (The same series of questions may be proposed for each element or component performing a secondary function of some kind.) Used by engineers, this kind of analysis has led to many design and manufacturing simplifications that not only reduce costs but often produce a better product at the same time. (The discipline was born as a result of World War II experiences, when it was discovered that substitute materials, whose use was forced by wartime shortages, often were better and cheaper than the materials for which they had been substituted.)

The method is not confined to saving money. The method may be used to conserve energy, time, materials, or other resources. The questions are modified to direct the analysis properly. What would that cost? may become How long would that take? When the Environmental Protection Agency found itself in difficulties getting its program to improve water-treatment facilities completed within the time schedule mandated by Congress when it authorized the program, the agency called on value engineering consultants to work on the problem. (The agency was to award $10 billion in grants to communities, but it was taking up to two years to approve applications by the communities.) The team of three consultants tracked the problem down through the analysis of each element required to process each application and found that the problem lay in the communities' slowness in writing final engineering reports that were required by law to qualify for the grants. More precisely, the problem was that the engineers waited until their engineering studies were completely and totally finished before even contemplating report writing, which could have been more than half completed by the time the engineering studies were finished.

Value engineers have developed their own special block diagramming method to assist in the analysis and presentation of functional analyses. A simple example of this is shown in Figure 15.1, illustrating the logic of an ordinary mouse trap.

In this presentation, the overall goal or need is expressed as "eliminate mice," whereas the main function is "kill mice." The distinction and the reason for it is an important one. The need is to get rid of mice, not necessarily by killing them, however. The device used and analyzed here is designed to kill mice. If another kind of device had been studied the main function might have been defined as trap mice, but the need would have remained the same because the need has nothing to do with the method, while the main function has everything to do with the method. How defines the relationship:

How to eliminate mice?

By killing mice.

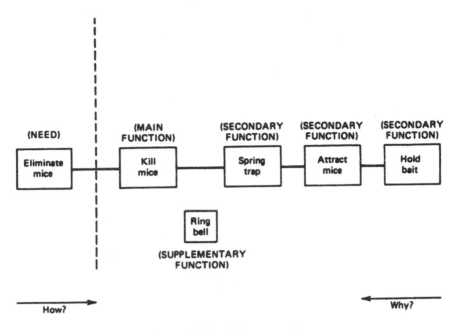

Figure 15.1. The mouse trap.

In this case there are secondary functions that are necessary to accomplish the main function, but there is one that is only supplementary—ring bell—and not necessary to accomplish the main function.

Brainstorming

Brainstorming is a useful way to reach agreement with clients in many cases, especially when an assignment requires working with, and often leading, the client's own in-house experts. This is almost invariably a disparate ad hoc group who often do not even know each other very well. They therefore require firm and positive leadership, and brainstorming fills the bill quite nicely in a great many cases.

The method was invented by advertising executive Alex Osborne, and the overall objective is to inspire a synergy of fresh, creative ideas through free association. Its session is conducted in three major phases:

1. The group is assembled, with a leader, who lays out the rules—throw any and all ideas on the table, spin-off on others' ideas, offer twists on your own ideas, and be entirely uninhibited—but no ridiculing others or their ideas: all ideas are to be recorded and considered. The leader then poses the basic question to be answered or the problem for which solutions are sought, encourages everyone to participate, and enforces the rules. Ideas are recorded on a blackboard or poster board where everyone can see them.

2. When the group runs out of fresh ideas the next phase starts. Here ideas are evaluated and thrown out, retained, modified, or combined with others.

3. Final evaluations and choices are made.

This is intended to be a group activity. Value engineering teams use the discipline, as do many other teams. However, it is possible to do this on a solo basis too. The creative process involves three stages also:

1. *Concentration:* Think intensively about the matter, seeking ideas consciously.

2. *Incubation:* Put the matter out of your (conscious) mind, after you have exhausted all approaches consciously, and go on to other things. (This is turning it over to your subconscious mind.)

3. *Illumination (or inspiration):* This is when your subconscious mind provides an answer, as when you wake up one morning with the answer to something that has defied conscious solution or when a word or name that has eluded you suddenly pops into your head.

Whatever the means, you must somehow manage to reach a clear and mutually understood agreement with the client.

Rule 3: Written Agreements Must Be Specific

You must never sign an agreement that is not absolutely specific in what you agree to do, when you agree to do it or have it completed, what you agree to deliver and how much of it, how much you are to be paid, when you are to be paid, and all other such important details. Whatever the agreement, it must be absolutely specific, and that usually means that it must be quantitative, as well as qualitative. The failure to be specific is a major reason for problems. When you write a proposal, you are in effect proposing a contract, for your proposal will probably become the key part of the contract, incorporated in it by reference. You thus have time to think things out and decide exactly what you wish to have in the contract.

It is rare that some kind of deliverable item is not involved in a project, even a project calling for services. At the least, there is usually a requirement for a final report and often for a series of reports. That is the only physical evidence that the client can show for the money spent, so it often assumes a correspondingly large importance to the client.

In many cases, the client has no firm idea of how to specify requirements for the report(s), and so it is not a good idea to press the client for specifications. Instead, you should offer your own specifications, making your own best guesstimates.

A 100-page report, typed double-spaced, as many clients prefer, will run to approximately 25,000 words, a not inconsiderable amount of writing. Ordinarily, you will want to include some charts or graphs. A few decades ago you would probably have had to rely on a commercial illustrator to do these for you. More recently you could have gotten much of what you needed in the form of excellent do-it-yourself art materials from local supply houses. Today, you can probably create all the charts and graphs you need with the computer on your desk.

What Should Be Spelled Out

There are no hard and fast rules as to what must be specified. In custom work, such as consultants do, each case is unique. But specify everything that is going to cost time or money, for you must be paid for your time and reimbursed for your expenses. Of course, you can't know in advance just what all those will amount to so you must cover these in two ways:

1. Plan all the chores and functions and estimate the time and money you will have to spend on them—travel, toll calls, printing, writing, research, interviews, and whatever else you can anticipate.

2. Write in general provisions specifying that you will be reimbursed in full for time and out-of-pocket costs for these items, being sure to list all the types of expenses you expect to incur.

The estimated costs are a must for the fixed-price contract, for the client is obligated for only a specific total of dollars. Therefore it is important that you estimate carefully, but it is also important that you fix limits. If you estimate a 100-page final report on a fixed-price contract you are obligated for that only. But if you had not specified the number of pages the client would feel justified in demanding 300 pages, and you would have no grounds for refuting the demand. On the other hand, had the client accepted your proposed 100 pages and later decided to demand 300 pages, you have a legitimate basis for renegotiating and amending the contract.

Such cases are not rare or unusual. Once, having prepared and delivered a training film and 50 copies of a manual, as required by contract, I was confronted with a demand for an additional 150 copies of the manual at no charge. Oddly enough, the demand did not come to me from the client, but from our own marketing vice president, who was relaying the client's request and who evidently shrank from telling the client quietly that we would have to charge for more copies. When I explained that I was not willing to have my department stand the loss, he indignantly demanded that I tell that to the client.

I did so. I had no difficulty explaining calmly to the client that while we would be happy to supply a few extra copies—we had a few on hand—we would be forced to charge for as many as 150 additional copies. (We did, in fact, have to go back to the printer to produce another 150 copies.) There was no problem. (There rarely is when you are calm and businesslike.) The client was quite willing to pay for what he wanted. I doubt that the client had ever expected us to provide additional copies free of charge. I have never found being businesslike in any way a problem or a handicap in doing business. Most clients respect your right to be as businesslike as they are. This is not to say that I never found a client unwilling to take advantage of me if I permitted it; it has happened, but those have been exceptional cases.

Verbal Understandings Are Important Too

I have found it conducive to good relationships with minimum problems to be open and honest from the beginning with clients while still trying to be diplomatic. I have not found many clients willing to retain me on a completely open basis—that is, sign a blank check for me by retaining me at a daily rate on an indefinite basis. Although such arrangements are made occasionally, as when an organization retains you as a technical or professional temporary, they are the exceptions. In most cases, the client wants some idea of what the entire commitment is likely to be. I therefore make it a practice to try to get enough information about the requirement to make a reasonable estimate of the cost and offer the client a not-to-exceed figure. I then try earnestly to live with my estimate. If the job runs slightly over, I absorb the difference normally, assuming that I underestimated the time required. If the job runs over due to the client adding work or to experience demonstrating that my estimate was based on inaccurate input from the client, I discuss amending our contract (or purchase order, which is a contract). I have rarely had a problem with this; most clients are reasonable about it if you have been careful to arrive at a clear understanding at the beginning. I work at making sure that the client understands exactly the basis for my not-to-exceed estimate. I do something to create that basis in writing—in a contact or purchase order, if we have one between us, or in a letter of understanding otherwise. However, it is equally important—perhaps even more important—that the client has been helped to understand that clearly in the beginning. The paper in the files is less than totally helpful if the client is not conscious of what it says and feels, somehow, victimized when you ask for an amendment to your agreement and more money.

In a recent case, a client retained me to help them prepare a proposal which was due only a week later. Obviously, I could not spend more than seven days on that task, and I agreed to do my level best to prepare a first-class proposal despite the time constraint. Near the end of the period my client's customer allowed an extension of several days for the proposal, and we therefore raised our sights a bit on the task, so that I spent two additional days on it. My client agreed that this was a change and issued me a second purchase order to pay me for the extra two days. It took a little conversation—it was really only conversation and did not merit the term negotiation—and several days to reach agreement, but there was never a question about my right to be paid for the extra days.

Specifying Rates

The daily (or hourly) rate you charge includes the salary you pay yourself, the overhead, and a profit margin. Although there are some exceptions, for most of us the overhead is a major element of cost in our daily rate. And a major overhead item is our unbilled time, especially that time we spend in marketing, finding clients and assignments.

That means that when we draw a long-term assignment, perhaps many weeks or even months of work without breaks or with only minimal unbilled time, our overhead costs plunge sharply during that period. Should we then favor the client who retains us for an extended period with a significantly lower rate reflecting that reduced overhead?

You are likely to encounter clients who will expect to be able to bargain with you about your rates, especially when they can offer long-term assignments or promise a great deal of work for the future. (They understand the overhead problem too!) Should you agree to negotiate your basic rates in such circumstances?

There are some consultants who will not vary their rates under any circumstances. (Many believe that it is beneath their professional dignity to bargain as though the scene were a middle-eastern bazaar.) There are some who will bargain and negotiate under special circumstances, such as those hypothesized here. And there are those who will negotiate whenever things are slow and they feel a need to win an assignment, even at a reduced rate.

This is a matter of policy and you must define it for yourself. But if you do negotiate special rates with a client, be sure to have a clear understanding of what the rates are and for what duration they are effective. It's a good idea in this case to commit the special rates to writing via a written agreement or contract of some kind, since it is a special case and an exception.

There are hazards in this arrangement. Suppose you agree to charge a special, reduced rate on the basis of a promise that you will be working a minimum of so many days per week or so many total days over the next three months. And suppose that most of the promised work does not materialize, and you are employed only sporadically for a day here and day there. (Even with the best of intentions on the part of a client, this can and does happen. As Samuel Goldwyn was alleged to have said, "Verbal contracts are not worth the paper they are written on!")

For such cases as these you must therefore protect yourself with written guarantees, guarantees that you will be employed for some minimum number of days over the specified time period or paid your full rate if the promised volume of work fails to materialize. If the client refuses to enter into such an agreement, the refusal speaks for itself.

Final Reports, Presentations, and Other Products

Consulting is a service, but that does not preclude creating and selling appropriate products. In fact, they may be the most important aspect of consulting. They reflect you, the consultant, how well you perform and how effective your services are.

—Herman Holtz

WRITTEN REPORTS: PRODUCTS OF THE CONSULTING PROJECT

Most consulting projects require development and delivery of some product, at least a written report and often items such as software, tapes, slides, and manuals. If the project is large or long term, you will probably be required to submit progress reports periodically, culminating in a final report. The progress reports permit various executives and technical specialists to monitor the project, judge how well it is progressing, and learn of any problems. The executive who authorized or inspired the project has need to maintain awareness of the project in its details. He or she is responsible for the program, and may have to report on it at staff meetings. You may therefore have to arm your client with informal memoranda and notes in preparation for those boardroom inquisitions. Even if you are yourself invited to visit the boardroom to make a presentation of and discuss the project status, at least one of the client's staff is expected to be able to answer all questions and provide all information called for about the project.

General Nature and Content of Reports

To satisfy the needs, written reports must be more than routine boilerplate. They must report accomplishment, problems, plans, and projections, and be lucid, informative, complete, and accurate. But they must also be completely dignified and discreet, and, as in the case of proposals and similar writing (see Chapter 13), they must be factual in tone and style. That is, they must be objective, scrupulously avoiding hyperbole. The tone should be definitely upbeat, reflecting confidence in the outcome of the project, but presenting unadorned facts.

Typical Formats

Progress reports are usually written in unvarnished narrative format, reporting events in chronological order, generally in forward sequence—the order in which they occurred, although occasionally a reverse chronology or even a different format may be necessary. Since the progress report is normally one of a continuing series it should present a link with the prior month's report, refreshing the reader's memory on the project status of that time as a baseline for the current report and a yardstick for measuring progress. The single most important consideration is progress or the lack of it and causes thereof. In the latter case, the report must identify the specific problems encountered, what is being done to cope with them, and what the plans are for solving the problems in the month to come.

A Common Mistake to Avoid

Only significant facts affecting progress belong in the progress report. Don't confuse effort with accomplishment. Effort that is fruitless because a problem is encountered might be mentioned in passing, but it is the problem and its solution or plans for its solution that are relevant and should be described and discussed. Suppose that by extraordinary effort and clever improvisation you acquired difficult-to-get information that proved to be worthless for your purposes. You have that understandable passion to tell the world about it. Don't. No matter how heroic or brilliant your effort was, no matter how hard you worked, the fact is that only progress or impediments to it should be reported. No one, including the client, cares about the storms you met at sea; they want only to know whether you brought the ship home.

Organization and Formats

Information can be organized in a large variety of ways, and each type of report or other presentation should be matched to the most appropriate organization. Here are some of the many ways in which information can be organized:

- Chronological, order of occurrence
- Historical—similar to chronological, but not necessarily in strict order of occurrence

- Reverse chronological—tracing events back to origins or first causes
- Order of importance—least to most important or vice versa
- General to particular or vice versa
- Syllogistic—beginning with premises and developing logical arguments
- Deductive—stating principles and analyzing facts, relating them logically with principles listed
- Inductive—examining and organizing facts analytically for logical inference of principles

Although chronological order is most often used for project reports, reports of any substantial size are generally broken down into a number of sections and each section has its own organization, according to need. However, some clients have their own, standard formats, and you may be asked to follow those. But even if the client does not have a preferred format, it is a good policy to describe the format you propose and ask for approval of it. The following is a detailed explanation of a recommended and typical 6-part format:

1. *Background information.* If this is a final or only report to be submitted, this first section would be a recapitulation of the objective of the project, general strategy, principal functions, and other data which would bring the reader up to speed. But if this is merely one of a series of progress reports, the introduction need merely furnish a brief transition from the prior progress report and introduce the general objective of this just-expired reporting period's effort.

2. *Narrative.* A narrative recounting of all events of the reporting period, usually in chronological order. Linkages to or transitions from the prior report may be included in introducing the various elements of the reporting period's efforts.

3. *Problems encountered.* This should include complete accounts of the problems and how they were overcome or plans for solving them next month. Usually includes follow-up report on projections made in prior report.

4. *Examination of results.* In projects such as studies and surveys, data collected must be presented in full detail, discussed, and analyzed. This is generally syllogistic, may involve mathematical presentations, must show methodology of analysis and rationale for using methodology chosen, and present results such as logical conclusions to be drawn for future investigation.

5. *Plans for next month.* Links from this report, problems anticipated and how they will be handled, and anticipated next month's achievements. Must be specific about next month's goals.

6. As an alternative to (5), if this is a final report, this section will probably be one of extending examination of results on a total-project basis and extending conclusions drawn in (4) to final recommendations.

The nature and objectives of each section dictates how the information in it must be organized and presented. Raw data, for example, may be presented in a straight chronological narrative, but when data are to be examined and analyzed, they must be arrayed, grouped, and processed to facilitate manipulations and the detection of correlations and other relationships. Hence the data may themselves dictate the organization necessary to achieve the goals of the report. In fact, it may be necessary to try several different organizations and reorganizations of the data to see which works best.

Syllogistic presentations are inescapable. The client wishes to know how you reached conclusions and on what basis you offer your recommendations. Where you must explain a premise or principle upon which you base some of your work, it may be necessary to make an excursion, which will require a presentation from-the-general-to-the-particular or even a reverse-chronology of effect-cause to trace something back to its source or origin.

Project reports tend to be speculative. Most have sections which ought to be confined strictly to factual reporting, while in other sections you may speculate—with syllogistic logic—on the meaning of the facts presented. Even here it is necessary to be objective in tone and method, and offer no conclusions, recommendations, or even general opinions for which you cannot demonstrate a logical chain of reasoning supported by facts. That is vital to the overall credibility of your report, and you must preserve that credibility. Once lost, it is difficult to regain.

One common error made by consultants is the assumption that his or her professional image and reputation are so impressive that clients must accept anything he or she says on his or her authority alone. Some clients will accept your pronouncements as self-evident fact or even wisdom. But it is hazardous to depend on this: You can never be sure that any given client is trusting enough to accept all your counsel without question or that your counsel will always prove wise. An inflated self-image can be your undoing.

It is not necessary to risk your reputation and image. It is quite easy to avoid the risk by qualifying your advice, especially when it is called for and delivered spontaneously under conditions of urgency, such as when a client calls in obvious distress, demanding an immediate judgment. Explain your rationale, why you advocate whatever you do, often pointing out that under the circumstances you have not had the opportunity to ponder the problem at length nor to consult any of your sources of information.

For example, when a client called me from the opposite coast to ask my help with the Postal Service which had denied him a second-class mailing permit for his newsletter and invited him to appeal, I probed the problem with questions for a bit and then ventured an opinion, but asked him to do nothing until I had time to do some checking to verify my spontaneous opinion. I was rather sure I knew what the problem was, but I played safe by speaking to a Postal Service official, after reviewing relevant regulations, and then offered my client final advice on how to straighten the matter out and get his permit. Had he acted on my early advice, he would have accepted my judgment without question and may have failed to get his permit, and I would have lost him as a client. Nothing was lost by asking him to wait a few days while I validated my spontaneous opinion, and I reduced the risk of looking foolish and incompetent.

To preserve your reputation, make it a practice to think syllogistically—logically—whenever you are speaking or writing "for the record" or in formal counsel to a client. Remember that few things are entirely predictable and no one is infallible. Report objectively, and avoid getting into a position where you may have to eat your words and lose face. For example, if a client asks me whether a federal contracting official will always bow to pressure from the General Accounting Office to allow protesters enough time to write a formal proposal, I can only answer that they should do so and that I have succeeded in persuading them to do so in the past, but I cannot guarantee that they will always do so. I qualify my answer because I truly cannot guarantee that others will always do what they are supposed to do. If you run into an exception to the rule—a contracting official who defies the General Accounting Office—your credibility is undamaged because you were not dogmatic or cryptic about your advice.

This runs counter to the principles and practices of some consultants who believe that they must always hold their cards very closely and appear to be immutably wise or even omniscient. Some fear that if they are open, the client will learn too much and not be dependent on them in the future. They see this policy as self-preservation. For that reason, many professionals develop and guard a jargon all their own, one almost indecipherable to those outside the profession.

Why does the insurance industry use the word premium to mean payment? Why do accountants say you are on a cash basis when you bill clients and expect to wait 30 or more days to get paid? And why does cost of sales mean, to an accountant, total cost of production, rather than cost of getting the order?

Consultants are no less guilty. I befuddled one correspondent by using the term *sign off* to mean approve. My client, thinking of radio broadcast jargon, interpreted the term to mean say good night and was irate with me for confusing him.

It is wise to avoid the use of jargon when communicating with anyone outside your industry, whether client or only prospective client, unless you take the time to explain or interpret the jargon carefully.

I reject the idea of preventing clients from learning what I know or how I achieve my results. I reject the idea of making them dependent on me. I could not admit, even to myself, being so insecure or fearful that I need secrecy. I am eager to reveal what I know to my clients and I am entirely open with them. I turn this to my advantage by conducting many training seminars in government marketing and proposal writing, earning highly satisfactory fees for doing so!

Aside from that practical consideration, this is an ethical question too: Is not the client, who is paying you the fees you ask, entitled to know what you are doing and how you are doing it? I think so, although others think otherwise. And aside from the fact that training seminars may constitute a substantial element of your practice and income, the basic fear that you may be giving away too much has little basis, in my view. Clients may be interested in learning something of your methodology and the rationale for it, but few want to do the work themselves. Quite the contrary, most want to call you back again if your work proves effective, and so be able to regard you as a valuable resource. Clients may interpret evasions and other efforts to avoid disclosure as mistrust on your part, and that is infectious: It may lead the client to become mistrustful of you.

This adds up to the need for writing your reports and other presentations carefully and with clear communication intended. It is more than likely that because you are an individual, probably a one-person enterprise, you will not have an editor on staff to review and edit your writing. But you can train yourself to edit your own writing, as professional writers do. It is a writer's article of faith that all good writing is rewriting and that with only rare exceptions, your first draft is greatly improved by rewriting. Many professional writers rewrite repeatedly to produce a half-dozen or more drafts before deciding that they have achieved a final draft. You must review your first draft, edit it, and rewrite it at least once.

Examine everything you have written in your first draft by studying your draft for ambiguities: Can anything you've said be interpreted to mean anything other than what you intended? Are any of your words special terms or jargon? If so, have you made provision to explain them?

One tip: Long sentences and "big words" are not as much the problem as are unusual words, words the average person is not likely to know. I once created a serious problem in communication by using the word *epitome* in the draft of a manual. To my surprise, almost everyone involved in a dispute that arose concerning my use of this word insisted that they understood the word and that I had misused it. There were many red faces when we were forced to turn to the dictionary to resolve the matter. I had to discard this word, not because it was the wrong word to use—it was exactly right—but because readers would probably misunderstand what I had written, as so many fellow writers and editors had!

Level of Detail

The matter of disclosure raises the question of how detailed your reports should be. Unless the client has specified a level of detail, what you reveal in your reports is dictated by your own judgment. Here are several factors to consider:

■ *Objective of the project.* If the objective of the project is a physical product such as a manual, computer program, or inventory system, it is usually necessary only to report on problems and progress towards the goal. If the project is aimed at making a study, carrying out a survey, or devising some new methodology that the client is to use, it is likely that the client will feel a need to have a great deal of detail formally documented and discussed.

- *Technical level.* If the client is a specialist in the same field as you, he or she will probably want technical data, but will usually not require painstaking explanations and interpretations of the data. You can use the special idiom and shorthand that the special jargon of your field affords you. Beware, however, of using any ultra-special jargon. An electronics engineer specializing in communications equipment may use technical jargon that is cryptic to an electronics engineer specializing in test equipment or missile guidance systems. For example, *byte* has a different meaning now, as used in personal computer technology, than it did when I first encountered it at IBM in upstate New York a long time ago.

- *Objective of the report.* Some reports are routine requirements and are hardly glanced at, except to verify that they have been rendered and to see if there is anything unusual or special about them. But some reports are themselves the objective of the project and constitute the end-products. For example, I was once awarded a contract to carry out a swift study for an official who needed the report to support and validate his budget request. In another case, the report incorporated a model for a training program evaluation, and that model was the objective of and justification for the project.

The Report May Be an Opportunity

A report can represent opportunity to generate new business. A government executive with whom I had done business approached me once about an idea he had. He was sure that one of the major operations carried out by his agency could be done far less expensively by contracting the work out to a private firm such as the one that employed me. His idea was to have me write an unsolicited proposal, which he believed he could get approved as the basis for a contract award.

I found the notion appealing, inasmuch as such a contract would have been for a national network supplying some $15 million worth of auto parts annually to the agency's many vehicle maintenance facilities, and we spent a day together visiting some of those facilities and getting some first-hand information. I then returned to my own office to study the matter.

I soon realized that the proposal would require extensive research, thus involving a large effort and great cost, with no guarantees that a contract would result.

This risk was too great, and I so advised the official. I suggested a reasonable alternative: If he awarded us a small study contract, the resulting report would furnish him all the data he needed to publish a comprehensive statement of work and invite proposals from everyone, including my own firm. That approach won many small contracts for us in the past.

This is quite proper, although a contractor who does such a study for a fee—under contract, that is—may be disqualified completely from bidding, but using consultants in procurement is not unprecedented. Many clients, especially government agencies, retain consultants to assist them in soliciting proposals and even in evaluating proposals and selecting winners.

This kind of opportunity for new, expanded, or follow-on business may arise at the initiative of clients, but arises more often from the initiative of the enterprising consultant who is always alert for opportunities. Writing a report and reviewing the situation overall, if you do so thoughtfully, ought to be a nearly ideal situation for searching out opportunities for follow-on contracts, for by this time you have had the opportunity to become thoroughly familiar with the client's needs and problems.

Report writing is therefore often a marketing opportunity. If you refer to the final item, item 6, of the suggested report format, you will note that in the case of a final report there is frequent opportunity to make recommendations as the final element. Where that is a logical and reasonable final step in the report, it is also the perfect opportunity to seek additional work from the client. You should have been alert from the beginning to opportunities for follow-on contracts, and the final element in your report is the place to begin selling it. (At the same time, when carrying out a project for a department or division in a large organization, don't miss the opportunity to get acquainted with other potential clients in other departments or divisions of the organizations.)

VERBAL REPORTS AND PRESENTATIONS

In the course of many consulting contracts, you will make frequent, informal verbal reports, reports that are actually dialogues, in which the client asks questions and makes observations. This is, in fact, often a crucially important element in achieving client satisfaction. However, it is also not at all uncommon for clients to request formal verbal reports and presentations, usually to an assembled group. Here, too, it is likely that you will be asked questions and expected to engage in dialogue after you have made a formal presentation.

These questions asked by listeners may be sincere inquiries, efforts to gain greater understanding or to make contributions to the project. But they may also be ploys by individuals, especially those who are relatively low-level staff, to gain attention and demonstrate their alertness, intelligence, perceptiveness, and many other admirable traits to the senior executives in attendance. Many sitting in on presentations feel the need to express themselves for such reasons.

That's not all of it. Sometimes there are those present who simply resent the introduction of consultants, inferring that the use of consultants impugns their own competence and credentials. Such individuals may pose antagonistic questions.

You must therefore expect an audience that may be friendly and sympathetic, but also may be antagonistic and predatory. Be prepared to keep your sense of humor and pretend that you do not perceive the barbs in some of the questions. You can deflect those easily with good humor and even sense of humor.

I once undertook to develop, for the Postal Service Training and Development Institute, a model evaluation system that was to measure training transfer: a qualitative and quantitative measure of actual improvements in job performance resulting directly from training programs. This was pioneering: No one had made a serious attempt before to do this. Perhaps the training professionals were reluctant to test their theories on the anvil of practical results, but in any case it had not been done before. Moreover, I had been cautioned by those professionals reputed to be experts in the field that it was an impossible task. Training and education professionals in my own organization had used dogmatic assertions to dissuade me from even attempting the project. But "can't be done" are "fighting words" to me; I happen to think that the word *impossible* ought to be banished from the language! In any case, I persisted and produced what I thought to be a reasonably respectable first effort to do something about this impossible task—to surmount what I sincerely believe to be a barrier of fear.

One thing I did not know was that there had been internal dissension in the organization: The Ph.D. assigned by the Postal Service to monitor the contract was one of those opposed to the effort because she happened to agree that it was impossible to make such measures.

The group of about 20 professional training and education specialists that I was forced to face were not all hostile, although several obviously were, but most of them were at least skeptical. They tended to believe the dogma about the difficulty of actually measuring training transfer and showed no reluctance to attack the model: As a first effort, the model had to be based largely on arbitrary premises, and so it was vulnerable to assaults. Still, we disarmed the critics largely by our smiling agreement with their skepticism and our frank admission that we had a Model T here, on which a great deal of improvement had yet to be developed and even that not possible until extensive testing and field tryouts had taken place. They had been prepared for pitched battles, for our arguments in defense of turf, not for complete understanding of their skepticism. At the same time, we—my own staff and I—could offer respectable foundations for our premises and projections, while we were also able to make them understand that our own accomplishment represented to all of us only the first step of a long journey. We made it abundantly clear that we had no illusions about this.

Interestingly enough, our sub-rosa champion, who was the driving force behind the project, was the head of the agency. Still, it would have been quite impolitic for him to have subdued critics by sheer authority of his position. It seemed obvious to me, therefore, that he asked for the unprecedented large-scale presentation to give all of us—the consultant-developer and the staff critics—our day in court. I felt certain that he had his fingers crossed in hope that we could defend our work adequately and silence the critics.

That raises an important point. As a consultant you owe allegiance to the organization overall, in one sense, but you owe special allegiance to the individual who has been responsible for retaining you and who is, in a very real sense your true client. In making reports and presentations, you are often really representing that individual and his or her own interests.

"Yes, but—" is an effective argument when you are meeting opposition because it is not a challenge to the other party. You cannot win arguments with clients because to win arguments is to lose clients. The more the other party defends an opinion, the more bitterly he or she resents any effort to rebut or discredit that position. Logic is not effective against passion. If it is necessary to resist a client's will—and only absolute necessity should lead to such resistance—you must offer only passive resistance and as much agreement on major issues as possible.

An interviewer once asked me if I could write a number in Boolean algebra. To have guffawed at this or even to have said something like "Boolean algebra deals with logic, not with numbers," would have embarrassed the other. Instead, playing dumb and saying, "I'm afraid I don't know how to do that, but I can write you the Boolean equation for any logic circuit," saved the day. He knew immediately that he had made a gross error—he obviously had not more than a vague idea of what Boolean algebra is—but since I gave no hint that I recognized his faux pas he was not distressed and the situation was thus not polarized. He merely shrugged, and we went on.

Preparation

Some people are fortunate enough to be able to speak well spontaneously with little rehearsal, but even they must prepare. Smoothly professional presentations are rarely spontaneous. While the appearance of spontaneity is a desirable trait in a presentation, it is an illusion resulting from careful preparation. This does not mean that you should memorize a speech; only a polished and experienced actor can make a memorized speech appear to be spontaneous. Instead, prepare to speak by knowing your subject thoroughly. Plan an organized sequence of information and arm yourself with a guide in the form of an outline or set of notes. (I prefer an outline, in classic outline format on one or more sheets of paper, but many prefer notes on a series of cards.)

The Importance of Visual Aids

Visual aids are helpful in even brief presentations for several reasons: They help your audience grasp the information quickly. They provide a change of pace and add interest for the audience. They lessen the reliance on your words alone and transfer attention from you to the visuals. They thus relieve you of much of the stress.

The question of what kinds of visual aids are most effective is controversial. You have, many possibilities: chalkboards, flip charts, posters, transparencies, slides, videocassettes, filmstrips, and movies. Since, as an independent consultant you are not normally going to undertake massive projects, you are not likely to go to the expense of preparing movies or even sets of slides. However, you may be able to use off-the-shelf films, videotapes, and slides; there are many large libraries of such materials, and it is often possible to rent such visuals or even borrow them without charge.

On the other hand, chalkboards, flip charts, and posters, and freehand illustration are usually quite acceptable for all but the most formal presentations. But there is today another resource quite appropriate to this need: the personal computer.

Computer Graphics and Desktop Publishing Programs

Desktop Publishing has come a long way in a short time, as have virtually all functions that you can carry out with modern computers. The great popularity and rapid proliferation of personal computers with large memory and storage capacities has made it possible to turn out many graphic aids in your own office. Too, there are a great many collections of clip art you can use in your computer to turn out graphic aids.

Handouts

Handouts—information in physical form, usually printed—are still another aid in presentations. Some presenters like to hand out such material piece by piece, throughout the presentation, while others hand out the entire package at the beginning. Most of this can be computer generated.

You can use handouts in addition to or in place of visuals such as posters and flip charts, since the effect is similar: Everyone can see graphically what is being discussed or referred to. In some cases, the handout is the most practical solution because the information is too voluminous for a poster or chalkboard presentation. Handouts offer another advantage: The attendees do not have to rely on memory or notes when they have handouts. Handouts are also useful in planting seeds for future business. Be sure that you and what you do are clearly identified somehow in your handouts and that the handouts are designed to be worth keeping for future reference!

OTHER PRODUCTS

Many consulting projects require the delivery of other products than reports and presentations. These may include manuals, instructional materials, audiovisuals, program tapes, designs, drawings, specifications, or administrative guidelines.

The common hazard of such requirements is that of disputes resulting from the failure to have clear understanding and agreement between you and your client when entering into the project. This problem has been mentioned before, especially with regard to proposal preparation—but it is such a common and serious hazard that it is worth mentioning again. It not only causes problems vis-à-vis the immediate project but also sours relationships and compromises both the possibility of future business with this client and sometimes your professional reputation.

The only sensible way to avoid this problem is to anticipate the probable need for an end-product and come to specific agreement on just what that end-product is to be. That means quantitative as well as qualitative definition of deliverable items. If you agree on the need for a manual as an end-product, for example, you must agree on estimates of its size, format, number and type of illustrations, content, physical specifications, and number of copies. Anything less—anything left undefined or left to chance—is an invitation to grief.

A common problem is the tendency to take what appears to be the easy way out, using vague euphemisms such as best commercial practice or good commercial quality as standards. That kind of phraseology leads to disputes and lawsuits. In a contract to produce a multimedia training system we stipulated each item to be delivered, and we specified that we would deliver camera-ready copy, a common enough phrase that is normally definitive enough.

The client was greatly upset when he inspected the end-product, the camera-ready copy. He objected loudly and unremittingly to the paste-ups and spliced corrections, totally rejecting our protestations that these were all standard practices even by the exacting standards of the military organizations. He was unmoved until I persuaded him to call on any printers he chose and have them inspect our camera-ready copy. Only when several printers assured him that the copy was completely acceptable and would produce clean printed pages did he finally yield.

This is an unusual case; admittedly, few clients are that difficult or reluctant to learn what they need to know. But not only clients can be stubbornly ignorant. In a case, where a firm was to conduct training operations on the client's premises, the firm was authorized to sell materials to their own on-site project, billing the client up to $75,000 for their own training manuals at prices "not to exceed those charged [their] most favored customer." The consultant organized a $75,000 project to develop and have manufactured such manuals, to be delivered to the on-site project, and billed the client $75,000 for the labor and related costs of producing those manuals.

The client refused to pay the bill, ruling it non-allowable under the terms of the contract. The contractor haggled and haggled, but the client was immovable on the subject, and the firm's chief was unable to understand why the item was not allowable. He thought the contract was clear enough, and even his attorney was unable to understand the client's argument.

Finally the firm brought in an expert to help. The expert spent only a few minutes studying the relevant clause in the contract.

"Here is the problem," the expert explained. "You are billing your client for R&D—labor and materials to develop this set of manuals. But the client authorized sale of off-the shelf, proprietary manuals at the best prices you offer anyone. He did not authorize the development of new, special manuals and won't pay for your R&D."

The solution was to set a retail price on the manuals, discount them properly, deliver them, and invoice the client for the books, less the discount—$75,000 worth. The client then paid the bill without a murmur!

Interestingly enough, the outside expert who came in and solved the problem did so entirely on the basis of interpreting the language of the relevant clause. He realized that the phrase identifying the maximum price to be charged could logically be applied only to proprietary manuals and so could not be interpreted to authorize R&D development of special materials.

Pyrrhic Victories

You can also win Pyrrhic victories, victories in which you emerge a victor nominally, but lose far more than you win. One consulting firm who did so charged a federal agency approximately $50,000 to develop two manuals, a student manual and an instructor's manual, for a training program. However, they failed to provide administrative guidance in organizing a program to use these manuals, and when the agency protested that the manuals were of little use without such guidance, the firm's representative merely shrugged and pointed out that they had satisfied the contract. The agency had to bring in another consultant to develop a solution to use the two manuals. The first consultant won the argument but lost the good will of the client. Ironically, the original consultant could have easily negotiated a follow-on contract or amendment to the original contract, while retaining the client's good will, but failed to perceive the opportunity to do so.

The Hazard of Completion-Percentage Reports

Some programs call for a progress-reporting device by estimating the percentage of completion each month. Theoretically, if all goes as it should, the percentage of completion should track the percentage of dollars spent. Spending proceeding at a faster pace than completion is an obvious danger signal. If a given project is scheduled for six months and $30,000, every percentage point of progress (completion) should reflect approximately $300 of the budget expended.

Unfortunately, this rarely works out. Typically, the consultant is likely to report on a six-month contract along the following lines:

Month	Percentage Completed (%)	Remaining Effort (%)
1	10	90
2	25	75
3	45	55
4	65	35
5	70	30

The trend is simply this: The consultant tends to equate time and/or labor hours—percentage of effort, that is—with percentage of completion. But the accountant finds the two, money spent and progress made, proceeding along these lines:

Month	Completion Reported (%)	Budget Spent
1	10	$4,500 (15%)
2	25	9,500 (32%)
3	45	17,000 (57%)
4	65	25,750 (89%)
5	70	28,000 (93%)

What is happening here is obvious. The consultant begins to perceive, as time goes on, that early estimates of progress were somewhat optimistic. As the scheduled delivery date grows closer the consultant begins to see just how optimistic those early estimates were. But in the meanwhile the accountant begins to scc thc fiscal disaster building up. In the early months, this does not appear to be a problem because the substantial budget expenditures are apparently balanced, at least roughly, by progress. But when the progress proves to be an illusion, it is too late to save the day.

The trap lies in trying to measure something by itself. The system is supposed to balance the budget against the progress, but it works only if progress is measured, not estimated, and measured by some objective means.

FINDING A MEASURING STICK

It is not easy to find an objective set of measures for most consulting projects. There are methods that do work, however, and in principle, the way to set up an objective measuring system is this:

- Break the entire project down into as many distinct, observable or verifiable steps as possible, trying to make them at least roughly equivalent to each other in effort or size. Let us assume, for example, that you can identify 50 such steps or elements. (Try for 50 as a minimum.)
- Assign each a pro-rated percentage value. In this case (50 steps), each represents 2 percent of progress.
- Monitor each step or element continuously (e.g., once a week).
- Score progress each month by assigning values to each step or element and adding them up, along this scale:
  —Step not begun is zero percentage.
  —Step begun but not completed is one percent.
  —Step completed is 2 percent.

These arbitrary measures—zero, 1, or 2 percent—will tend to average each other out, very much along the lines of a series of approximations. The more elements you have the greater the accuracy will be. But even if the accuracy is less than perfect, it is far, far better than the almost pure guesswork that those typical percentage-completion methods involve, for it is based on measurement, not estimating, once the measures arc established.

Fees and Collections

We pay for our education, especially the practical one. Here are just a few ways to avoid that special consultant's hazard of being tricked or duped into working for nothing.

—*Herman Holtz*

CASH FLOW IS A PROBLEM FOR EVERYONE

I make it a practice, as a result of costly early experience, to require one-third of my total estimated fee in advance, another one-third at some identified and agreed-upon midpoint, and the final one-third upon final delivery and acceptance. Most businesses doing custom work—printing, for example—follow the practice of requiring a substantial retainer or deposit when accepting an assignment. The main reason is ensuring payment, but it is also an effective way to qualify a prospect and a great aid to your cash flow. This is a must when dealing with clients who are small and unknown. If you do business with the government or large and well-known corporations such as IBM and General Motors, their purchase order or letter of agreement is security enough, but often even these large corporations will agree to provide a retainer.

The cash-flow problem affects even large organizations, but is especially painful for independent entrepreneurs. Moreover, if you charge expenses to clients without markup, you allow cost-free use of your money. If you try to overcome the cash flow problem by discounting your paper—borrowing against your receivables—you will find that this is not easy to do in practice. Banks are reluctant to lend to service businesses because service businesses usually have few tangible assets to act as collateral.

Learning that you have been providing free services is an unpleasant surprise. If you are unwary, you may not realize at first that some who appear to be serious prospects as clients will waste huge quantities of your time in discussions during which they are busily milking you for information, but never retain you. They pick your brains, manipulating you into free consultation, at least for advice and information. You may even be unwittingly encouraging them to do this by being all too eager to cooperate in furnishing up-front information free of charge. But the other case is even more serious. Here is a typical scenario:

> You visit the client in a well-furnished office suite in a modern building. Secretaries and others are busily engaged in tasks in the reception area and other offices in the suite. You are favorably impressed with the businesslike atmosphere of what appears to be a successful company.
>
> The well-dressed, affable client greets you cordially, invites you to sit in a comfortable chair, while he offers you coffee and takes an adjoining chair. He smiles, calls you by first name tentatively—"George—may I call you George?"—assumes your consent and goes on: "We have lots of work here, and I can send a lot of business your way." And he is off on a discourse of what marvelous things await you as a result of the good fortune of meeting him.
>
> Once you have reviewed the requirement, you estimate the probable size of the fee you will require, and you mention it as tactfully as you can, although the new client has not asked you about the cost. (This is itself an unwelcome omen.) You are encouraged but because you've been warned you ask, somewhat reluctantly—you don't want to offend this new client—about a retainer. "Sure thing," you're assured, "no problem. Take a few days for the paper work, of course. But in the meanwhile we have to get started on this right away."

Maybe you will get that promised retainer. And maybe you will not. Maybe you will get evasions, excuses, and stalls until it dawns on you that you really have absolutely no assurance that this client can or will pay the bill after you have done the work. In fact, it may be that the client owns absolutely nothing in the office except his briefcase. (I have known substantial office suites to be furnished entirely with rented furniture, fixtures, and equipment.) If you sued and won a judgment, you couldn't collect your money. You may make the unpleasant discovery that it is much easier to win in court than to collect what you won.

WARNING FLAGS

Trouble overtakes the unwary. But how can you be wary unless you know what to be wary of? Here are some signs that should alert you:

Client Indifference to Cost

It is unnatural for any buyer under any circumstances to be indifferent to cost. The client who asks you what your services are going to cost is revealing a serious interest in and probable contemplation of retaining you. Even if the client is asking your price to compare the cost with that of competitors it still reflects acceptance of you technically and as one of the prospective consultants worthy of serious consideration. Most clients do not waste time discussing costs with a consultant who is unacceptable to them.

The client who never asks the cost is usually uninterested, and you can adjust your actions accordingly. However, if you run into the paradox of a client who shows definite desire to retain you but is uninterested in the costs, something is very wrong. I would be alarmed by that. Clients who agree too readily to my terms and do not even attempt to negotiate alarm me. Perhaps they do not worry about my charges because they have no intention of paying me. One example:

> A prospective client called me from California to discuss his need. We chatted a bit and I suggested he send me some of his material by mail so I could discuss his need more intelligently. He did so, I studied it, and we talked again. He displayed great eagerness to get on with the job, and I waited with a growing sense of unease for him to raise the question of cost. (Good sales technique dictates waiting for the prospect to raise the question.) When he did not, I raised it, and he assured me that cost was not an object; he would pay whatever was necessary.
>
> That convinced me that we would not do business. But I played out the hand: I stipulated a retainer I would require before going further.
>
> I never heard from the gentleman again, which did not surprise me at all.

Beware the prospect who professes no interest in cost. Be sure to demand a substantial retainer before proceeding with such a client.

Handshake Contracts

A written contract is not a guarantee, nor is the purpose of a written contract to guarantee anything. Contracts are disputed in courts every day, a certain indicator that they guarantee nothing. The sole reason for a contract is to submit the agreement to writing in the hope that this will help you to avoid disputes later as to what you and your client actually agreed to.

If either you or your client is not acting in good faith—does not mean to live up to what you agreed on verbally—no written contract is worth signing, and you should not be doing business together.

That does not mean that you should not have a written agreement. Many of us learn the hard way that a lengthy contract in Latin legalese is likely to alarm a client and end effort to close a sale, but a simple letter agreement is an adequate contract. It commits your agreement to writing and relieves you of relying on your memory if you have disputes later on.

The actual signing of such a simple letter agreement is less important to me than is the willingness of the client to sign. That indicates the client's intent and sincerity. The client who balks at signing a simple letter agreement issues a warning, and I would then insist absolutely on a substantial retainer if, indeed, I agreed to continue the relationship at all. (The prognosis for the relationship is not encouraging in such a case.) But that isn't all of it: The letter of agreement or confirmation is a useful marketing tool in many situations that might be difficult to handle otherwise.

Handshake contracts can be treacherous. My suspicions are aroused by the hearty and bluff prospective client who assures me that his word is his bond and that all we need between us is a handshake to seal our agreement. I am especially put on guard by the prospect who says, "Trust me." Those are two words that signal danger. When I have allowed clients to overcome my fears and persuade me to vary my policies I have usually come to regret it.

Verbal contracts are *not* worth the paper they are not written on. There are exceptions. I do not always insist on a written agreement. There are old clients with whom you've done business in the past, or situations where you have good reason to have no fears—where a handshake agreement is entirely acceptable. In fact I generally ask the client whether he or she will issue me a purchase order or prefers a letter of agreement. However, even this is not necessary in many cases. Large organizations such as many of those with whom I have done business—the Salvation Army, Control Data Corporation, federal agencies, Dun & Bradstreet, H&R Block, and many others—usually issue purchase orders or letters of confirmation as a matter of course. It is the smaller organizations with whom you have to raise the point specifically. But the written agreement is useful in another way, especially in those sticky situations just described.

When you find a client who shows no interest in the cost side of the problem, raising the question of a written agreement helps you tactfully introduce the question of advance payment as a retainer, midpoint payments, and other matters. Perhaps the individual with whom you are talking is not truly authorized to commit the organization. Asking for a purchase order or letter brings that matter to a head and resolves it quickly.

Choosing a Midpoint?

If you choose to try to arrange a one-third advance retainer and one-third midpoint payment, you must find some means for defining or identifying a nominal midpoint. That is not always easy to do, important although it is. In my own case, I try to set it at the point when I have completed the rough draft of a proposal and gotten the client's agreement that it is a good draft.

That leaves me with some leverage: The client still needs me and my services to complete the job properly, and he has too much invested in me at this point to make it a good risk to try to finish the job without my services. It is important to set that midpoint, the point at which you are to be paid a second one-third of the total estimated fee, with that consideration in mind: It should be a point at which you have reached a significant milestone and yet a point at which the client still needs you and your services to get the job finished properly. If you succeed in doing this, you are protected for at least two-thirds of your total fee.

If you have difficulty finding a midpoint, try identifying a series of milestones or objectives. Then try to select one that comes close to these criteria:

- It occurs well after the beginning and before the end of the project in time. (It is a midpoint in a general, not literal sense.)
- It represents a major step toward final achievement of the main goal of the assignment.
- It leaves you with adequate leverage—the client has a substantial investment in the project, still needs you to finish the project.

Overtime

Some consultants charge a flat daily rate and do not count the hours. Others do count the hours and charge premium overtime rates when they work more than eight hours in a day or on weekends and holidays. Whichever you do, you should have a clear understanding with the client about it, and any written agreement between you ought to note this carefully.

Progress Payments

For some types of assignment division of the payments into thirds is not practicable. This is the case, for example, when you are retained on a long-term contract or one of indefinite duration, such as when you are virtually a contract employee, working on the client's premises.

That is not the only situation where the assignment may run into many months or even into several years. It is impossible to estimate the total cost or to fix a midpoint in these cases, and you could hardly wait for many months to collect your fees. In such situations, you must arrange to be given progress payments regularly, at least every month, although weekly or biweekly payments are more usual in such cases.

CREDIT CARD CONVENIENCE—AND INCONVENIENCE

We have become accustomed to using credit cards of many kinds for our convenience in purchasing. With a Visa or MasterCard in your purse or wallet, you don't need to carry much cash or a check book: You can almost always use your bank credit card. (I have used my own for major purchases, in fact.) Most merchants—retailers, restaurants, motels, and other establishments, large and small, accept them without hesitation and without the occasional hassle that you must undergo to have your personal check accepted.

Not all cards are true credit cards. Visa and MasterCard are bank cards and are true credit cards: They give you a line of credit and you can pay back on a schedule. Some others (e.g., American Express) are charge cards and charges against them must be settled in full each month.

Both kinds of cards are extremely convenient for you and the seller when you are buying something. It's a simple transaction for the merchant, simply depositing the credit card slip as cash. The account is credited immediately; with no waiting to clear, as in the case of checks.

On an average, most retailers consummate from about 30 to 70 percent of their sales via credit cards, and in some businesses (e.g., the hospitality enterprises), the percentage approaches 100.

The credit card business has changed drastically over the years. It has grown to many billions each year, is almost totally electronic in its processing today, and does not require your signature, thus enabling the expansion of credit-card buying by mail, telephone, and computer.

As an independent consultant, you may or may not have need to accommodate your clients with credit card convenience. If your work is all on substantial projects for larger companies and corporations, it is not likely that any client will ask you to charge the work to a credit card. On the other hand, if you sell your services to private individuals, sell products (books, tapes, newsletters, seminars, etc.), or sell by mail, it is probable that your clients are going to want you to charge their credit cards for payment. And that is where you run into trouble. Few banks will approve merchant status for home-based, one-person, or small and independent mail-order businesses. Small business owners report various problems and various results in winning merchant status for credit card transactions. Many report being forced to buy expensive equipment—a terminal for entering credit-card information and getting approval for the transaction. Others report lengthy delays, far beyond original promises, in getting approval and permission to start processing credit card orders.

There are individuals who promise to get merchant status for you, for a fee. Often, that individual is a broker who is floundering trying to find a bank who will accept his client.

On one occasion, when I had moved my office from a downtown Washington, DC, office building to my own home in Maryland, I gave up my credit-card setup because it would have been inconvenient to bank in downtown Washington when my office was in Maryland. (That was before electronic banking and before changes in the banking laws.) Since I continued to get orders with credit-card charges, I asked a friend in Georgia to help me. He agreed. I sent him my charge orders, and he processed the orders for me through his own system and sent me his own check. This is a service you may wish to turn to, if processing credit-card orders is a problem for you. There are services who will handle your credit-card orders for a fee.

There are banks who will approve you for merchant status if you persist. (One consultant told me that he got his merchant status 15 minutes after he stamped his foot.) Some banks may wish you to post a collateral account, perhaps a CD, to serve as a security bond. For the average independent consultant, probably $1,000 will usually serve to satisfy the bank's uneasiness.

If you prefer to turn to some service to help you, it will cost you a fee of some sort. Often that includes buying a terminal for entering your credit card information and getting an approval of the charge. That is an expensive investment, and an unnecessary one, I have been assured by specialists in credit card operations. There are many banks who will grant merchant status to entrepreneurs who may not be approved by other, more conservative banks.

Credit card merchant status is not without its problems, such as charge-backs, when a client contests a charge and the bank withholds payment to you, pending settlement of the claim. However, if you do business by mail and telephone and sell commodities of any sort, it will cost you sales and client good will to be without merchant status.

COLLECTIONS

If it is your good fortune to do business always with clients blessed with AAA credit ratings you may never have a collection problem, although even those with AAA credit ratings can cause you much grief by being agonizingly slow in paying their bills. I have been the victim of well-known large corporations whose bill-paying habits make even the federal government appear to be a fast payer. Fortunately, there are a few things you can do that usually help speed the process.

Large organizations become musclebound for a variety of reasons, including ponderous paperwork and archaic procedures. Those procedures grow up over many layers of management, and the procedures in a large organization tend to become enormously detailed and bureaucratic. But that is not the entire problem. Another is the indifference of workers who become bureaucratic in any large organization. Unfortunately, in bureaucracy, the means is all-important, and the end must often be sacrificed to the means. Still another bureaucratic problem is that only those at the highest levels may exercise initiative. If the procedure requires three copies of your invoice, but you have supplied only two, the invoice may never move from the in-basket to a payment schedule. Don't expect the clerk to make a copy or to call you; such things happen only rarely. (I once waited eight months for a bill to be paid because of such a problem, unaware that it had not been paid. It would probably have never been paid had I not suddenly discovered the unpaid invoice in our files.)

If you are doing business with a large organization, ask in advance exactly what you must do to get paid and follow the procedure. If at all possible—and it usually is—personally hand your invoice over to whomever you are dealing. By knowing how the system works you can track down problems of nonpayment much more rapidly than you can when you are groping blindly. In any case, here is the typical series of steps when you are having trouble getting paid, including those unfortunate cases where you must start getting tough with a client who refuses to pay:

1. Normal billing: submittal of your regular invoice.
2. Statement of money due issued at regular interval, usually first or fifteenth day of the month.
3. Courteous form collection letter requesting payment.
4. More insistent, less diplomatic letter.
5. Telephone inquiry, courteous but firm.

6. Severe letter, stipulating firm action, such as legal measures or collection agency, if bill is not paid soon.

7. Matter turned over to collection agency or lawyer.

You don't want to come to these latter situations, although if the client is resistant to paying, you've nothing to lose, and you don't want to do business again with such a client. My experience has been that there are few such problems when you exercise the precautions suggested here. Still, you can never tell what will happen, even then. You may be the victim of another kind of depredation, such as this:

A client came to my office and retained me to prepare a sales brochure for him. We agreed on a price of $600, and he paid me $300 in advance as a retainer. I prepared several roughs, as I do in such assignments, and we reviewed them together, coming to agreement on which should be developed to its final stage. Shortly after that the client called me and advised me that he had sold his business and wanted to abort the brochure effort. I agreed reluctantly to settle for the money already paid, although I had already done about three-quarters of the work. But the client demanded a refund of the advance retainer! When I refused, he sued me in small claims court. The case lasted about 10 minutes, the judge advising the gentleman that he was lucky to get off for one-half the total fee, under the circumstances. (He, not I, had breached the contract.) Still, the whole affair cost me most of a day sitting in the courtroom waiting for my case to be called, so I was a loser in the whole affair after all, despite being the victor in the case.

It is a good general rule to avoid all litigation, and even all legal expedients. Even when it is you doing the collecting, you may win a limited victory. If you turn the matter over to a collection agency or retain a lawyer and sue, it is going to cost you one-third or more of whatever is collected for you, and often that is less than the full amount. And in civil court, the court cannot and will not try to collect for you, even when you win. The court awards you a judgment, a hunting license.

Judgments

When you sue and a judge or jury finds for you—enters judgment for you against the defendant—it does not mean that the defendant will then pay you the money you have won. You have won a legal battle, but you have not yet won the war. Probably a well-established firm will pay at that point, but you may be up against a defendant who will refuse to pay willingly even then, and may think that he or she is judgment proof. That means that the defendant thinks he has his assets so well hidden or protected by legal dodges that you will not be able to use that judgment to seize the funds or property of the defendant. (I have reluctantly allowed some debts to go uncollected because I knew that I could win a judgment but would be most unlikely to be able to satisfy it, and in some cases I settled for far less than the total amount for the same reason.) It is certainly far better to take any steps possible to minimize the probability of having collection problems.

Credit Ratings

You can subscribe to a credit rating service and get a rating on any client with whom you wish to do business. There are two problems with that: You are likely to find that some of your clients or prospective clients have no ratings established. But you may find also that a client who enjoys a good credit rating is a slow or reluctant payer of bills or one who makes a practice of contesting every bill—especially one for services—and regularly succeeds in bullying vendors into settling for less than the full amount. Again, getting a retainer in advance is a far better credit rating than any reported by any agency or bureau.

Mechanic's Lien

In general, the law provides that a mechanic (using that term rather loosely), may hold your property that he has repaired pending payment of your bill. If you fail or refuse to pay, he may sell your property to satisfy the bill.

You could conceivably be in the position of the mechanic, with the client's property (e.g., a computer program you have been working on) in your possession. This does not give you the right to seize a client's property, however, or to reclaim property that you have returned to the client. You need to consult a lawyer in the specific case.

COLLECTING FROM GOVERNMENT CLIENTS

A common complaint about doing business with government agencies is that the government takes too long to pay its bills. That complaint has finally resulted in legislation designed to compel federal agencies to pay more promptly. How well it has succeeded in doing that is questionable, for the typical delays in being paid by government agencies are not the type of ills corrected by legislation.

The Prompt Payment Act has helped a bit, but the delays are almost invariably the result of bureaucracy. However, there are other measures that produce results. I was able to get reasonably prompt payment almost always because I took direct action when I was not paid in 20 to 30 days. All it normally takes is follow-up, telephone calls in which I insist on learning where my invoice is at the moment and why it has not been processed for payment. I have invariably found bureaucratic sloth: My invoice is still gathering dust in someone's in-basket because they wanted my invoice in triplicate or quadruplicate, rather than in duplicate but were too lazy or indifferent to make copies in their own offices, they have lost the invoice somewhere in the chain, there was some petty detail out of order, and so on. A little outrage, sometimes a duplicate invoice sent directly to some individual, or other action usually produces results within days.

The cure for the disease is this: (1) Ask what the payment procedure is—who is in the chain of approval and what are the steps before the check is cut, what information must be included in the invoice, how many copies of your invoice are required, how long should the process take normally, and so on; (2) Go back to the individuals in that chain if you do not get your check within that normal processing time and ask blunt questions. This usually produces results. It has for me, almost without exception. And in those exceptional cases, I still managed to get paid without more than an extra couple of weeks delay. Once, I was required to submit two additional copies of my invoice, and the government insisted then on paying me three times! In the other case, I had to finally write a letter of complaint to the agency head, whereupon I was finally paid.

One of the advantages of dealing with government agencies is the objectivity of the government as a client. You can be very blunt, indeed, when pursuing something such as overdue payment and not offend anyone. On the contrary, the government client recognizes your right to be paid on schedule and is likely to be apologetic about delay. The largest advantage to you is the statutory protection and preference you can enjoy, especially as a small business. For one thing, the law says clearly that as a small business you are entitled to receive progress payments, whereas a large company might be expected to wait until the project is completed before submitting a bill. It is common practice on ongoing contracts to submit your invoices each month, and in most cases contracting officers will accept and process invoices from small businesses as frequently as every other week. So there is no reason to be at all bashful about demanding payment without delay, nor need you be hesitant about your need for progress payments.

Consultant Skills You Need: Making Presentations

An inherent anomaly of consulting is that clients want your services as a specialist, and yet, as an independent practitioner, you must rely on yourself for all the ancillary skills and functions, which then requires you to be a generalist!

—Herman Holtz

CONSULTING: BUSINESS OR PROFESSION?

We who are independent consultants must face the reality that consulting is a business. We provide professional services to clients, but we also handle business functions—marketing, accounting, invoicing, management, and administration. But the complexities of independent consulting go beyond that.

Three sets of skills are necessary: technical, managerial/administrative, and entrepreneurial. In some respects, entrepreneurial skills are the most significant. Independent consulting is an entrepreneurial adventure. Your entrepreneurial skill is going to be the principal influence and probably the decisive factor in the future of your venture.

Success as an independent consultant depends as much on your managerial/administrative skills and your entrepreneurial vision as it does on your technical/professional skill: You need the managerial/administrative skills to deliver your consulting services and to conceive, organize, and operate those ancillary functions that broaden your income base. Remember that the failure to establish and build up a range of income-producing activities is often cause of failure in independent consulting. Writing and public speaking are essential in delivering your basic consulting services, but they are also important in adding profit centers to your practice. Again and again we find enterprising independent consultants who have done this with great success, not only building successful practices but often expanding them into even

larger and more ambitious ventures. Here are just a few examples of entrepreneurial successes:

- J. Stephen Lanning, a Maryland marketing consultant, founded the popular newsletter *Consulting Opportunities Journal,* which became the
  centerpiece of his activities, including other publications and services
  for consultants.
- Dr. Jeffrey Lant, a Cambridge, Massachusetts, consultant, has written
  and published so many thick tomes on the how-to of consulting and its
  related activities as to make it astonishing that he finds time to build up
  his varied and growing Internet business ventures.
- Hubert Bermont, a Maryland book publishing consultant, now devotes
  most of his time to running his association, The American Consultants
  League, and his duties as a senior member of the faculty of The Consultant's Institute, which offers consultant training and certification by
  means of a correspondence course.
- My own consulting service expanded rapidly into seminars and writing,
  especially the latter, which now occupies most of my time as natural ex-
  tensions of and integral to my consulting service. I have, in fact, been
  compelled periodically to go to much larger computer and related resources to support my expanding writing activities.

PUBLIC SPEAKING

A great many people shrink from writing as an unpleasant and difficult task.
Even more shrink from public speaking, many in absolute fear of it. Many of
the most successful executives, and professionals are terror-stricken at the
thought of facing an audience. Even some professional speakers and performers confess to fear and nervousness every time they must mount the platform,
and they must somehow drive themselves each time to face an audience. So
you may or may not get used to it. That is, you may or may not get completely
over your fears of facing a large room full of people intent on your words, gestures, and facial expressions, although most people do eventually conquer the
fear. However, you can learn to handle things and become a good public
speaker.

THE NOTION OF BORN SPEAKERS

You may have had the notion that there are born speakers, as there are born
salespeople, born artists, and so on. If there are any, they are in rare supply;
the most successful speakers are those who have worked hard to learn to
speak well. Probably the notion of the born speaker arises from the fact that
some individuals are blessed with naturally good voices for public speaking—

strong, resonant, clear, and pleasant-sounding voices. And yet some quite successful public speakers have voices that are not at all inherently well-suited to speaking. One prominent broadcaster (Barbara Walters) who is probably best known for her ability to persuade public figures to allow her to interview them has a reedy, shrill voice and a pronounced lisp, for example. Dave Yoho, a successful professional speaker with a marvelous speaking voice, struggled to overcome his speech defects as a youngster. Stuttering has not prevented actor James Earl Jones from becoming successful. Here are a few key points:

- Anyone can learn to speak well; even natural handicaps do not prevent the determined individual from becoming successful on the platform.

- The key to overcoming fear of speaking lies in first identifying its basis. If you fear appearing foolish, take steps to ensure that you cannot appear foolish by being sure that you have something to say and are well prepared to say it—that you know your material and how you will present it. That does not mean a memorized speech. It does mean knowing your material, and you should carry cue cards or an outline listing your main objectives and key points, in some logical order—with a beginning, middle, and end—that leads to your main point, so that you do not lose your way. You will almost always do far better speaking extemporaneously with such aids than you would reading a written speech or reciting one from memory.

- Be enthusiastic and don't be afraid to show that enthusiasm; it's contagious, and it compensates for lack of polish and experience.

- Make sure that you are dressed properly, and the best insurance is to be conservative. Wear quiet, conventional clothes, with a minimum of jewelry.

- Don't try to be a comedian. Comedians make it look easy because they worked hard for years to learn their craft. Trying to emulate them is likely to bring you a great deal more grief than acclaim. Just be you.

- Have a proper feeling for your audience. They are not your enemies. Quite the contrary, they want you to succeed. Don't be afraid to gesture freely, smile, scowl, pause, shout, whisper, and otherwise act out your material. That, manifesting your enthusiasm, is the real secret of being a smash hit on the platform. You are a performer, or you should be, and your audience wants to be diverted as much as they want to be informed. Even not having a great deal to say that is worth hearing will be forgiven if you are enthusiastic and forceful enough to energize your audience.

Planning the Presentation

Murphy's Law states that anything that can go wrong will do so. I found that disasters happen spontaneously: They need no help to bring them about; the gods are only too eager to visit them upon you.

Good things happen only when we *make* them happen. This applies in full measure to presentations. Whether you write out your presentation in full text, memorize it, use notes, carry an outline, or use a set of cue cards, preparation is effective in making things go right.

I do not use the same method for each situation. That is partly because I do not always deliver the same material, and quite naturally I need more planning, preparation, and guidance material for a presentation that I have not delivered before. Usually, I need only the sketchiest of notes and those primarily to ensure that I do not, in my enthusiasm, forget to make key points. But, I have sometimes prepared a full lecture guide for myself when I am breaking in a new program.

That's a good plan if you are new to speaking. If you get so nervous that you forget everything your notes were supposed to remind you of, you can at least read your presentation. That's better than stumbling along aimlessly. Some public speakers—Franklin D. Roosevelt, for one—could do this quite well, as can many professional performers and public officials. Of course, they have usually invested time in rehearsing carefully, and some even make notations on paper of where and when to pause, make gestures, whisper, shout, smile, and otherwise supplement and dramatize the material. But if you are truly enthusiastic about your subject you will probably not need such cues. Enthusiasm causes you to forget about yourself and all your anxieties, and you make all the gestures and inflections unconsciously. That is by far the most effective way to make any presentation, but planning is still necessary.

Goals and Objectives

Presentations fall into certain broad categories, defined by a general goal or theme, such as the following:

- How to solve a problem of some sort
- How something works
- How something came about—history, causes, origins
- New developments in a given field of interest
- How to do something
- Arguments for or against something
- Reporting on a project, new developments, new views
- Organizing a group or an effort
- Leading a discussion
- Offering a demonstration
- Introducing another speaker
- Presenting an award
- Warming up an audience

You need general goals reflecting broad categories, but you need a specific objective or set of objectives when you plan. When I offer a seminar on marketing to the government, for example, my general goal is to teach my audience both the basic philosophy of marketing successfully to government agencies and the art of preparing bids and proposals. But I have many specific objectives outlined, each of them a milestone marking progress along the road leading to the goals. (This is how I visualize the relationship of objectives to goals—the objectives representing an orderly sequence of steps defining the path that leads to the goal.)

The Beginning

You must let your audience know what your goal is and how you will approach the subject. You should do so as early in the presentation as possible. Your introduction should make that clear. For example, when I present a seminar on proposal writing, I start by defining what a proposal is so as to make the philosophy and theme apparent. I make it clear that a proposal is a sales presentation, and that we will keep that definition clearly and unequivocally in mind as our standard. I stress that the chief ingredient of success in a proposal is sales strategy, and that excellent writing skill helps greatly, but there must be effective sales strategies and techniques. I make it clear that we are going to talk about winning and whatever is required for that.

It is thus not very many minutes into the presentation before my listeners know, in general but clearly characterized, what the goals and the themes are to be. There will be no confusion about where we are headed and what kinds of things they are going to learn about.

An Opening

This is not to say that you must start with "This is what I am going to talk about." An oral presentation benefits from an opening attention-getter just as a written presentation does. Many performers and professional speakers open with something humorous or novel. But that does more than get attention. It also assures your listeners that you are not going to be dull and so creates a receptive mood, which is a decided asset.

It is not necessary to be a comedian, but not hard to be humorous. I announced to a group that I would talk about the USP. Dead silence and blank stares prevailed. I paused, deadpan. Then: "I gather you would like to know what the devil that is." A long moment, then laughter, as the group appreciated the put-on and relaxed. There are other ways to start:

- Ask a key question, addressing the heart of your presentation. It can be rhetorical, one that you are going to answer yourself, such as "What is a proposal? Let's think about that."

- It can be a question that you wish attendees to respond to with their ideas. Lead with an example, if necessary to prime the pump.

- Starting with an amusing or novel, but relevant, anecdote is a good opening. Do a little research and try to come up with such an anecdote or two.

- You can use what I call startling statistics as an opening. Did you know, for example, that there are 79,913 governments in the United States, according to the U.S. Census Bureau? Or that nearly one-third of all our citizens receive some form of federal assistance?

- Use the unexpected, perhaps startling statement: I get gasps and chuckles when I tell an audience that I can show them how to *appear* to be the low bidder, even when they are not.

- Reveal or promise to reveal inside—little known—information about your subject, especially information that has been deliberately kept secret.

- Reveal or promise to reveal the very latest information on the subject, information too recent to have reached conventional information channels.

- Open with an apparent anomaly, such as this: Charles Kettering knew that the self-starter for automobiles was an impossibility. But when Ransome Olds, builder of the Oldsmobile, hired him to invent one, Kettering set out to find a way to do the impossible.

- You may use a gimmick, a device that can be effective in the right hands, but be careful: It can backfire. If you place a wrapped package or an apparently strange object on a table with what is quite deliberate and great care before you begin to speak and then carefully ignore it during the early stages of your presentation, you'll arouse a great deal of curiosity. But you must not wait too long to reveal what it is, for it is a distraction that can weaken your presentation if it goes on too long. It must also be related directly to your presentation or your audience will feel that they have been tricked, and they will not like that.

The opener must lead smoothly into your theme. That's the introduction, a preview of what is to come with a few items defined in advance to avoid confusion later. The introduction thus gives your listeners a road map helping them to follow you.

The Middle

Now that you have prepped your audience by previewing your presentation it is time to get down to business and deliver on the promise. The level of detail and the kinds of details vary, according to your goal, the amount of time you have, and the scope of the subject. In my case, I would focus on bids and federal supply schedules, rather than on proposals if I were addressing a group of suppliers who would rarely be required to write proposals in competing for government business, and on special programs for minority-owned ventures if addressing a group of minority businesspeople. So the body of my presentation and even the introduction, in many cases, would include both generalized information about government procurement and specialized information relating to the special interests of my audience. I make it a point to learn as much as possible about the audience I will address when I am preparing a presentation. When I am to address a group who develop training programs, I find training-program examples. I ask questions of whomever is arranging my appearance, and I collect annual reports, brochures, and other literature about the organization.

There are excellent reasons for this: It is far more useful and interesting to your audience to talk to them in terms of their direct interests. I could use generalized examples to illustrate what I am explaining, but that would compel the listener to translate that into his or her own need. Your address has much more meaning when you do that for your listeners.

My public speaking engagements are almost always how-to presentations, while yours may be something else. But the principle is the same: Do what is necessary to learn the direct interests of your audience and relate your presentation to those.

Ending

Closing your presentation is similar to your opening because the conventional close summarizes and reinforces your key point. However, a great deal depends on what kind of presentation you have been making. A logical argument for or against something is generally ended by summing up the facts presented and offering the logical conclusion. An emotional argument is ended by an emotional exhortation that iterates the primary pro or con positions. A how-to is often ended by inviting questions from the audience. However, whatever the case, it is proper form to thank your audience for their attention and patience, and if they choose to applaud, thank them again when the applause subsides.

A FEW PRESENTATION PRINCIPLES

Language is a first consideration in all presentations, whether written or oral. Unless you are understood clearly—unless the message received is the one you wanted to send—your presentation cannot be a complete success.

Fortunately, with today's communications—telephone, radio, TV for both voice and data, modern e-mail—and the greatly expanded traveling we do today, regional differences in our American versions of English are fewer than they once were. As a native of Philadelphia, I had to learn to ask for a sweet roll in Chicago when I wanted coffee cake. A soda was a pop in New York and a phosphate in Chicago. And if I were in some place where hardly anyone is a native, such as Miami, the complications in such matters multiplied.

These are minor difficulties compared with the general uses and misuses of English in America. It is a remarkably rich language, with extensive borrowing from other languages. There are about one million words in the language, divided into two rough equal halves, one of general words and the other of technical terms. The size of the average individual's vocabulary ranges roughly between 12,000 and 15,000 words, with 20,000 words considered to be quite a large vocabulary. (However, it is not at all unusual for individuals to have vocabularies of less than 10,000 words.) Some scholars, writers, and others have vocabularies ranging to 40,000 words and even a bit above that. These are unusually large vocabularies, and considering these statistics, individuals with large vocabularies must avoid using much of their vocabularies in writing and speaking if they want to be understood completely by the average reader or listener.

Most of us have two vocabularies, our speaking/hearing vocabulary and our reading vocabulary. Our reading vocabulary is normally quite a bit larger than our speaking vocabulary, however, and you should keep that in mind and be even more careful when preparing an oral presentation than when writing.

This does not mean that an unusually large vocabulary is a disadvantage or handicap. A large vocabulary is a marvelous tool for reasoning. We use both words and images in our thought processes. But it is also a marvelous tool for organizing information to be presented. Prepare your draft with whatever words come to mind as most suitable generally, without regard to your prospective reader's or listener's vocabulary. When you edit and revise your draft into the final document, you can eliminate all those big words, those terms more likely to prevent communication than to further it. But remember that most people can handle more words in reading than in listening because of the greater size of their reading vocabulary and because they can reread written material and infer meanings from context.

In both cases, during editing and revision processes, try to find and use the simplest words and terms, and try to eliminate all the pompous and unnecessary phrases. Here are just a few examples, the original words or terms in the left-hand column, and suggested replacements in the right-hand column:

in order to	to
comprise	contain, include
epitome	essence, representative
mendacious	lying, untruthful
luminous	glowing
for the purpose of	to, for
utilize	use

Avoid clichés, words and phrases that have been so overused that they are stale and are considered bad writing. Some of them are also incorrect (point in time, which is redundant, since point means the same thing). Here are just a few clichés to avoid:

bottom line	point in time	state of the art
along these lines	cutting edge	safe to say
fallout	few and far between	mind over matter
goes without saying	in-depth	be that as it may
richly rewarding	matter of course	all in all

Be careful to use words correctly. Just a little carelessness—not necessarily ignorance, but even absent-mindedness—can produce ludicrous and embarrassing results. One technical writer, for example, referred to the duplicity of the circuits when he meant duplication or redundancy, and assignation when he meant assignment. Keep a good dictionary at hand and use it whenever you are not absolutely sure that the word you are using is the right one. Keep a basic grammar text at hand, too, for swift reference when you are not absolutely sure about your constructions. Today, the word processor in your computer is likely to include a dictionary, thesaurus, and grammar checker. If possible, use a professional editor. It will save you time and help you produce a more thoroughly professional result.

Understanding versus Belief

Most of us suppose that we believe what we understand, and we therefore try to persuade others by rational explanations and arguments. We find it rather frustrating when others stubbornly refuse to believe our conclusions, and we often say in exasperation, "Look, you don't understand this," perhaps without realizing how right we are. Belief and understanding are so closely related that it is by no means clear which follows which. For example, although we have seen photographs of Earth from thousands of miles in space and perceived the globular shape, most of us never doubted that Earth and other celestial bodies are all at least roughly globular. We took it on faith as a premise. Yet, there are flat-Earth proponents who interpret those photographs as showing merely that Earth is a flat disk; they refuse to believe that Earth is globular and so they do not understand the photographs and all the other evidence of Earth's shape. They do not even understand (read believe) those physical laws that compel all those spinning rotational bodies to be globular because they could not spin on their axes, be balanced between and among many gravitational fields, and be otherwise than globular.

Even in conventional logic and argument, the conclusions reached—understanding—must stem from acceptance of the premises.

There is much that we can verify with our own senses, but there is much that we cannot so verify, and we validate our understandings of that which we cannot see, hear, smell, taste, or touch by logic and authority. We accept certain things as fact because we accept the authority of those who present it—teachers, scientists, and clergy, for example—or we accept because it is common belief, accepted by almost everyone, apparently, and so must be correct.

Communication Is Really Persuasion

It seems clear from this that belief must come first, and that it is difficult to define the line between belief and understanding. It seems also clear that if we wish to communicate clearly we must understand the art of convincing others—inspiring their confidence and persuading them to believe as we believe. In short, to write (communicate) effectively, you must be persuasive first, logical second. Yes, most people want logical explanations—rationales—to support what they wish to believe, but they will reject logic that is contrary to that which they wish passionately to believe. Only persuasive techniques stand any chance of overcoming bias. Logic will not.

Most people are strongly biased about only a few things, and even those are often predictable. It is predictable, for example, that a factory worker, a truck driver, a stevedore, and many other specific kinds of workers are most likely to be biased in favor of labor unions because they believe it to be in their interests to be so biased. But they are probably not strongly biased about most other things, and are willing to listen or read and be convinced—persuaded, that is.

The basis of all persuasion is to make the other party perceive it as in his or her interest to believe you, to *want* to believe you. Many people will believe the most extravagant promises, even with questionable evidence, if your presentation is attractive enough. If they like you and your promise does not conflict with any strong biases, they will want to believe what you promise.

That latter factor is not trivial. If an audience finds you offensive in any way—and that applies to your written presentations, as well as to those you deliver personally—they tend to reject what you say. I have witnessed quite excellent speakers with good material strike out with audiences because they somehow managed to come across as arrogant, sneering, boorish, or otherwise offensive. One man overdid his use of the first person, for example, which made him appear boastful and vain. Another came across as smug and condescending. Even if you do not appear offensive, failing to gain their respect has the same devastating effect: One speaker was so deliberate and measured that he appeared to be cold or hesitant, out of his depth on the platform.

That is one reason that efforts to be a comedian are so dangerous. Any humor that makes a class or type of person the butt of the humor by denigration is dangerous. Even expert comedians are on dangerous grounds when the laugh is at the expense of any identifiable group or kind of person—ethnic, religious, political, or other. A humorous anecdote about your own mother can bring down on your head the wrath of those who think you are insulting mothers generally.

Presumably, you can tell funny stories about some mythical stranger or relative who isn't representative of anyone else, but the hazard still exists. If you must try for laughs, avoid making anyone but yourself the butt of your humor. I do occasionally relate humorous stories, but the joke is always on me. I'm the expert who got to be that way by making all the stupid mistakes, and I gleefully relate a few of my most humorous blunders. I tell audiences about how contracts are sometimes wired for favored bidders, but to demonstrate that this is not foolproof, I sheepishly admit that I managed to lose a contract that was wired for me, and I explain how I managed to be so inept.

A story of this type has a positive effect. It tends to make you likable because you admit your human weaknesses and you are not ashamed to laugh at yourself. How can anyone hate a guy who makes jokes about his own stupidity?

A Few Dos and Don'ts

Here are a few things you should and should not do when you are facing an audience:

- Don't display nervous habits such as fidgeting, pulling an ear lobe, playing with keys, drumming your fingers on the lectern, or other such little habits. Aside from what they can do to your image generally, they can become both distracting and quite irritating to an audience who must hear and watch you for several hours.

- Don't slouch, lean against the wall, or show other signs of boredom or weariness.

- Don't try to explain with words alone. Make use of a blackboard, posters, slides, transparencies, models, handouts, or whatever other aids are suitable and available. They are a stress-relieving change of pace for your audience, as well as for you.

- When the presentation is to last for hours and the choice is yours, make your audience more comfortable by using a classroom style—chairs at tables—instead of theater style—rows of chairs. (Remember to give breaks, too.)

- Meet people's eyes as you speak, but do not focus on any one in particular nor dwell on one individual for long (despite some bad advice to the contrary). To do so is to make that individual uneasy and to mystify and quite possibly offend others.

- Don't try to speak in public as you do in private. (That is also bad advice often given by those who ought to know better.) Most of us speak disjointedly in casual conversation, often with such interjections as "Y'know," "uhhhh," "uh-huh," and sentence fragments. Those are taboo in public speaking.

- Show your respect and affection for your audience. They want you to succeed in being a good speaker. Relax, smile, and enjoy talking with a roomful of friendly people.

- Learn how to stop when you are finished. Stick to your schedule. Don't allow the one-hour lecture to become two hours. Let the audience know that you have finished, ask for questions if appropriate, and thank them. (If you are given applause, it may be because you have finally finished, but it is still appreciation!)

You will be pleasantly surprised at how soon you will begin to feel comfortable on the dais and actually enjoy being there and talking to those who came to hear what you have to say.

Skills You Need: Writing

*The ability to write well is even more frequently needed
in your work as an independent consultant than is the
ability to speak publicly and make presentations.*
—*Herman Holtz*

WRITING SKILLS FOR THE CONSULTANT

We refer to certain address delivered orally as *presentations*. But many more of our presentations are in writing, although we may use other terms for them. Most of what you read about public speaking in the previous chapter applies to or has its counterpart in writing. You may avoid or at least minimize making formal presentations from a dais but you will probably have to write a great deal in pursuing your career, unless you are an atypical consultant. Hardly anyone in the business world today can escape the frequent need for writing. The information explosion and paper explosion are not something that happened to someone else; they happened to you and me, and they continue to happen and influence what we do. Do not underestimate the enduring role of paper as the principal medium, although computers had enormous impact on how we do things. Still, despite the proliferation of computers and archives of information stored in computer files, storing data in paper archives continues. Computers on desks everywhere are responsible for swelling paper records. Knowledge and its distribution are growing exponentially in every field. Millions of word processors spew out printed reports, manuals, proposals, specifications, books, and other texts, recording, reporting, informing, educating, and documenting.

The Meaning of Print

The computer era has stimulated publishing in general. Computer books and periodicals alone represent a vast amount of printed paper, but the computer has added new dimensions and meanings to publishing. On the Internet alone, you find thousands of electronic publications—books, periodicals, catalogs, proposals, and other information that is read on screens rather than paper. What is said in this chapter applies to both electronic presentation on computer screens and to inked impressions on paper. You may do all or most of your writing for the computer screen, but the practices and principles apply in any case.

Important Differences

A vocal presentation reaches a limited audience, even if repeated many times and broadcast electronically; it is transitory. A written presentation can be reviewed and studied repeatedly and is permanent. There is no limit to the number of people who can be reached with written presentations, and no limit to how often one can review the material without equipment of any kind.

Even the information archives that exist on computer disks and tapes suffer by comparison: They are useless for practical purposes of transmitting information to people until projected on screens or printed out on paper, both limitations in their utility. The written word on paper is still the most efficient way to disseminate information, as well as to record it, study it, and use it, even if not the most efficient way to store it.

Details and Precision

Written accounts must be accurate and precise, more so than vocal presentations. The written account is a permanent and unchanging record. Misstatements and inaccuracies in a written account will return again and again to haunt you, whereas they are forgiven and often unnoticed in an oral presentation. This is especially true of a formal written record, such as a technical manual, progress report, or textbook. Readers expect to find gross inaccuracies in newspaper accounts, for example, given the nature of newspaper data gathering and writing, and they forgive these. They are far less forgiving of errors or lack of precision in the permanent medium of the book or manual.

These details were not of special importance when we discussed the writing of informal documents such as press releases and newsletters, which were adjuncts to your main activity of direct consulting services. Now we are going to discuss those more formal applications of writing skills where writing is an integral part of the consulting service, and therefore affects the quality of your service. There is also the matter of the kind of impression made on the client by your writing—the effect on your professional image, that is. That has great significance in terms of how it affects the probability that clients will recommend you to others. In many cases, your client will judge your professionalism and competence as much by what and how you write as by what you say and how you handle yourself in face-to-face exchanges and the actual results of your work.

This does not mean that you must be a master of polished and elegant phrases, but it does mean that you must be able to construct well-organized writing to produce documents that accomplish your purposes. It is necessary to master basics of usage and know how to organize a written presentation of each type. And the two reasons for stressing this latter point are:

1. Most who are natives of the United States or other English-speaking country and have at least a high-school education are reasonably familiar with the basics of English-language usage, and can easily consult dictionaries and other references if in doubt. The finer points of usage are rarely a serious problem. We can also turn to a skilled editor for help, which is a good idea in any case, and which I recommend to you. (Most of my own writing is sifted through the screen of professional editors, to its betterment.)

2. Editing can correct weaknesses in usage—spelling, grammar, punctuation—but it cannot correct defects in basic planning and execution, in concepts, organization, and construction. That requires rewriting, not editing. Not even heavy editing will salvage poorly planned or poorly executed writing. Therefore, the emphasis here is on those subjects, rather than on the mechanics of English-language usage. Incidentally, it is not necessary for most purposes to keep a separate text on usage at hand; many good dictionaries include excellent articles on usage and related subjects, features that are usually adequate to help you find the answers to questions of usage. Too, many modern word processors, such as Microsoft's popular WORD program include help with a few basic problems of grammar.

Even so, it is necessary to know what planning well means. That may mean remembering who your client (or your patron) is. But to discuss the significance of that, let's digress for a moment to consider an important problem in marketing: fear of consultants.

Fear of Consultants

Perhaps, you will recall that a great many employees of organizations have a fear of consultants. Or you may have sensed some hostility from employees when working on the client's premises alongside employees but never realized that the hostility is caused by fear.

This is a marketing problem facing you in doing business with organizations. Employees fear that when management hires a consultant, management has doubts about the staff's capabilities. The sales manager tends to feel threatened by a sales consultant who can help train a salesforce for higher productivity. The comptroller resents the presence of a financial consultant on his or her turf. The same thing is true for the production manager and other staff people. They see consultants as threats. And so many executives and others are hostile to the idea of hiring consultants, insisting stubbornly that the consultants cannot supply anything that they, the employees, do not already provide the organization. Understanding this problem and its causes helps you cope with it.

Clients, Nominal, and Immediate

When you do business with an organization, especially a large one, the organization is your client. Ordinarily, you will be expected to support some element in the organization, such as a department. You may win a contract as a total stranger through competitive bidding or you may have someone who endorsed or sponsored you and so helped you win the contract. Either way, you will be supporting the group, usually by interfacing directly with whomever is responsible for that group and what they do. Whether that individual is the patron who helped you win the contract, someone to whom you owe gratitude, or a total stranger you now meet for the first time, you must regard that individual as your true, immediate client.

That must be a consideration in your reporting, formal or informal. You must consider the interests and concerns of that individual. You will be wise to give full credit to that individual for any achievements resulting from your work. That is very much in your interests for future work and to make it clear that you are not only not a threat to any individual on the staff but you actually enhance everyone's image of the organization. You will be a judicious consultant if you are self-effacing and maximize the importance of your immediate client in preparing reports and other documents that reflect the project you have been working on. When the head of marketing in one company retained me to help with a proposal, he was my patron and my client, and my job was to be virtually his alter ego, doing a fine job which would reflect credit on him. And when an engineer in that same firm was assigned to develop a proposal later and arranged to have a purchase order issued to me for services, he became my client, and I worked at giving him the best proposal and making sure that he saw, reviewed, and approved all copy before it went to management for review and approval. (Interestingly enough, that engineer was one involved in the earlier proposal and expressed some opposition in that project, but subsequently asked for my services to help him with a proposal assigned to him, and was much easier to work with then.)

Consider, then, in the initial stages of planning any writing, both the nominal purpose of the document and how that may affect your client and your relationships with your client. Even a client on whom your services have been imposed against his or her wishes can be won over if you are wise enough to do every honest thing possible to further your client's interests.

Nature of the Deliverable Item

Every project has a deliverable item. In some cases the deliverable item is itself tangible and the entire purpose or goal of the project, while in other cases the deliverable item is intangible—usually a service—but there is a required tangible item that represents that deliverable.

In most of my own consulting projects there is a definite tangible, physical product required, which is itself the purpose of the project: a proposal. On the other hand I am also called on sometimes to deliver training seminars, and it is the presentation of that seminar—the information I provide—that is the deliverable item. But the client requires something tangible too, something that justifies the cost. (In industry, as in government, executives must always be prepared to exhibit what the organization got for the money; hence, the need for tangible items for files.) In the case of my custom seminars that is the substantial seminar manual I provide. It is as useful for the authorizing executive's official files as it is for future reference and refreshment by those who attended the sessions. (And there is occasionally a requirement to simply study something and render an opinion, which I do, but always substantiate it in writing for the record, that is, for the client's files.)

A computer consultant may be asked to produce and deliver a specific program or improve an existing one. The deliverable items in that case will be at least two: the program itself, as a tape or disk, and the documentation, probably in both tape or disk and hard copy printout.

In many cases, such as one in which I assisted an EPA contractor to value engineer EPA's municipal water-treatment grants program, the value engineering assistance was the deliverable service, but the client required a written report as a tangible item to file (if not to use) to document and justify the project.

In some other cases, as the one in which I assisted the Postal Service Training and Development Institute in updating a transportation-rate manual, the deliverable item was an updated manual.

Most consulting projects thus require writing something as the final deliverable item or as representative of it. Long-term projects often require interim written products, such as progress reports or drafts of final reports.

Purposes, Real and Nominal

Some suggestions as to true purposes of written documents have been offered already: organization executives and staff specialists must be able to document their expenditures and so justify them when and if they are audited. They usually require something tangible—reports, manuals, or other paper—for the purpose and, as in government bureaucracies, the reports and other documents may have no other purpose or utility. On the other hand, the written product may be itself the purpose of the project. That would be the case most often with proposals, manuals, computer programs, specifications, training programs, and custom-developed systems for inventory, purchasing, accounting, and other functions. Sometimes that written item is both a backup for the executive who authorized the project and a functionally useful end-item.

Important Basic Truths

Writers and editors have their own platitudes reflecting their conventional wisdom. Several reflect the philosophy that good writing is invariably rewriting, that really good first draft is the rare exception.

That is the basis for a distinguishing feature of the professional writer's attitude: Professional writers accept and operate on the premise that everything they write must undergo the draft/edit/rewrite phases for at least one such complete cycle (and many writers are not satisfied with only one cycle of editing and rewriting, but go through several or even many such cycles). The belief that one can write well in a first draft is usually the hallmark of inexperience, often of a novice who does not write well. There are occasional exceptions, but it is optimistic to expect those exceptions.

Editing, as used here, refers to editing by another person than the writer, preferably a fully qualified and experienced professional editor. Careful writers do a great deal of self-editing and rewriting of their copy before the editor sees it, but it is difficult to be objective about your own copy. So self-editing, although it is necessary and should be routine for all writing, does not take the place of full-scale, formal editing.

A truism of conventional wisdom holds that good editing almost invariably reduces the bulk of the draft manuscript by about one-third—that is, that most writers overwrite in their first drafts, and one of the functions of a good editor is to tighten up the manuscript be filtering out the unnecessary redundancies, unneeded and irrelevant details, and other excess verbiage.

In actuality, overwriting is a good practice and is encouraged, with the proviso that it must be followed by rigorous editing. It is a good practice because it permits both writer and editor to study the material and decide, in a second look, what to keep and what to discard. That is, writers do well to get it all down on paper and decide later what is most important, most useful, and most effective in meeting the goals and objectives. You can't select the best of a dozen of something without seeing the entire dozen.

There are many writers who do write tight first-drafts. Usually, when that is the case, it is because they do scrupulous self-editing continually, as they write, and so have far less to do when they review the finished draft.

This is one of the functions in which a writer comes to appreciate word processing: The processes of self-editing, rewriting, and even extensive reorganization and revision are so facilitated by word processing that I often wonder how it was ever possible to produce a serious work without this marvelous tool. What computers and word processing software do in automating repetitive, tedious chores is helpful but insignificant when compared with these much greater capabilities and contributions to writing excellence. The practice of writing by hand and then using typists to enter the manuscript is almost tragic in its underuse of the tool. Writers must work at the keyboard to gain the true benefits of word processing, which improves the very quality of writing when used well. The common excuse of some that they are not trained typists is not a valid one. I and many others turn out a stream of books and other manuscripts with two-finger keyboarding!

Good writers understand that writing is not confined to words alone, but includes all aids to communicating the information. Providing needed illustrations is the writer's responsibility, for a good writer does not illustrate his or her words, but uses whatever is the most effective or most efficient communication medium. The writer must decide where illustrations are necessary—

where words alone cannot do the job or cannot do it nearly as well as an illustration of some sort can—and conceive or find suitable illustrations, make sketches, or otherwise define the need to a specialist, such as a photographer or artist. (Illustrations include photographs, line drawings, renderings, charts, graphs, and even tables and matrices.) In self-editing a draft, the writer ought to keep in mind whether additional illustrations would be helpful. One more point about illustrations. Good illustrations do not merely *supplement* extensive and tedious text passages; they *replace* such difficult to write and difficult to read text. If an illustration cannot displace its own weight in words, it is not a good illustration; it does not do the job. The quality of an illustration as a contributor to meaning and communication is in inverse proportion to the amount of text needed to explain it; the best illustrations require little supporting text. You should use that as a yardstick in evaluating and using illustrations.

Writing, then, is an all-inclusive word that involves far more than writing per se. Writing itself is probably not more than one-third of the total effort and is often a far lesser portion of the total than even that. There are planning, research, illustrating, editing, and production to consider. Moreover, much of it is iterative. Even with a well-thought-out and detailed plan, initial research may turn up information that compels you to revise your plan, or you may have to do research before you can even begin to do any serious planning.

Steps in Development

The development of any written instrument follows the logic of any kind of development, beginning with need or purpose: What do you wish the written instrument to be or do? That can be any of a wide variety of things, including the following:

- Log the project chronologically and logically
- Justify the effort and its cost
- Guide future researchers
- Provide useful information derived
- Report specific advances
- Provide how-to guidance
- Provide reference data
- Inform stockholders
- Inform the public
- Provide input for a prospectus
- Study a problem

That is a first step. You must progress through the development of a hierarchy of definitions before you can do much actual work on the development of a manuscript. You must identify both your overall goal (train, advise, argue, document) and product (e.g., manual, proposal, report). That done, you must move on to develop a working plan, preferably in formal outline format, to include the following main items:

- Set of objectives
- Content outline
- Format
- Illustrations
- Schedule

The schedule should include projected times or dates for at least the following items:

- Start
- Draft completion
- Review of first draft
- Revision, rewrites
- Second review
- Final reviews
- Production and delivery

Execution

Writing can be relatively easy or difficult, depending on how thorough and detailed your research and the planning have been. The more thorough and well thought out the planning, especially the research, the easier it is to stitch all the information together coherently. If you have not thought things out, planned carefully, and especially researched your subject thoroughly, you will be forced to do much improvising and patching. This will affect the continuity of the final product and make it difficult to produce an acceptable product without extensive editing and revision. Time spent in planning and preparation usually saves more time later, while it also helps you produce a better product. In fact, it is quite likely an antidote for that stubborn resistance to and perhaps fear of writing that characterizes so many people.

The true difficulty in writing and almost certainly the most common cause of bad writing is the lack of preparation. That includes not only the failure to do most of the things just outlined, but applies even in the case of writing on a subject in which you are already an expert, that is, developing a manuscript for which you require little or no research. Even in cases such as that, too often you can be overconfident in your expert knowledge and neglect to think the project through.

Again and again in leading writing groups, I have found that "bad" writing was not due to any basic inability of the writer to use the language effectively, but was due to the failure to know just what he or she wanted to say: The writer had simply neglected to think about the subject and identify a goal and a set of objectives, and so was floundering and improvising, despite having a general outline of required coverage and specification. But even these do not help if you do not take the time to think the subject through completely. It is quite easy to deceive yourself into believing that you know the subject so well that you do not have to waste time in research or planning. Wishful thinking makes it easy to persuade ourselves to believe things that are not so. Sometimes we even lure ourselves into believing that the ability to memorize and recite certain facts or to use certain jargon demonstrates understanding and mastery of the subject.

A Test of Understanding

A reasonable test or proof of understanding is the ability to explain the concept in lay language to a lay person—someone totally inexpert and unfamiliar with the subject. Perhaps it is necessary to use jargon to demonstrate that you are a professional and an expert, but make sure that the use of jargon is incidental and not essential for understanding the document.

This problem is particularly abundant in technical fields, where jargon is quite thick and mystifying to even those who work with it daily. (For example, once an unexpected failure of a computer program resulted in a dump of data; now the program crashes, and who knows what it will do next year. Improvisations in radio were once referred to as haywire wiring and outboard circuits. In computer software, at least in software for personal computers, improvisations are kludges. But certain other changes or modifications to programs are known as patches.)

There is a tendency in many cases to explain things by labeling them with terms that are not necessarily definitive even to those in the technical field, let alone to others. In fact, another test of true understanding is the ability to translate that jargon accurately into everyday English and into concepts that anyone can understand. That is the job of the writer and often the main goal of the document.

Don't be misled by the frequently heard advice to use short sentences and short words, either, for many short words are uncommon words, and being short does not help anyone understand them. Tell the average individual that the earth is an oblate spheroid, and it is not likely that you will paint an accurate image in many minds. Tell them, rather, that the earth is a globe, but slightly flattened at the top and bottom—at the poles—something like an orange, and they will get the picture quite easily.

Use your ability to translate jargon and concepts with verbal illustrations as a yardstick by which to measure your own readiness to begin writing. If you can't make the translation easily, it is probable that your understanding is less than perfect. Do a little more research into the subject and think it out a bit more. You may discover that you did not know the subject quite as well as you thought you did! (I am skeptical when someone says, "I understand it, but I can't explain it," or, "You wouldn't be able to understand this.")

There are cases where the publication is a small or informal one—perhaps a proposal of only a few pages—so that there is no occasion for all the formal paperwork of developing book plans, outlines, schedules, and research plans. Rather, most of that is done mentally and spontaneously. But that, too—thinking the matter through thoroughly—is planning and preparation and is as important for the small writing project as for the large one.

Many professional writers do their thinking on paper. They start writing down various ideas, notions, and bits of knowledge almost at random, thinking out the organization of the product en route and often in the process discovering gaps that need to be researched and filled. Ultimately, they reorganize and rewrite all the material. The writer who works this way is developing an introduction, while thinking the thing out generally and planning the rest of the work.

That introduction is known as a lead, and the process is working from the lead. It is a perfectly legitimate way of working for those who have learned to work that way and prefer it. It is most effective for short pieces, and difficult to do for a lengthy manual or book. Even with detailed outlines prepared in advance as guides in starting a new book, I have written leads of as much as 50 pages and then discarded them completely because I decided I was on the wrong track. That's not easy to do. In fact, it is quite painful. But it is the kind of discipline you must exercise if you are going to turn out quality writing.

I use that method, planning and outlining primarily in my head and writing from a lead for short pieces, and combining methods for longer ones, such as books and manuals. That is, I plan a book by developing a formal outline and planning the content, chapter by chapter and subject by subject, along with at least some general ideas for illustrations. But I work from a lead to develop each chapter, although I am guided generally by the original outline.

It is probably not a good method for those to whom writing is difficult or distasteful. It takes a long time to learn to work that way and be comfortable and effective with it, and it is probably most appropriate for the professional writer because it usually means a great deal of self-editing and rewriting. If you go through careful and painstaking formal planning and preparation, on the other hand, you will surely minimize the amount of writing and rewriting you must do later.

Reading Level

It may surprise you to learn that relatively few people read with great facility above the eighth-grade level, which is well represented by the popular *Reader's Digest* magazine. You can do much worse than emulate that style. In fact, if you succeed in writing in that style and reading level, you need not worry about your reader's general reading level; you can hardly go wrong.

However, as a consultant you are probably working in some specialized or technical areas, and so cannot entirely avoid the use of jargon. The important thing is to know to whom you are writing and to judge accurately your reader's probable knowledge of the jargon. That means discriminating effectively between the general jargon of the field, which most people in the field know, and the special jargon that requires explanation.

In general, follow this rule: It is not the reader's responsibility to understand what you write; it is your responsibility to see to it that you can be easily understood. One wise editor told me that it is not enough to write so that you can be understood; you must write so that you cannot be misunderstood.

Using this philosophy, I try to review my own copy while asking myself whether it is at all ambiguous—whether it can be reasonably interpreted to have more than one meaning. If so, it must be changed to minimize that possibility. I do not knowingly permit my writing to be even marginally ambiguous.

Outlining: Two Kinds

References to many kinds of outlines may be found, but I know of only two kinds that have any true significance: an outline of what you intend to write about and an outline of what you intend to say. Somehow the difference between these two appears to elude a great many people. Here is an example of the first type, followed by an example of the second type. The subject is a symptom diagnosis of a malfunctioning TV receiver.

Outline Type One: What you will write about

1. Visual and aural inspection of picture and sound
   - (a) Video symptoms
   - (b) Audio symptoms
   - (c) Raster
   - (d) White noise
2. Functional checks
   - (a) Front panel controls
   - (b) Rear panel controls

Outline Type Two: What you will write

1. Visual/aural inspection, picture and sound
   - (a) Raster present? Video information present?
   - (b) Audio present? If not, white noise present?
   - (c) Conclusion as to probable trouble indicated by symptoms—high-voltage problems, loss of video, loss of sync pulses, loss of input RF, other
2. Functional checks
   - (a) Rotate brightness control: Response? Significance?
   - (b) Rotate contrast control: Response? Significance?
   - (c) Rotate volume control: Response? Significance?
   - (d) Rotate automatic gain control (agc): Response? Significance?
   - (e) Conclusions from above (probable cause) and/or logical next trouble-check

Note: Use one or more logic trees to illustrate trouble-shooting rationale and analyses.

The difference between these two outlines should be apparent. The second outline could be developed further and be even more detailed. The first outline may serve in an early stage of planning, but you are not ready to proceed to writing a first draft until you have developed an outline of at least the second level of detail. It is foolish to believe that you are ready to write before you have reached that stage of planning and preparation.

You may have to do some fairly extensive research to be able to produce an outline of that level of detail, but that is a positive effect: The need for more research shows that you were not ready to begin writing. That first outline should therefore be a preliminary step, exploratory planning.

Organization

Writing is a process with a logical progression of ideas and information. There is a natural or logical order to all materials. One reason that it is not always immediately apparent is that writers and other planners of writing sometimes fail to have a clear view of who the reader is to be. Consider the outline just presented, for example: Is it apparent for whom this is intended? Is it part of a training program for electronic technicians? A do-it-yourself program for householders? An orientation for students? None of that is apparent, but obviously the translation of the outline into text would be quite different for each case.

Identifying the Readers

You must know who your intended readers are: students, lay people, technicians, or other; how little or how much they know about the subject before beginning to read; and, finally, why they want the information: what they will do with it. Be highly specific here so that you can translate that into guidelines. Those will tell you how technical or nontechnical your explanations should be.

Logical Charting

Once you have a well-defined goal, you can turn to a simple block diagram, a flow chart, for direct help in thinking out all those intermediate objectives that will lead you logically to the goal. Such a diagram is actually a generalized outline in chart form and is an excellent first step in outlining. In fact, it actually precedes outlining, since it helps you think out the problem and organize the basic phases and functions logically.

Designers of computer programs tend to draw their charts vertically, from top to bottom, while designers of equipment tend to draw charts horizontally, from left to right (the way we read). I favor the second method, but you can use either. Whichever method you use, begin with the one thing you know (or should know) for sure, the final block, which represents the overall goal.

In this case, I will assume that the publication is going to teach handyman TV service to the nontechnical person, and my goal is to enable the reader to do what is stated in the box:

Make
simple
repairs

That established, I can begin to perceive the objectives necessary—the progression of things the reader must learn to do in order to reach that goal of making simple repairs. The obvious major steps in the process are these:

- Observe symptoms
- Analyze symptoms
- Reach conclusion (diagnose)
- Verify diagnosis
- Make repairs

There is a preliminary objective: The reader must gain an understanding of the basics of TV operation, enough at least to understand the simplified procedures to be presented. So my set of objectives is to teach the reader how to do the things illustrated in the following logical block drawing:

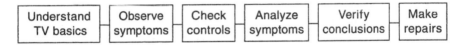

| Understand TV basics | Observe symptoms | Check controls | Analyze symptoms | Verify conclusions | Make repairs |

"Check controls" is added because that is part of observing and analyzing symptoms. Actually, many more details will be added in the full outline because each of these is a major topic that must be expanded and explained in the outline.

Outlines and charts are not developed in one pass. Both go through rough-draft and revision stages before you become satisfied with the result. These are the stages in which to do the bulk of your thinking, drafting, rethinking, and revision—long before you attempt to do serious writing. The more you do here the less editing and rewriting you will have to do later and the easier the writing will be. One advantage of charting your thoughts as an early step are that doing so compels you to think out the steps and the sequence. We can easily ramble on in writing and deceive ourselves into believing that we have said something when we have actually evaded saying anything because it is too much trouble and too difficult to think things through. Words are abstractions and for some uses far from the best tools. But charting, even with blocks containing those abstract symbols (words), evasion becomes difficult, as visualization becomes easier. Two, it is much easier to perceive the logical flow in even a primitive chart than in text, and thus the whole process of developing the full chart and detailed working outline is facilitated. An excellent technique is to print the logical blocks on 3×5-inch cards and lay them out on a table, where they can be shuffled around, seeking the most logical and effective flow. Cards may be added also if and as necessary.

There is a third benefit: The chart itself becomes an asset you can use directly or via adaptation as an illustration in the written presentation, thereby further simplifying writing.

You can verify the logic and validate your diagram by reading through it in either direction. Reading from left to right, the boxes reveal the why of the flow. A feedback loop is provided from check controls to observe symptoms because checking the controls provides some of the symptomatic information. Even this drawing is cursory, and many more blocks could be added as guidelines to the development of the working outline, which should be much more detailed than the diagram. The outline ought to answer the how of each block and of each transition from one block to the next. If it does not do so, it is probable that you ought to add blocks or otherwise revise the chart to rectify the deficiency. In this manner you can use the why and how questions to help in developing the chart, as well as in validating it and generating the working outline.

Functional Divisions

Organization means separating the document into functional sections or groups, and presenting them in a consistently logical sequence. The designation of such sections varies, as a consequence of the size and nature of the end-product. If the end-product is to be a book-sized document—say 100 or more pages—it is almost inevitable that it will be divided into chapters, each titled in a manner that identifies the focus of the chapter. If the simple drawing shown is to define the coverage of a book-sized product (admittedly, if that is the case, the drawing is a bit too primitive to be anything but a very early approximation of coverage), each block might identify the focus of a separate chapter, or perhaps of even more than one chapter. On the other hand, if the drawing describes what is to be only a relatively brief report, article, or chapter of a book, each division would normally be identified and introduced by a headline of some sort.

Thus the divisions would be physically different, but functionally they would have the same needs and treatment: Each division would require an introduction at its beginning and a transition to the next division at the end.

RESEARCH AND DATA GATHERING

The quality of the research is a key factor in the quality of the written product, and the quality of the research is determined by its completeness, accuracy, and selection of the best material:

■ The information that is most germane to your overall goal and the objectives you have as the itinerary for reaching the goal.

- The information that appears to be most complete, and most accurate, and most reliable.
- The information that appears to be most up-to-date.
- The information that provides you, as a writer, the greatest opportunities for drama, excitement, or other interest-arousing angle.

A clue to when your research is probably complete or nearly so is the point at which your research is turning up little that is new—when the resulting information has become repetitious. However, this is also a tool for judging accuracy: If most accounts agree, that supports the idea that what you have is accurate. But if there is serious disagreement among the sources, you are wise to search for ways to validate one source or the other.

Sources of Information

Despite all this, you are still faced with the need to rely largely on your own judgment, even when you have drawn information from official records. Court records, for example, may be legal truths, but they are still reflections of claims and opinions, and certainly not always factual.

The biggest problem is not how to find information—we live in an age of superabundance of information, with Internet the latest and greatest—but how to process, compile, organize, filter, analyze, and otherwise assimilate and utilize it. Among the many sources, most readily available, are the following:

- Public libraries
- Newspapers (Modern libraries usually have microfiche copies of old ones, and actual copies of recent ones, but newspaper morgues—in-house libraries, that is—will often allow access to their files of back issues.)
- Other libraries, including those in government agencies, universities, civic nonprofit organizations, and even large corporations. Many of these will allow you access to their files.
- Public-information offices (also known as public-affairs offices and by other names) of all those organizations mentioned here.
- Government agencies generally, especially those of the federal government.
- Publications of the U.S. Government Printing Office (GPO). Usually you can quote directly from these and use illustrations and other material that is in them because most of the GPO publications are in the public domain: anyone can use the material in them. But there are exceptions: Some government publications include copyrighted material, for which permission to use has been granted the government. But that permission does not extend to anyone else; you must be careful and make sure that what you use is, indeed, in public domain.

- Press clipping services. These search many newspapers and other print media daily, clipping items on subjects you name, charging a fee for each clipping.

- Historical societies

- Foreign embassies, consulates, and tourism bureaus

- Public databases, information you can access via your personal computer and modem. These are rich sources and some can even help in selecting the specific data you seek. (I once carried out a complete research job for a client by having such a service do my search of their files, and send me the data via our telephone and modem link, which I then needed merely to edit and print out to complete the task.) The public databases are an outgrowth of the desktop computer. They specialize, so that there are such databases for legal, medical, marketing, and almost uncountable other identifiable subject areas.

- The Internet is the modern miracle of technology, similar to the public databases in principle, but a giant step beyond them. The Internet is the ultimate in information availability, dwarfing all other sources. Probably most of our knowledge is available somewhere on the Internet, which is a network of millions of computers, interconnected by telephone lines and links, and accessible to everyone with an Internet connection. It is incredibly rich in information, and there are many search tools available to guide you to whatever data you seek. It has long been my own first recourse for information. It is a jumble of roads and lanes with no distinct pattern, but every unit of information has a unique address that identifies the computer in which it is stored and the file(s) in that computer, and you can address and reach them, although some data is reserved to those who have special authority to read that information, and in some cases there are fees charged for access.

The Internet is an excellent place to start many kinds of research and will often identify other sources and guide you to them, although the library and the telephone directory are also a great help when properly used. For example, if the information you want is industrial or technological, you may be able to get what you need from industrial or business firms. Moreover, you may even be able to get reproducible materials—news releases, specification sheets, tables, charts, and photographs, for example—with permission to use these directly. You normally must promise attribution—a line acknowledging the source and identifying the product or process. You should have written permission to use the material—a release form.

Some organizations and individuals, particularly in those cases where you seek permission to quote directly from copyrighted material, will require you to specify exactly what you wish to quote and may even demand the right to review your manuscript and approve or disapprove of your use. And some require payment, especially if the quotation is a lengthy one. I refuse to go along with giving the copyright owner the right to edit and approve or disapprove my

RELEASE

Permission is herby granted to Herman Holtz and his publishers to reproduce, cite, comment on, and/or quote briefly from material supplied herewith, with the understanding that full attribution will be made.

_____   _____
(Typed/printed name/title)   (Signature)

_____   _____
(Company/division)   (Date)

Figure 19.1.   Simple release form.

work, so I generally drop the matter when that degree of control over my writing is demanded. I will find a way to get along without the material.

Some organizations will include a letter granting permission to use their material (and in the case of news releases and accompanying material, such as photographs, formal release is not necessary because the permission to reproduce is implicit), but it is more practical to supply a release form of your own. I use a rather simple one, shown in Figure 19.1. It has served me well enough in most cases, and rarely have I found it necessary to use anything more elaborate than that. (I do, however, send a courteous letter of request making it clear that I will use the material supplied objectively and will be scrupulously fair in any case where I find it necessary to make a critical comment. But I try to avoid the necessity for criticism, since I generally use materials to exemplify good practice, rather than to recommend for or against any proprietary.

THE DRAFT

The focus in this chapter is on usage and writing practices, although summarily because it is not my purpose to attempt to teach the basics of grammar, punctuation, spelling, and other such academic subjects. But there is one point I must make: Contrary to what other writers and lecturers on the subject suggest, expert knowledge of grammar, punctuation, spelling, rhetoric, and other mechanics of usage is not the skill of writing any more than the ability to use a hammer and saw are the skills of cabinet-making or even carpentry. They are the tools of writing, and you must have at least a reasonable mastery of them, but that mastery, no matter how great, will not of itself make you a writer. Moreover, you must have a good dictionary and you should have a good grammar text at hand if you are not completely at ease in matters of usage. What I think is more useful here than a brush up in usage is a discussion of some practical problems in writing.

First, a general caution about writing a draft: Even if you do everything recommended here as constituting thorough planning and preparation, expect to write a rough draft as a first step. Don't fall into another trap that inexperienced writers often do: That is the trap of being careless in writing the first draft, reasoning that "It's only a draft, so I can fix things later." Too many carelessly conceived drafts never do get fixed, but haunt the writers for a long time after the event. The more care you exercise with the draft, the less change you will have to make later and by far the less danger that something totally wrong will appear in the final document. The convenience and encouragement of word processing induce me to more self-editing and revision than I have ever done before, so only a small portion of what I finally print out now has to be rewritten later, even after scrupulous editing by my publishers. It's the ounce of prevention eliminating the pound of cure.

Introductions

Every subject and every functional division must be introduced, whether it is a sentence, a paragraph, a chapter, or an entire volume. With a paragraph the introduction is the first sentence, and it is referred to as the topic sentence.

Introduction, as applied to writing, is not a mysterious term, nor is it jargon. In fact, it is simplicity itself. It means merely telling the reader what you are going to discuss or reveal. Check some of the paragraphs in front of you and verify that that is the case: Each one starts with a sentence that telegraphs what is to come, directly or indirectly. And the rest of the paragraph is about that topic, or it should not be in that paragraph. For when you have said all you have to say about that topic, it is time to end the paragraph and introduce the next one. Glance back (or forward) at the paragraphs here and see whether or not each paragraph was introduced with a sentence that telegraphed what the paragraph was to be about.

The same philosophy applies to the chapter, if you have chapters. The opening paragraph ought to introduce the chapter in the same way. Check the opening paragraphs of the chapters in this book and see if that is not so.

Transitions

Introductions to new material and new subjects, whether they are presented in new paragraphs or new chapters, are actually made or at least strongly suggested in the preceding paragraph or chapter. That is known as a transition or bridge. It is a clue to what is to come to provide a continuity of thought and keep the reader oriented.

Somehow, writing effective transitions appears to be difficult for some writers, and the ability to write smooth transitions should be cultivated. One tip is to use key words as transitional links. That is, introduce a key word or topic at the end of a paragraph and use that same key word in introducing the next paragraph. Note, for example, the word tip so used in ending the last paragraph and introducing this one and the next one.

Another tip is to make sure to telegraph the next theme or subject, even if you do not use a key word to do so. Theme is a part of writing. My theme in this section of this chapter, for example, was that the mechanics of English-language usage are the tools of writing, but they are not the art of writing, and becoming letter perfect in all those rules will not, itself, make you a writer.

I did not set out to prove that idea, but offered it as a theory, asking you to accept it on my authority as an experienced professional writer. And here, in this paragraph, I deliberately avoided using that word "theme" in making this transition because I wanted to demonstrate another means for making smooth transitions: I used another word—idea—instead of theme, knowing that since I was continuing the discussion you would have no trouble following the train of thought by recognizing that I used idea as a synonym for theme.

There are many cases where you are breaking off or concluding a discussion and preparing to set forth on an entirely different topic. But even this calls for a transition, although of a different kind. In such a case you must let the reader know that you are making a change. In some cases, you need only an appropriate transitional word or phrase such as *however, on the other hand,* or *in comparison.* In other cases, such as when you are concluding a chapter and preparing to take up a quite different and not directly related subject, you might require an entire concluding paragraph to prepare the way for the introductory paragraph of the new chapter. But, again, the final paragraph or paragraphs will be of that "however" and "on the other hand" philosophy.

There are other methods for achieving good transitions, but all are based on the same idea: guide the reader to the new subject by linking it directly to the subject you have just summarized when the new subject continues a theme or alerting the reader to the change of subject or theme and providing an introductory orientation to the new subject or theme.

Readability

Readability is difficult to define because it means different things to different readers. On the one hand many people really mean understandability when they use the term. And there are no really good, scientific measures, despite many efforts to create standards.

A measure often used is grade level, with the *Reader's Digest* a de facto standard, as noted earlier, suitable for everything except possibly certain scientific and technical materials. Other ideas about readability concern the length and complexity of sentences and words, with some writers on the subject insisting that to be highly readable the words should never have more than two or three syllables.

The problem with all of these standards and guides is that there are too many exceptions for them to be truly useful. For example, there are many difficult or uncommon words that are quite short, while there are many common, easily understood words that are relatively long—have more than two or three syllables. *Ted,* for example, is quite a short (one syllable) word, but few people (other than crossword-puzzle fans and possibly farmers) know the word. On the other hand, most readers would have no trouble with the polysyllabic *managerial* or *insomnia*. Semanticists can account for this quite easily in technical terms, explaining the existence or absence of suitable referents on the part of the reader. And because of this, systems designed to help writers determine the grade level of any writing must include vocabulary lists.

In the end, as a practical matter, you must be able to judge which words are common words, easily understood by most readers, and which are uncommon words, not so easily understood by the average reader—provided that you, as the writer, have a good idea of who the average reader is and what he or she is likely to be able to understand easily. (And provided, also, that there is such an entity as an average reader.)

But all of this applies to sentences and their length also. Contrary to some of what has been written on the subject, long sentences are not necessarily difficult, nor short sentences easy to understand. Stops in a sentence—full stops, such as semicolons and dashes—are as effective as periods in permitting the reader to pause and digest what he or she has read so far, but even short pauses, such as commas, are helpful. The important thing is not the total length of the sentence, but the organization of information. If a sentence has one central idea, and the information is presented in a logical sequence, readers are not likely to have trouble with it. Readers have trouble with sentences that are guilty of one or more of these sins:

- Tries to present more than one central idea
- Fails to get to the point
- Fails to make a clear and unequivocal statement
- Uses an irrational or illogical order of presentation
- Evades the issue by using obscure euphemisms
- Works hard at saying nothing

Readability also refers to other aspects of written and printed materials, having to do with format and related matters. Here are some tips to make your writing more highly readable in these respects:

- Solid, unbroken blocks of text are formidable and may make unreasonable demands on the reader to retain large amounts of data before reaching a summary or conclusion. Keep paragraphs reasonably short and summarize key points often.
- Use bulleted or otherwise listed items to make points.
- Don't rely on text alone, especially when you want to paint an image. But even for presenting and explaining abstractions and broad concepts, analogies and drawings help. Readability is not concerned with words alone, but with total communication.

Imagery

Illustrations are not necessarily drawings or photographs; they can be verbal illustrations, imagery or images drawn by words. "As strong as an ox," and "a bear of a man" are two examples. Simple word descriptions that help the reader or listener understand are also imagery.

For imagery, use comparisons that the reader is likely to be familiar with. It does not help to describe something to be as complex as a tracking equation when the reader or listener is not likely to have any idea of what a tracking equation is. What you refer to as a simile, metaphor, or simple comparison, must be something familiar to be effective.

Do It Yourself Artwork

It is not always necessary to turn to professional illustrators for artwork. Most modern art-supply stores and office stationers can help you with templates, transfer (decal) type and drawing symbols, and clip art. If you have a modern personal computer there are many desktop publishing programs that include all these things in forms and configurations you can transfer to paper via your printer. Do-it-yourself illustrations are a reality.

Level of Detail

The amount of detail you should include in anything you write should depend, logically, on two things: the reader's need—and that should equate with the goals and objectives you are addressing in writing the material—and the reader's ability to absorb, appreciate, and utilize the detail.

A most common problem in technical publications is offering readers far more detail than they need or can use, often more than they can understand, in fact. As a writer you do not need to report everything you know about the subject. Make an objective evaluation of what the reader needs and can use, and restrict yourself to that. And if you conclude that your reader needs technical detail but is not trained in even the rudiments of the technology concerned, there are still ways to provide a limited and almost painless education in the salient facts by providing tactful explanations as you go.

One problem is that you often have a mixed audience or readership. Some are technical/professionals, while others are lay people. It is necessary to present the information so that both understand, and yet the technical/professional readers must not feel that they are being talked down to. Consider the following alternative ways of explaining a multiplexed interface as an example of achieving this goal:

■ The interface is multiplexed, permitting the equipment to carry on concurrent exchanges of information with several dozen sources and destinations.

- The interface is multiplexed, sampling each of several dozen inputs at 50-microsecond intervals in turn so that for practical purposes, several dozen transmissions are received concurrently.

- The interface is characterized by multiplexing or ability to handle a number of inputs and outputs in such rapid succession that it is virtually simultaneous.

- The interface has a multiplex characteristic (ability to handle a number of inputs and outputs in such rapid succession as to appear to be simultaneous).

These are in a descending order of technical detail or an ascending order of technical explanation. Anyone can learn from this what multiplexing means, at least in a general sense. And yet no one should be offended, not even the knowledgeable engineer or technician who reads this.

Making Slides and Transparencies

With today's 35-mm cameras almost anyone can shoot good-quality slides at a reasonable cost. Unless you have quite special needs, you can usually make up your own set of slides to use in presentations from the platform. However, you may find transparencies more convenient for several reasons.

You can make transparencies on most office copiers and computer printers. Even if you do not have a copier of your own you can generally arrange to have a nearby copy shop do this for you. But even that is not the whole story on this; there are other resources.

One of the other resources is the personal computer. Today's computers, with their large memories and sophisticated software, can turn out the copy you need, with an abundance of typefaces, headlines, banners, forms, and clip art, and even print out the actual transparencies, as well. The word *independent* in independent consultants has greater meaning than ever before.

Technological Assets for the Independent Consultant

There was never a time when the independent consultant was as independent and self-sufficient as today, with the facilities and resources available now for even the most modest office.

—Herman Holtz

THE NEW MEANING OF INDEPENDENT

There have always been independent practitioners in every field, including consulting. Never before, however, has *independent* meant as much as it means today, when the humblest office has a computer with all the peripheral items and access to the whole world via Internet. Independent now means *self-sufficient.* Today, your reliance on printers, copy shops, stationers, and other local suppliers and services—even travel—is reduced or even non-existent. Properly equipped, you can be seated at your desk and transmit files, reports, proposals, invoices, general correspondence, quotations, and even payment— carrying out in minutes what once would have taken hours.

If there is a drawback, it is the need to keep up with what is available and how to use it. New advances require new learning. Installing a new monitor for my new computer proved to be a problem because the new computer included many monitor adjustments new to me. Fortunately, an IBM consultant helped me get the job done, finally.

Few new developments have caught on and developed as swiftly as the personal computer and its peripheral items—printers, monitors, fax machines, modems, and software. It developed so rapidly that government and big corporations have less and less need for the big computers now called mainframes. Desktop computers are used in millions of offices today, often linked to other computers in the office via a local area network (lan), and in an even newer development, an intranet, which is an internal mini-Internet with internal Web-type sites.

The computer and its companion equipment is the greatest boon yet to office efficiency in general. Modern takes on new meaning here because in the case of personal computers it refers to equipment of the recent 3 to 5 years! The personal computer has evolved so rapidly that I retired my first computer, vintage 1983, in 1986 and today I am using my fifth computer. I find it necessary to invest in a new computer about every three years.

What used to be peripheral and separate (stand-alone) equipment items, such as modems and fax machines, are now standard internal elements of computers. Virtually no one today sells bare computers. Almost all come with a number of current software programs already installed. The instruction manuals have shrunk greatly, with more reliance placed on internal help files and menus in the software systems. The computer you buy today includes capabilities for joining an online service and getting access to the Internet. You will probably find Internet access a business necessity. It is the best possible medium for many purposes, including networking, research, advertising, and doing business internationally.

The term *networking* has a number of meanings. The Internet is a worldwide communications network, and within the Internet are many other communications networks. However, networking is also word-of-mouth advertising, finding business and winning clients by making yourself and what you do well-known and respected. Many businesspeople once joined clubs and associations as a means of networking. But today, going online and participating in cyberspace activity on electronic bulletin boards, message boards, newsgroups, mailing lists, Internet, and other activities in cyberspace is the way to network, and is the most efficient method. The personal computer gives you a window on the world in the communications capability it provides, with the Internet a global system. On the Internet, it is as easy to chat or do business with someone in Capetown or Singapore as with a neighbor down the street.

DATABASE AND SPREADSHEET FUNCTIONS

Word processing and e-mail have been the most used functions of computers, although another popular computer facility is the database. Database functions and designs are highly flexible and can be shaped to suit your needs. A database is any collection of information, and you, the user, decide what belongs in the collection and what are the common factors that make the information a collection. Thus, a database may be a simple list of names and addresses, a client list, a list of invoices, a file of letters, combinations of these, or any other information you wish to record and preserve. If database needs are simple and the collection of data not especially large, the simple flat file database will probably serve. However, a relational database is even more fluid: It can search for and summon information from other files and databases. It is a more suitable database system for large and complex data collections.

Database software allows you to design your files to suit your own preferences. Each individual data item (e.g., name, address, telephone number) is known, technically, as a *field,* and the entire set of fields for a given entry— for a client or a project—is a *record.* You decide (within the bounds of the software) how many fields you can have in a record and how large they can be, thus establishing the size of a record, how data will be entered, and so on. That determines how you can search the database and retrieve information. You thus do your own design, and the database is a flexible vehicle that permits you to shape it to your own needs.

Spreadsheet software is also most popular, enabling you to make projections, make correlations, do modeling, and conduct "what if" studies (e.g., see what the total effect on business is likely to be if you raise your rates or make some other changes in how you conduct your practice).

Archives

One of the folders I keep in my system disk I call ARC, which stands for "archives." In that folder I keep materials I use again and again in my work, either directly or with modification and adaptation. Here are descriptions of a few of these files:

- *Trademarks and registered trademarks.* The list, to which I add as the occasion arises, is a great time-saver for me.
- *Charts and graphs.* Many of the charts and graphs I have developed rather laboriously, can be modified and adapted to new uses far more easily than new ones can be created, so I store many of these as basic models.
- *Glossaries of special terms.* These can be adapted to new needs. In fact, it is necessary to update and upgrade these, since some terms survive, while others perish. For example, "user friendly" was once a popular term, but one rarely hears it today. "Wysiwyg" (pronounced "wizzy-wig") stood for What You See Is What You Get when that was a rather new idea. But today, with huge memories and huge storage disk capacities, it is usually a given that you will see what you are going to get, so the term has vanished.
- *Bibliographic listings.* Again, a file that is maintained and from which I draw what is appropriate to the occasion. It is more than book and magazine titles today, however; it lists also computer program titles, e-mail addresses, and Web addresses. That is most definitely a list that ages, and the list must be kept up-to-date to be useful.
- *Useful text passages* (such as marketing notes, various formats, and other texts).

PRINTERS

Printers have gone through a great deal of evolution, from dot matrix printers to laser printers and inkjet printers. Both the latter types are in widespread use and both do an excellent job.

MODEMS

As noted, the modem, that device necessary to communicate with other computers (electronic bulletin boards and public database systems), is normally supplied as a standard part of your computer, a circuit board. The most popular today is the 56K, which is now replacing the 28,800 baud (28,800 bits per second) modems.

FACSIMILE MACHINES

The fax has become commonplace: There are few who do not know what it is and what it does. It has also become inexpensive enough for most of us who are in any kind of business venture to have one of our own. You normally get an internal fax on the circuit board with the modem. The disadvantage of an internal fax is that you can't use it to send printed text and illustrations unless you have a scanner to convert it into a computer file. I keep a stand-alone fax machine, along with my fax modem. That gives me flexibility in sending and receiving faxes in whatever ways are most efficient and most convenient.

TAPE DRIVES AND BACKING UP

The random access memory—RAM—is volatile: When you turn your machine off, whatever is in RAM disappears. The disks, both floppy and hard or fixed disks, retain what has been stored and is available the next time you turn your computer on. However, hard drives wear out, as do all things, and sometimes they fail suddenly—crash. Then all your stored data is lost. (Some experts can retrieve much of the data on a crashed disk, but for most of us, it is a lost cause.) Because of that possibility—and many computer experts say that every hard disk will fail eventually—it is necessary to make copies of whatever is on the disk that is otherwise irreplaceable.

Many people back up their data by making copies on floppy disks. That becomes a less and less practicable idea as the size of your hard disk and the volume of data stored there increases. There are several ways to address the problem, and today one solution available is to store the data on tape, using an internal or external tape drive. But another method is the high capacity zip disk, a system that will store 100mb on a removable disk, and may be used as backup. It is also possible to have a CD ROM unit that will write on CDs as well as read them, and you can store up to 650 mb of data per CD. Still another way is to use a backup service, one that stores each day's data on your hard disk. Still another possibility is to have a second hard disk duplicating what is on your main disk.

THE COMPUTER AS A GENERAL AIDE

Relatively few owners of desktop computers in small offices—especially one-person offices—use computers with true efficiency and effectiveness. Not the least of what my own computer does for me is act as my general assistant; an efficient secretary could not do a great deal more, and could not do many of the chores nearly as quickly as the computer does. For one thing, it is un-likely that any secretary or assistant could find an address, telephone number, file, or note as quickly as the computer does when properly organized and prompted. In my case, with the press of two keys, my telephone list is on the screen in alphabetical order. The same is true when I want to review my ap-pointments, logs (diaries), correspondence, purchase orders, and other notes and lists I keep in various files. I have not quite achieved the paperless office, but I have made a great deal of progress toward it: I rarely have to scratch fran-tically through paper on my desk, looking for a note; it is in one of the several scratchpad files I keep in my computer.

FINDING SOFTWARE

Software has become incredibly abundant, and with that growing abundance has come competition and more modest prices. But it is a complex market, with more than one kind of competition and more than one influence driving down prices. Here is a brief, familiarization survey of the software market.

Prices for commercial programs have long been discounted by retailers, so that street prices or over-the-counter prices are far lower than the list prices. A program for which the publisher lists a price for approximately $500 will usually be available for not much more than one-half that list price. There are, however, increasing numbers of more modestly priced programs, ranging as low as $19.95 for many, with the result that they are far less heavily dis-counted and frequently not discounted at all. The more modest list prices do not leave a great deal of room for discounting.

There is today some public-domain software (also sometimes referred to as *freeware*); programs written by individuals who generously donated these to the world at large often through the Internet. In many cases, the author re-tained copyright but generously licensed everyone to use it for personal use—specifically not for commercial use—free of charge.

Today, most of these freelancing programmers offer their software as *shareware*. The author copyrights the program and makes it available to all on a trial basis, with the proviso that he or she—the author—expects payment for continued use of the program beyond a trial period. The payment is voluntary, of course, although the author suggests a specific figure (usually quite modest) for "registering" (and paying for) the program and promises some additional benefits, including a printed user's manual and free updating.

Much of the shareware is of poor quality, much is highly specialized, and of little interest to the average user, but much of it is quite good, sometimes better than the expensive commercial versions. There are many excellent utilities, programs for copying files, displaying directories, recovering erased files, and other such tasks. One that I use enables me to store short items, such as my name and address or a brief note, and insert it into a file or e-mail with a code of two key presses. The authors of shareware encourage free distribution to encourage trial by new users, and much of it is made available through the thousands of electronic bulletin boards and Web sites, from which anyone can download the files to their own computers. Today, although many bulletin boards still exist, much of the distribution of shareware is done via the Internet.

Keeping up with it all is a challenge, but I find the investment of time well worth making. I constantly discover newer and better ways of accomplishing more in less time and with less effort.

Index

HU6CY

MRTXX

Y2HDJ

KUGHT

YK6UD